Praise for *Vanishing Frontiers*

"Andrew Selee brilliantly chronicles the forces that have redefined our relationship with Mexico over the past quarter century, covering trade, immigration, security, and so much more. His intimate knowledge of Mexico and its people shines through as he tells the story, in a highly readable fashion, of why Mexico matters to the well-being of our nation. As our government is currently renegotiating the North American Free Trade Agreement, *Vanishing Frontiers* is a must read for all Americans, who will find it a book once started, very hard to put down."

> —Carla Hills, former US trade representative and
> secretary of housing and urban development

"While some politicians talk about walls, Andrew Selee tells us about the bridges that bind Mexico and the United States together. Few relationships will define our future as much as the one we have with the country next door. From energy and innovation to film and food, this book captures the many linkages that tie us together and shows why Mexico truly matters for our future."

> —Bill Richardson, former governor of New Mexico,
> US ambassador to the United Nations, and
> secretary of energy

"Drawing on his deep bicultural background, Andrew Selee narrates in colorful and fascinating detail how economic integration and demographic change are blending Mexican and American societies. Given the ongoing and heated public debate about NAFTA and US-Mexican relations, this is a most timely work."

> —John Negroponte, former US ambassador to
> Mexico, deputy secretary of state, and
> director of national intelligence

"In nativist times, Andrew Selee's *Vanishing Frontiers* is a spot on, vivid, extraordinary, ground-level view of the key players quietly building bridges between the United States and Mexico. This wide-ranging, painstakingly well-researched, and sharply written account provides a much-needed human face to grasp the seismic changes sweeping both countries. *Vanishing Frontiers* adds much needed context and splendid insight to today's complex conversation. Selee takes us on a personal journey and bluntly reminds us why walls are obsolete and ties inevitable. You cannot understand the future of both countries without reading *Vanishing Frontiers*."

—Alfredo Corchado, border correspondent,
Dallas Morning News, and author, *Midnight in Mexico*

"This beautifully crafted work is an extraordinary account of the deep and complex relationship between Mexico and the United States, sharing the same qualities as Richard Reeves' bestselling *American Journey: Traveling with Tocqueville in Search of Democracy in America*. Like Reeves and Tocqueville, he has travelled throughout the United States, speaking in-depth with Mexicans and Americans from all backgrounds and ages, in order to shed light on the degree to which the two countries have become integrated economically and culturally, presenting fascinating stories of successful individuals whose professions range from restaurants to film, sports to journalism, and technology to politics. Their personal experiences are woven deeply through the fabric of both societies, allowing readers to identify and clearly understand numerous trends in their deepening integration. The degree to which Selee effectively combines fascinating personal accounts with in-depth recent data revealing significant trends in the relationship will appeal to and deserves the broadest readership."

—Roderic Ai Camp, Philip McKenna Professor of the
Pacific Rim, Claremont McKenna College, and
author, *Politics in Mexico*

"*Vanishing Frontiers* offers fascinating insights into the ways that ordinary people—and some extraordinary human beings—continue to shape US relations with Mexico. Outside the glare of politics, citizens of both countries are bringing their nations together in myriad ways. Selee's optimism is more than wishful thinking; it is based on years of personal observation and empirical research. And it offers a welcome corrective to the anti-Mexican rhetoric exuding from Washington DC these days."

—Peter H. Smith, distinguished professor emeritus,
University of California, San Diego, visiting professor,
University of Denver, and author, *Talons of the Eagle:
Latin America, the United States, and the World*

"In this fascinating collection of fact-based stories, Andrew Selee draws on his deep and personal knowledge of both the United States and Mexico to reveal to us how, underneath today's choppy waters, the strong combined currents of economy, geography, demography, and culture are inexorably driving our two countries together into a synergistic production and social platform and a closely interwoven destiny, transforming both countries along the way. This is a must read for anyone interested in learning more about an indispensable and strategic neighbor and in visualizing and harnessing the shape of things to come in North America."

—Jose L. Prado, chairman and CEO,
Evans Food Group, and former president,
Quaker Oats North America

VANISHING
FRONTIERS

VANISHING FRONTIERS

THE FORCES
DRIVING MEXICO *and*
the UNITED STATES
TOGETHER

ANDREW SELEE

PUBLICAFFAIRS
New York

PublicAffairs
Hachette Book Group
1290 Avenue of the Americas, New York, NY 10104
www.publicaffairsbooks.com
@Public_Affairs

Printed in the United States of America
First Edition: June 2018

Published by PublicAffairs, an imprint of Perseus Books, LLC, a subsidiary of Hachette Book Group, Inc. The PublicAffairs name and logo is a trademark of the Hachette Book Group.

The Hachette Speakers Bureau provides a wide range of authors for speaking events. To find out more, go to www.hachettespeakersbureau.com or call (866) 376-6591.

The publisher is not responsible for websites (or their content) that are not owned by the publisher.

Library of Congress Control Number: 2018939586

ISBNs: 978-1-61039-859-6 (hardcover); 978-1-61038-902-6 (Ebook)

LSC-C

10 9 8 7 6 5 4 3 2 1

To my wife, Alejandra,
for her inspiration and guidance, and to our children,
Lucia, Elena, and Alexander,
for their future

Contents

Introduction

- -

Intimate Strangers

One of Demetrio Juárez's proudest moments was when Joe Maddon came in to his restaurant to order food. In some ways the two men couldn't have more different lives. Juárez, born and raised in Atzompa, Puebla, a hamlet of roughly three hundred families in the mountains of central Mexico, came to the United States as a migrant worker in the 1980s, at the beginning of a new wave of Mexican migration northward. After living in New York City for many years, he settled in Hazleton, Pennsylvania, a small city in the breathtaking Pocono Mountains of northeastern Pennsylvania, where job opportunities were increasingly plentiful and rent was cheap.

Maddon, on the other hand, was raised in a large, boisterous Italian American family in Hazleton, only a few blocks from where Juárez lives today. He went on to play major-league baseball and eventually become the manager of the Tampa Bay Devil Rays, where he won two American League Manager of the Year awards. He was later recruited as manager of the Chicago Cubs, where he led the once hapless team to its first World Series win in over a century, breaking the curse—real or imagined—that had hung over it.

1

Maddon has stayed connected to Hazleton, and much of his family still lives here. But Maddon wasn't in town to see his family or talk baseball the day he came into Juárez's restaurant, El Mariachi. As on many of his visits to town these days, he was there to try to heal a city torn by divisions between longtime residents and newcomers.

A century ago, Hazleton was a magnet for people leaving poor, isolated pockets of Ireland, Italy, and eastern Europe. The city still has a wide variety of ethnic restaurants, along with churches of every denomination imaginable, from Italian and Romanian Orthodox to Welsh Primitive Methodist. Hazleton once even boasted the nation's only Tyrolean Catholic Church, which catered to a small population from the Italian and Austrian Alps, as well as the Western Hemisphere's first Slovak Catholic congregation. "Hazleton is like a miniature Brooklyn, a diverse urban landscape in a semirural, mountainous region," says Charles McElwee of the Greater Hazleton Historical Society. "In the city, the past remains visible in the present."

Over a decade ago, in 2006, Hazleton found itself at the center of the national debate about illegal immigration and America's relationship with Mexico. Faced with a new influx of immigrants, many from Mexico, it became the first city to pass local ordinances that banned hiring or renting to unauthorized immigrants. The city became ground zero for protesters against immigration, and national news cameras camped out in the city for weeks to follow the debate. Protesters were fond of shouting "Go back to Mexico" to express their outrage at the growing Spanish-speaking population in town, and Juárez remembers getting angry phone calls at the restaurant telling him to go home.

The courts eventually struck down the local ordinances; yet the conflict over who should live in the city continues to smolder beneath the surface, as it does in many cities and towns around the United States. Hazleton, almost 2,000 miles from the border with Mexico, became a bellwether for many of the tensions Americans feel in their relationship to the country next door.

Today the debate about Mexican immigrants that tore at the seams of Hazleton has become a national one that increasingly touches on the larger issue of America's relationship with Mexico. Donald Trump won the presidency in part by promising to deport unauthorized immigrants, renegotiate the North American Free Trade Agreement (NAFTA) that ties the Mexican, American, and Canadian economies together, and build a "big, beautiful wall" on the border between Mexico and the United States.

Polls show that these positions are not actually popular with most Americans—majorities register positive opinions of Mexico and even more so of immigrants—but they do appeal to a quarter to a third of citizens. That's still a large percentage of the country, and it's the source of Trump's most passionate support, some of it in places like Hazleton, Pennsylvania, and its surrounding towns. And while most Americans may not share these specific positions, deep down many do harbor doubts about the country next door and how we should relate to it.

But if Hazleton and much of the rust belt are at the center of Trump's rise to power, they have also been at the center of two equally surprising changes going on in the relationship with Mexico. The first is the dramatic drop in Mexican immigration, which actually started a decade ago in 2007. Since then, the number of Mexicans crossing the border illegally has slowed to a trickle, and the number of Mexicans in the United States without documents has fallen dramatically. It's hard to tell this from the current debate on immigration policy, since our frameworks for understanding what's happening haven't yet caught up to reality.

Mexicans continue to enter the country through the visa system—increasingly many of them with college degrees—but the age of mass Mexican migration across the border appears to have ended. And Chinese and Indian immigrants now actually outpace Mexicans in new arrivals.

In Hazleton, too, the number of Mexicans has stayed steady or perhaps dropped a bit over the past decade, but new groups of Dominicans and other Latin American immigrants, as well as Puerto Ricans, many of whom had been living for years in the New York area, have moved in.

The other change—perhaps even more unexpected—is that just as Mexican immigrants stopped flowing north, another flow took its place. Mexican companies started investing north of the border, and financial capital started flowing from south to north.

Bimbo, a Mexico City–based company, now owns two major plants in Hazleton. Few Americans have ever heard of Bimbo—the name is a play on the Italian word for child, *bambino*—but we all know its popular brands, like Entenmann's, Stroehmann's, Friedhoffer's, Sara Lee, and Thomas' English Muffins. Bimbo is now the largest baked goods company in the United States—and in the world—and makes over a quarter of the fresh bread we consume in the United States.

About ten minutes from Hazleton in Mountain Top, another Mexican-owned company, Mission Foods, has set up a major plant making corn and wheat tortillas. And Arca Continental, a midsized Mexican company, owns Wise Foods, the makers of Cheez Doodles and Wise Potato Chips, in nearby Berwick, Pennsylvania. Since Arca Continental acquired Wise Foods, the company has expanded operations and hired more workers. Its chips have also become the "Official Potato Chip" of both the New York Mets and the Boston Red Sox, a fascinating connection between Mexican investment, American workers, and America's national sport.

As it turns out, more and more of the products Americans depend on are made by Mexican companies in the United States using American workers. These include not only bread, tortillas, and potato chips but also hot dogs, lunch meat, milk, and yogurt. And Mexican companies also provide much of the cement and nails that anchor our buildings, the cell coverage that connects us, and the commercial ports that bring goods into the country. These companies, which hire American workers to produce goods in the United States, dominate or are among the top two players in each of these industries, but this trend has gone almost completely under the radar in American life.

And it's not the only hallmark of change underway in the relationship between the two countries. Today it would be almost impossible to ride in a car, plane, train, or bus in America that doesn't have parts made in Mexico, the United States, and Canada, since almost all vehicles sold in the United States are assembled in nearly seamless production processes involving the three countries.

While it's true that some jobs making American cars and car parts went to Mexico, other jobs actually came to the United States when German, Japanese, and Korean car companies decided that it was more cost-efficient to build their cars in North America, sourcing parts and assembling vehicles across the three countries. Auto production in the United States—as well as in Mexico and Canada—has actually increased over the past two decades at a time when most people predicted a long decline for the American auto industry.

Energy too is flowing like never before. Mexico is the fourth-largest source of crude oil for the United States, but it also buys more than half of America's exports of natural gas, using it for electricity generation. Both countries are now collaborating on renewable resources to supply increasing electricity demand in communities on both sides of the border.

Silicon Valley too has developed its own close ties in Mexico, sourcing talent and placing some of its operations south of the border. And Mexican tech companies have taken off, often with the backing of American venture capital, and they frequently service markets on both sides of the border.

Even the film industries in the two countries are tied together. Movies popular in Hazleton and across the United States—such as *Gravity, The Revenant, Miracles from Heaven, Harry Potter and the Prisoner of Azkaban, Hellboy,* and *Pacific Rim*—have been made in Hollywood by Mexican filmmakers, while others, like *Night at the Museum, Brokeback Mountain,* the *Twilight* saga, and *Spy Kids,* have been filmed by Mexican cameramen. And for true cinephiles, there's no missing that some of the most celebrated independent films seen at American and international film festivals are coming out of Mexico these days.

Near the border between the two countries, these connections are often quite visible. Tijuana and San Diego, for example, now share an international airport—on the Mexican side of the border—and they have developed a common blueprint for their future together as a shared metropolitan area. San Diego city leaders, including the Republican mayor, regularly refer to the two cities as a "single region," one that's large enough to compete with Los Angeles and San Francisco and one day might host a binational Olympics or World Cup.

Further from the border—in places like Hazleton and Pittsburgh, Pennsylvania, Poplar Bluff, Missouri, and Knoxville, Tennessee—the cooperation between the two countries is often harder to see, but it's no less important for the day-to-day life of average Americans and Mexicans. This book chronicles the irresistible changes that have redefined the relationship between the two countries and made Mexico part of our daily lives—even though that relationship is not always visible on the surface.

On the day that Joe Maddon came into his restaurant, Demetrio Juárez had been impressed not by the star power of the city's most famous resident but rather by what his own teenage son, manning the cash register that day, had said when Maddon asked where he was from. Juárez's son replied matter-of-factly, "I'm from Hazleton."

At that moment, Juárez, watching from the kitchen, knew he'd achieved what he always wanted. His children, who had been born in the United States and grown up in Hazleton, knew exactly where they were from. They might still love Mexico—he took them back there once a year to Atzompa, and they reveled in the attention of grandparents, uncles, aunts, and cousins—but their home was here in the Pennsylvania mountains, and the United States was their country.

Maddon burst out laughing and said, "We should make a T-shirt out of that: 'I'm from Hazleton.'" Maddon is known for capturing phrases he hears and putting them on T-shirts—one of the many quirks that are part of his persona as a successful baseball manager. Juárez has no idea if Maddon ever made that T-shirt, but his comment captured a moment of understanding between the new and old Hazletons, between the young son of Mexican immigrants, who was born there in the 1990s, and the grown grandson of Italian immigrants, whose family settled there almost a century ago.

Since 2010 Maddon has been on a crusade to bring the older and newer residents of his hometown together. That year he spent Christmas in Hazleton and was shocked to find the city he had grown up in so angry and divided. The next night he joined his cousin, Elaine Curry, a local community leader, for dinner with one of the Spanish-speaking families in town. He remembers thinking that his experience that night was just like what he remembered from their family dinners when he was a child, where there were always three or four generations present, children running around, and two languages spoken. "My god, this is exactly what my house used to look like in the fifties and the sixties," Maddon has said. And he realized that night that history was repeating itself—that the immigrants who had come to his hometown were there to revitalize it in the same way his grandparents' generation had done a century ago when they arrived from Europe.

But by the 1990s that Hazleton—the dynamic city that had once boasted a thriving downtown with restaurants, a theater, and a streetcar and had been among the first three in the United States to get electric street lights—had become a shadow of what it once was. When the mines closed in the 1950s, the city had entered a long slide, shedding jobs and losing population steadily for decades.

Then, in the mid-1990s, the city hit a home run. A group of business leaders, calling themselves CanDo, built three industrial parks and began attracting major national and international companies to put warehouses and factories there. State tax breaks and a successful marketing campaign convinced the companies that Hazleton was strategically located on two major highways and had a competitive workforce.

Amazon built a major distribution center in Hazleton. Cargill built a slaughterhouse. Bimbo Bakeries took over the old Stroehmann's bakery facility and then built a new, even larger one for its many other products. By the early 2000s, the city's economy—and its population—were expanding again for the first time in decades.

But the companies weren't from Hazleton, and many of the workers weren't either. Mexicans and later other Latin Americans living in New York and New Jersey moved in to take some of the jobs. They were attracted by the steady wages and the city's low housing costs. In 1990 only 4 percent of the city's residents identified as Hispanic or Latino in the census, but by 2010 it was 37 percent, and today it's around half. It was a massive wave of change, not unlike what the city had experienced a century earlier when Italian, Irish, and eastern European immigrants poured into the city to take the expanding mining and textile jobs.

And the newcomers did not come to work only in the factories and warehouses. Many took their savings and started small businesses, often Mexican restaurants, Dominican grocery stores, Puerto Rican bodegas, and even a Peruvian American-run newspaper, alongside the few pizzerias, diners, and retail stores that remained. Hazleton's old business corridor, Wyoming Street, mostly boarded up at the end of the 1990s, sprung to life again with small shops and eateries that had Spanish names. When developers restored a few of the stately old buildings on Broad Street, the city's main artery, most of the new commercial tenants were enterprises with Spanish names. After all, immigrants drive much of the growth of small businesses across the United States, since they are more than twice as likely as native-born Americans to start a small business.

And even the largely shuttered Alter Street Business Corridor, a few blocks away, came back to life with ethnic markets and restaurants, including Demetrio Juárez's restaurant El Mariachi. When Juárez first rented the building, he found old movie posters in the basement—John Wayne, Marilyn Monroe, Frank Sinatra—his own personal connection to the past of his new hometown. It turns out that the boarded-up building he had just rented had been a thriving movie theater during better days.

But the backlash came quickly. After the killing of a young man born in Hazleton, apparently by two Dominican immigrants, the mayor at the time, Lou Barletta, decided he would take action. Partnering with national advocates who were trying to restrict immigration, the city council passed this century's first municipal ordinance aimed at outlawing anyone from renting to or hiring someone who lacked legal papers. Some residents would later question why he focused on immigrants rather than crime, but Barletta was clearly channeling a deeper sense of unease running through the community.

Crime usually drops in communities when immigrants move in, and national statistics suggest that immigrants—and Mexican immigrants in particular—commit far fewer crimes than native-born Americans. In fact, they have incarceration rates only a fifth to a tenth that of native-born Americans, according to some studies. But Hazleton was a bit unusual. Many of the immigrant families moving in had children born and raised in New York City, and they brought big-city ways to the small town in the mountains. Crime rates never became particularly high in Hazleton—and they were always below the average for the state as a whole—but they did go up for a few years in the early 2000s before dropping back again recently, and the increase was enough to raise legitimate concerns in the community.

Violence was a two-way street, as it turned out. Soon after the killing that sparked the local legislation, a group of white teenagers, in 2008, beat a twenty-five-year-old Mexican immigrant to death in the small town of Shenandoah, right next door to Hazleton, while yelling, "Go back to Mexico." For both sides, real violence, not just economic and cultural fears, defined the rocky encounter between longtime residents and newcomers and left deep scars that have only now begun to heal.

Over the past decade, Hazleton has evolved, and the two sides have begun to encounter each other in new ways. Joe Maddon and his cousin Elaine Curry, with her husband, Bob, played a major role in this change. After the fateful night when Maddon understood the forces tearing his community apart, he and the Currys, convened a group of residents—some native-born and others immigrant—to create the Hazleton Integration Project (HIP) to build bridges in the community. "In the middle of a city that was torn apart by racial tension," says Bob Curry, "we needed to do something." He adds, "If not, this city is going to die, it's going to blow away."

Today HIP runs a community center for children and youth in what was once an abandoned school building. After school each day, young people gather there for science classes, computer training, and basketball games. And when in town Maddon holds occasional gatherings that bring together old and new residents of the city to celebrate "unity"—the rallying cry of the Hazleton Integration Project. Occasionally he brings other baseball greats, like Cal Ripken Jr., to these meetings to attract the city's residents. One year HIP even sponsored a Unity Walk through the city, drawing one of the most diverse groups of town residents ever to come together.

Still, a huge gulf remains. Newcomers and longtime residents mostly eat in different restaurants, often shop at different stores, and attend different church services. Even at a recent HIP celebration, the distance was visible: mostly white residents gathered to watch a folk singing group, while three blocks away a Mexican dance troupe performed for a mostly Latino audience on the steps of the Catholic Church. Amilcar Arroyo, a member of the HIP board and publisher of the city's Spanish-language newspaper, says that Hazleton today is "like a river that seems calm on the surface but has strong currents below."

But beneath the surface things are changing too gradually. A few eateries, like Frankie's Pizza, a local institution, have figured out how to cater to both newcomers and longtime residents. The owners have a new Spanish-language menu, which has helped draw in a new clientele and boosted business. El Mariachi too is filled with both English and Spanish speakers every day, and Demetrio Juárez notes with pride, "Even city council members eat here." And the schools, the local YMCA, and even the annual Hazleton Day celebration have increasingly become key spots where new and old residents find themselves in the same place, if not always truly together.

Most longtime residents of Hazleton recognize that the city is growing again—both in population and economically—for the first time in decades, but they are not always comfortable with the way it is changing. It may be more dynamic now than before, but it's not the same city they grew up in, and they often find themselves in the minority when they walk down the streets. Perhaps the original settlers

of Hazleton, themselves the descendant of German and English immigrants, didn't feel much different at the beginning of the twentieth
century when the Italians, Irish, and eastern Europeans arrived. History may not repeat itself, but often it rhymes.

Something similar is taking place across the United States. Many
of the country's small cities and towns are now growing thanks to
the influx of immigrants and their American-born children. Almost
all population growth outside of metro areas in the 2000s came from
the arrival of foreign-born residents and their families. This may help
reverse the decline of these cities and towns, but it doesn't guarantee
that the growth will take place without stresses and strains between
older and newer residents.

In Hazleton city leaders are still trying to figure out how to harness the city's diversity—the heritages and cultural traditions of both
its older and newer residents—as an asset that will attract investment. The Downtown Hazleton Alliance for Progress, a relatively
new nonprofit supported by CanDo, several other civic groups, and
private companies, is now leading a revitalization of downtown, hoping to attract new retail shops, university programs, high-tech companies, and creative professionals. So far it has attracted sixty small
businesses to the downtown area in five years, a good start. Alliance
director Krista Schneider notes that the city's mix of old and new diversity is part of its calling card for the future.

The city hopes, in particular, to attract businesses in the innovation economy. So far, it's been a hard sell, but one high-tech company
has set up shop in Hazleton already, and it's run by a dual citizen of
Mexico and the United States, Francisco Torres-Aranda. He and his
late father, a Mexican businessman and chemist, patented a process
to make environmentally friendly sealants for oil and gas pipes, and

they've hired three dozen local residents to manufacture the product. Torres-Aranda lived most of his life in Mexico, but he and his family chose to move to Hazleton because it was close to the Pennsylvania hometown of Francisco's mother, and they found a beautiful place to build a house on a mountain top just outside the city.

Torres-Aranda has now become a major proponent of Hazleton's development and the benefits of bringing its newer and older residents together. And he's convinced that economics will eventually do what goodwill alone can't accomplish. "The barriers you can't break through with human interaction are sometimes broken by the wallet," he says knowingly.

Even with economic breakthroughs such as these, Maddon and the leaders of the Hazleton Integration Project still believe it is crucial to keep working on the power of human interaction. They are betting that the more people get to know each other across ethnic and linguistic boundaries, the more they will see themselves as part of the same community and recognize similar goals for their future together.

Their latest project is to build a park for the city's young people to learn about gardening and the environment, something that children of new and old families can do together.

And perhaps in a sign of things to come, the donation for the park came from one of the city's largest employers, Bimbo Bakeries, the US subsidiary of the Mexican bread maker.

Demetrio Juárez feels lucky to have made his home in Hazleton and that his children are truly American, but he also can't help feeling a twinge of pride when he thinks back to his brothers and sisters in

Mexico. Most still live in Atzompa, the rural village of three hundred homes where he grew up, or in one of the other small towns nearby, but all of them lead lives they could barely have imagined when they were growing up.

Back then, Atzompa was an isolated rural village, connected to the slightly larger town of Tulcingo De Valle by dirt roads that were hard to cross on a good day and almost impassable when it rained. Located in the verdant mountains of the Sierra Mixteca, which join the states of Puebla, Guerrero, and Oaxaca, this was—and still is— one of Mexico's poorest regions.

Juárez remembers that he first understood how poor his family was on the day that his mother sent him to the store to buy rubber flip-flops, the most rudimentary footwear, because she couldn't stand going barefoot on the dirt roads any longer. He had to buy them on credit because they didn't even have money for such a basic item.

By then Juárez's father had already left for the United States, crossing the border to wash dishes and deliver food for a diner in New York City. Mexicans from states further north had long been crossing the border to work in America, but Juárez's father was one of the first pioneers from his hometown to do so in the early 1970s. By the 1980s and 1990s, a slow outflow had turned into a flood of desperate men and women heading north to try their luck in the United States in order to help their families.

Juárez had managed to finish high school by sleeping on the floor of a school a few towns away, and he wanted to go to college, but, as the oldest son, he realized that he could only realistically help his family get ahead by joining his father.

It was a risky bet, but it paid off. Juárez shared a cramped apartment with his father and a dozen other men in New York and worked long hours delivering food on Manhattan's streets, but he learned English, discovered a passion for food, and eventually was able to send money home by working as a cook in a string of small restaurants.

During a fortuitous encounter, the owner of a restaurant he had once worked for in New York invited him to come open a new diner with him in Hazleton, two hours away. Juárez leapt at the chance. In Hazleton he could afford to rent an entire house for a fraction of the price that he had paid to share a small New York apartment. He was now married to his childhood sweetheart, and they would be able to start a family. And small-town Hazleton even reminded him of Atzompa.

But by then Atzompa was changing too. The success that Juárez and his father enjoyed north of the border was beginning to pay off for the family back home. The money they sent year after year enabled every one of Juárez's brothers and sisters—six in all—to finish high school and five of the six to go to college. The family now includes a lawyer, an accountant, two orthodontists, a dental assistant, and a doctor, his youngest sister, who chairs the surgery department at a regional hospital. It's a gigantic leap in the space of a single generation.

Today a major highway now connects Atzompa to the larger city nearby, Tulcingo De Valle—now just an eight- to ten-minute journey. The village even has a modern school, a small church, a basketball court, electricity, running water, and paved streets. Some of these were built with money sent home by the village residents who migrated abroad, like Juárez and his father. But in other cases, citizens managed to pressure the government to get the services they lacked because they increasingly had the means to worry about their quality of life, not just their survival.

Today Juárez's father lives in Atzompa again, surrounded by his children and grandchildren, who almost all live nearby. The father still can't believe that after all the years working long hours in a foreign country, he can now afford to live comfortably in his hometown and near his family. And the rest of his children—Juárez's siblings—have made good lives for themselves without ever having to migrate. Some have even chosen to live in Atzompa itself, since it's so well connected to the cities where they work.

In fact, relatively few people still migrate from the Sierra Mixteca. But, as in Hazleton, it's impossible to miss the imprint of migration on life in Atzompa and the surrounding region, though in reverse. Over the summer, large banners over the highway welcome back the *paisanos* who live in the United States. Summer and Christmas are times for family reunions, baptisms, *quinceañeras*, birthdays, and weddings, paid for by relatives who live abroad and return to celebrate awash in dollars.

Mexican migrants played a huge role in the region's improving fortunes, but so did other factors. Mexico's transition to democracy in the 1990s gave people a chance to pressure their government for schools, clinics, roads, and public services. Social spending in Mexico almost doubled as a percentage of public expenditures in the span of two decades, as politicians felt obliged to respond to citizen demands.

Demetrio Juárez's next older brother, Salvador, has become one of the region's most important political party leaders, playing a role in getting municipal and state authorities to bring services to the village. While their father, in his younger days, took part in peasant organizations to pressure the government, the children have flexed their muscle at the ballot box—and in the local political parties—to bargain for public investments.

Mexico's decision to open its economy to the world in the 1980s and 1990s also played a part in the country's changing fortunes. Over the past two decades, Mexico has built a dynamic manufacturing sector, tightly linked to the US market and American manufacturers. In contrast to the image of American factories moving to Mexico, many of Mexico's most important industries—including the auto and aerospace industries—manufacture together with American plants, often building different parts for the same final product.

Initially most Mexican factories featured low-wage, low-skilled work for American companies, but increasingly Mexican plants are involved in advanced manufacturing and often include their own research and development facilities. And now many, if not most, of them are Mexican managed and sometimes Mexican owned. Today Mexico produces more engineers per capita than the United States, a major reason for the country's rise into higher-skilled industry.

Since the early 1990s, average income in Mexico has increased by about a third and educational attainment by more than half. Today a quarter of all young people in their teens will end up going to college—three times the percentage of those who did in the early 1990s. The Mexican economy is now the fifteenth largest in the world and is projected to become the seventh or eighth largest by 2050.

Mexico is gradually becoming a more middle-class society as well, with somewhere around 40 percent of all Mexicans—and a majority in most big cities—part of the middle class. In many ways, Americans in the 1950s and 1960s took a similar journey in the postwar economic boom. Life expectancy—a useful indicator of healthcare access—has expanded by four years over the past generation and is now only two years less than that in the United States. These are gigantic changes in just a generation or two.

But not all the changes in Mexico have been good ones. Only fifteen minutes away from Atzompa, the Mexican state of Guerrero has become a hotbed of gang warfare between rival groups that supply illegal drugs to American consumers. Mexico's homicide rate, which had declined steadily from the mid-1990s, tripled between 2007 and 2011. It began to decline after that, as Mexican and American cooperation to dismantle the organized crime groups ramped up. But since 2016, there has again been a spike in violence in Mexico, as the growing demand for heroin in the United States has driven a fight for control over poppy production in Mexico.

And the rise in violence has highlighted another, perhaps even deeper malaise: Mexico's persistent government corruption, which has helped facilitate the rise and survival of the drug gangs. And corruption goes beyond just drug trafficking. It seeps into every form of government activity, from small bribes to get a driver's license to large payoffs to win lucrative government contracts. Corruption undermines public confidence in government, diminishes rule of law, and essentially levies a giant, unseen tax on the country's productive capacity. Mexico has achieved much over the past generation, but it would have accomplished even more if not for this all-pervasive drag on the country's progress.

Mexicans have now been rising up against corruption and starting to hold their government leaders accountable. It's a long, slow process, but all signs indicate that average Mexicans are no longer willing to tolerate business as usual. Civic groups, courageous journalists, and business leaders have all challenged—and begun to reveal—corrupt practices, often at great danger to themselves. And voters have increasingly turned to candidates who make rooting out corruption their top priority, creating the first real wave of elected leaders who feel accountable to citizens to follow through on these promises. There is still a long road ahead—and no guarantee that old practices will disappear—but the battle for a different future in Mexico is underway.

Yet, even with these very real and persistent problems, Mexico has managed to transform itself over the past generation in surprising ways, and this transformation is a big piece of the puzzle of why Mexicans suddenly stopped migrating to the United States in large numbers a decade ago and haven't started again since. Mexico may have a long way to go to become the country most Mexicans want it to be, but few, if any, could have predicted the dramatic turnaround it has made in a generation.

No one is more surprised by—or pleased with—these changes than Demetrio Juárez. Now when he visits Atzompa, he revels in seeing how well his family and his community are doing since he left. And he's even built his own home in the community, an elegant brick house across from his parents, which they use when he's away and where he and his family stay when in town.

But his biggest pride every time he visits isn't that house: it's seeing that his family has managed to make a good life for themselves without having to leave the area. His decision to migrate along with his father ultimately helped the rest of the family stay in Mexico.

Hazleton is in many ways a microcosm of the relationship between Mexico and the United States, both the one that exists between the two countries across our shared border and the one that exists within our own society. After all, Mexico has become both an intricate and intimate part of American life and a proxy for our own hopes, expectations, and frustrations.

Donald Trump's campaign prescriptions for the relationship—a border wall, more deportations, and withdrawal from NAFTA—may be at odds with reality, but they struck a note with an important segment of the American population because they captured the fears of change—and some of its painful realities—that Americans project onto Mexico and Mexicans.

In Hazleton, as in many of the other smaller cities and towns across the United States, Trump's message about Mexico quickly caught on. Voters in Hazleton, who had supported Barack Obama in the two previous elections, gave Trump a comfortable majority in the city, and Trump won by an even bigger margin in the surrounding county.

In many obvious ways, Trump's Hazleton supporters were voting against their own self-interest. After all, the influx of immigrants from Mexico and elsewhere in Latin America has rejuvenated the city, both literally and metaphorically. And some of the area's biggest employers today are Mexican, their presence closely tied to NAFTA. And now they are becoming part of the city's still limited philanthropic and innovation landscape too.

But Mexico has become, in today's America, as much a symbol as a real country next door. Polls show that a quarter to a third of Americans consistently dislike Mexico and see it as a source of unfair trade competition, illegal drugs, and harmful immigration. Mexico and NAFTA have become shorthand for concerns about global trade more generally and whether the American economy is on the right track. Americans also see Mexico's role in the drug trade as an extension of their fears about addiction and overdoses in the United States, an increasingly pervasive reality in many of America's smaller cities and towns. And Mexico often becomes a proxy for all debate about immigration. Even though the era of large-scale immigration from Mexico actually ended more than a decade ago, its effects continue to shape communities across the country.

Mexico has also become a symbol for those on the other side of these issues. A Gallup poll in February 2017, shortly after Trump's inauguration, showed that Mexico's favorability among all Americans had risen to its highest level in recent years, 64 percent. This jump of nine points in two years appeared largely driven by Democrats and Independents who disliked Trump's attacks on the country next door and expressed their opposition to the president by reaffirming their support of Mexico.

Much like those who dislike Mexico, those who appreciate it are also often projecting domestic concerns onto the neighbor next door. Sometimes it seems that Mexico has become more an emblem of Americans' hopes and fears for our own future than a real country that we deal with on its own terms.

Today, with Donald Trump as president, political discussions of Mexico have become focused, above all, on his promise to build "a big, beautiful wall" to keep Mexicans from jumping across the border into the United States. It's sold as a way of stopping illegal immigration and the flow of drugs into American communities, but it's also a powerful symbol of how he wants to deal with the larger forces shaping American society. For Trump and some of his most ardent supporters, the wall is less about effective policy than about making a statement.

Yet the contrast between Trump's symbolic promise to build a border wall and what's actually going on between Mexico and the

United States is dramatic. For more than a decade, Americans and Mexicans have been building bridges across the border—often in very new and creative ways. Some of these bridges are quite literal— like the new bridge that connects San Diego residents to the Tijuana airport, allowing them to use it for international flights as easily as if they were in the United States. The bridge started as a practical solution to San Diego's search for an international airfield that would help connect the city to global markets, but it's also become an affirmation of the growing connection between the two cities.

But most of the bridges are metaphorical. These include the bridges between American farmers and Mexican consumers and those that connect workers in the auto and aerospace industries, who make cars, buses, trains, and airplanes together. There are also strong and expanding bridges between tech innovators in Silicon Valley and Mexico's technology capital, Guadalajara, and still others between Mexican filmmakers and Hollywood producers, who are pushing the boundaries of filmmaking together.

Then there are the bridges among law enforcement officers on both sides of the border who work together, usually out of view, to track and dismantle drug trafficking rings that operate in both countries. A wall would do little, if anything, to stop drug trafficking, which depends mostly on hiding illicit substances in vehicles passing through border ports of entry, not in the vast expanses between them. But cooperation in sharing intelligence across the border and coordination in takedowns of organized crime cells have played a huge role in challenging the hold of these criminal enterprises.

And, of course, there are the migrants, like Demetrio Juárez, who are living bridges, helping develop their communities back home in Mexico while raising their American families in the United States.

And though few Americans yet realize it, this flow is now going in both directions: today around a million Americans live in Mexico, almost as many as in all of Europe, and they too are becoming transmission belts between the two countries.

My family is one of these bridges. My wife, Alejandra, was born and raised in Mexico, not far from where Demetrio Juárez grew up, though she has now spent most of her adult life and professional career in the United States. She has also become an American citizen, though she also remains deeply grateful to her country of origin and proud of its traditions.

I was born and raised in the United States, the son of a Danish immigrant mother and a father from rural Colorado, but moved to Mexico after college, spending several years living and working in low-income communities on the outskirts of Tijuana and engaged with community projects around Mexico. I later went on to conduct research in Mexico, trying to understand how the country next door was changing, and then afterward in the United States, trying to understand how we were changing through our relationship with Mexico. I've been fascinated watching these transformations firsthand, both as a researcher and someone whose family is immersed in them day to day.

By the time Alejandra and I met in the United States, we were both bilingual and bicultural and trying to figure out each other's country—so it was no surprise that friends who knew both of us tried very hard to get us together. That may not have been the spark that actually made us fall in love and eventually marry, but it's certainly what prompted our friends to introduce us the first time.

Since then, we've been privileged to move back and forth easily between the two countries, mostly living in the United States but spending as much time as we can south of the border. Our three young children, all born in the United States, have both countries as part of their heritage and their identity, and they remain close to family on both sides of the border.

But in this, we are only one family among many millions claiming a piece of their lives in each country. Indeed, if economics and common sense are driving Americans and Mexicans together—despite the political rhetoric—the personal ties between people on both sides of the border will likely build the strongest bridges between the two countries. It would be hard to find a Mexican these days who doesn't have family in the United States or an American who doesn't know a Mexican. And with the demographic changes in both countries, these ties are becoming increasingly personal and close, as they are in our own family. It's a relationship of increasing intimacy, not merely of economic convenience.

In the late 1980s, *New York Times* journalist Alan Riding wrote a book titled *Distant Neighbors* to explain how two countries as different as Mexico and the United States could live side by side and yet barely interact with each other. This was before trade, immigration, and the growth of border communities transformed the relationship. People on both sides of the border knew little about those on the other side, and the economies and societies were, in most ways, quite distant from the other.

But today, after more than two decades of rapid change, the reality on the ground is transforming. The United States and Mexico are increasingly integrated and interdependent, far more than most people on both sides of the border could ever have imagined back then—or perhaps most people realize even now. Today we are no longer "distant neighbors," as Riding aptly labeled us, but rather "intimate strangers," deeply connected to each other yet with few of the tools we need to understand our growing intimacy.

This book is a journey through the inevitable forces that are transforming Mexico and the United States and the way we relate to each other—forces that are far more powerful than political rhetoric and that have profound consequences for our daily lives as Americans. It's a chronicle of how Mexico has changed, but even more, of how we in the United States are changing as a result of the encounter with our neighbor next door. It's a story not about a wall but about the bridges we have been building between us and how they will shape our future.

1

"We Built a Bridge Across the Fence"

San Diego and Tijuana Become a Single Metropolitan Area

For more than two decades, politicians and business leaders in San Diego struggled to find a way to build a bigger airport. They knew that without a bigger airfield—one that could accommodate the larger aircraft needed to connect to cities in Asia—theirs would always be a second-tier city, far behind Los Angeles and San Francisco in economic potential. Unfortunately, Lindbergh Field, the city's principal airport, was located next to downtown and couldn't expand beyond a single runway. So while San Diego had emerged in the 1990s and 2000s as a hub for innovation in biotechnology, software, communications technology, and sound equipment, the airport remained an obstacle to the city's economic growth. And even though the city had a burgeoning Mexican-origin community and strong trade links with the country next door, there were few flights to anywhere in Mexico except the capital.

Eventually city leaders hit on a solution: instead of trying to build their own new airport, why not just connect to the much larger airport next door in Tijuana? After all, Tijuana's airport was located right at the border, in clear sight of San Diego, and already had the kind of long runways needed for big airplanes. And not only that, it already had flights to China and Japan.

What if they just built a bridge across the border wall?

The project took a few years to negotiate and bring to fruition, but in December 2015, the two cities inaugurated the pedestrian bridge that now connects San Diego to Tijuana's airport. Passengers coming from the United States park in an American parking lot, check in at a small terminal on the American side of the border, and then walk across the bridge, passing through Mexican immigration and customs on the other side, before heading straight to their gate to catch their flights. Built by private investors from both countries, the bridge was a gamble: no one was quite sure if people living in the United States would really use an airport in Tijuana to travel internationally.

Yet it has been a resounding success: the number of people using the US-side terminal and the pedestrian bridge has far surpassed expectations. The bridge has generated healthy profits for the original investors, as well as paid for its own upkeep and the cost of the extra border inspectors. It's also become an example of how the private and public sectors can work together to solve a pressing problem across two cities and two countries.

But perhaps equally as important, the beautifully designed bridge, which looks like something out of a *Star Wars* set, has become a monument to the new relationship emerging between the two border cities, which increasingly resemble a single metropolitan area. The bridge soars majestically over the rusted border fence below, creating a powerful symbol of how the two cities have been overcoming the distance that once existed between them.

"We built a bridge across the fence," says Denise Moreno Ducheny, a former Democratic California state senator from San Diego who helped promote the project. "It has become a visually powerful symbol of the integration of two municipalities and two states across an international boundary."

Kevin Faulconer, the Republican mayor of San Diego, highlights the bridge as one of many examples of the ongoing cooperation between the two urban areas. "We don't talk about two cities; we talk about one region," he tells me.

Increasingly, he observes, San Diego and Tijuana are planning their future together as a single metropolitan region with economic-development planning taking place in tandem. Many of the industries that are most important to San Diego today are the same ones that are essential to the economy of Tijuana, and many companies have plants on both sides of the border carrying out different parts of the same production process. And cultural offerings, from music to food to wine, increasingly attract people across the border in both directions, as citizens of both countries get to know the offerings on the other side.

This development would have been hard to imagine two decades ago when I lived in the region, first in Tijuana and later in San Diego. Back then, San Diego residents feared the city to their south and saw little advantage in crossing, unless it was to go drinking in one of the tourist bars on Revolution Street, the city's main downtown drag.

Tijuana residents, in turn, envied San Diego's beautiful beaches and cultural offerings but agonized over the time it took to cross the border to take advantage of them—if they even had visas to cross in the first place. The two neighboring cities were actually much further apart than the distance on the map might suggest.

But Tijuana has risen from the ashes of violence and disorder to become one of Mexico's most livable cities, known for its exquisite culinary offerings, its well-respected orchestra and opera, and the successful vineyards that stretch out for miles just south of the city in the Guadalupe Valley. And Tijuana has become, increasingly, a middle-class city. The economy now rests not on piecework factories but rather on advanced manufacturing in medical devices, electronics, and communications equipment—industries with strong counterparts in San Diego—often with research and development (R&D) in both cities.

As Tijuana has transformed itself from a chaotic border town into an increasingly modern city on the rise, its relationship with its northern neighbors has changed too. Once a backroom industrial base for US-owned businesses and a cheap place for an adventurous night out, today the city is an integral part of high-tech supply chains, the home of innovative new businesses, and a cultural mecca for people in Southern California.

San Diego–Tijuana is the world's largest binational metropolitan area, with a population of at least 5 million, and leaders on both sides of the border have started to plan for a future together, with shared production chains, joint proposals to host international events, and a large international airport on the Tijuana side of the border. Today the two cities are the combined hub of a shared cultural and economic space that stretches all the way from the vineyards of the Guadalupe Valley to the production studios of Los Angeles.

Javier Plascencia began planning his restaurant in Tijuana in 2008. That year more than eight hundred people were murdered in the city as rival cartels fought for control of the drug trade. Bodies were decapitated, burned, and hung from bridges. Gangs fought gun battles in broad daylight and funded themselves with kidnappings. "We knew we were opening up in a period in which there might be only five clients," Plascencia admits. "But we were making a statement that we were going to invest."

There were, it turned out, considerably more than five clients. By the time Misión 19 opened its doors three years later, cartel violence had declined dramatically. Star chef and television personality Rick Bayless visited. So did CNN's *No Reservations* star Anthony Bourdain, along with contributors to the *New York Times*, *San Diego Magazine*, the *New Yorker*, StreetGourmetLA.com, and *All Things Considered*. Now on any given night, Plascencia's customers are a boisterous mix of local Tijuana diners and American visitors.

Patrons come for Chinese-style roasted pork with cilantro, chilis, and tortillas and for risotto with wild mushrooms, huitlacoche, and epazote. Plascencia's dishes, presented with artistic flair, fuse the flavors of Mexico—especially Tijuana's smoky street food—with those of the Mediterranean and Asia. "That's what Tijuana is," Plascencia says, "this mix of cultures."

Some know this eclectic but emphatically *Tijuanense* style as Baja Med, and Misión 19's executive chef has become its most visible ambassador. Plascencia, whose talent in the kitchen and movie-star good looks sometimes seem at odds with his natural shyness, grew up cooking in his parents' Italian restaurant and chain of pizzerias scattered around Tijuana. He attended high school in San Diego, where he learned to surf, play golf, and speak fluent English, before coming back to Tijuana to take over the kitchen in a new upscale Italian restaurant his parents had just started.

Then he decided to branch out and start Misión 19, focused on Mexican food. "Halfway through my career I changed and went into Mexican food," he says, "back to my roots." At Misión 19, most of his ingredients travel no more than 120 miles to the restaurant. The bulk of the wines are from the nearby Guadalupe Valley, whose vineyards produce some of the earthiest and most flavorful wines in the Americas.

Misión 19 may be Tijuana's best-known restaurant, but dozens of sit-down establishments, street stands, and even food trucks attract culinary tourists from north of the border. This city previously known for its gritty industrial complexes and seamy tourist traps has undergone a dramatic cultural transformation in the past decade.

Tijuana now has several popular art galleries and an expanded cultural institute. The city even holds an annual opera festival, part of which takes place in the streets of Colonia Libertad, a working-class neighborhood that overlooks the border fence. It was originally the inspiration of a local man in the rough-and-tumble neighborhood who loved the opera and started it as a street fair.

Nowhere are these changes more visible than in downtown Tijuana, where visitors once encountered kitschy souvenir shops, cheap bars, and brothels. But the violence that overwhelmed the city from 2007 to 2009 drove out the tourists who used to frequent Revolution Street and ultimately led to the establishment of new businesses that catered more to Tijuana's own population. Today a street-food market, two craft breweries, and dozens of small restaurants line the thoroughfare, catering mostly to locals as well as a handful of well-off tourists from the United States. On weekends one of the buildings becomes a market for local artisans, whose small stands spill out onto the street. A few bars and table-dance places still dot the area, giving downtown Tijuana the feel of a transitional neighborhood, but it's abundantly clear which way things are transitioning.

The anchor of the new downtown is, not surprisingly, another of Plascencia's restaurants, Caesar's, the place where the Caesar salad was invented in the 1920s, either by Italian-immigrant owner Caesar Cardini or by his chef and compatriot, Livio Santini. If Misión 19 is Plascencia's vision for the future of his hometown, Caesar's—which the Plascencia family reopened in 2010—is his homage to the city's past. "It's an icon of the city," he says. "It's one of the few pieces of cultural history that we have here."

In a city where everything seems to have been built yesterday—and often on top of whatever was there before—Caesar's was a constant in Tijuana from the 1920s through the early 1980s, entertaining Hollywood stars, politicians, and gangsters. After the owners closed it in the late 1980s because of labor and financial troubles, it was turned into a dive bar and table-dance venue separated by a gaudy red curtain. I remember visiting once in the 1990s, attracted inside by a small plaque on the wall that explained how the Caesar salad had been invented there. I was shocked to find how seedy it had become and left even before ordering a drink.

Plascencia's brother, a jazz musician, first spotted the opportunity. Passing by Caesar's after an all-night gig at a downtown club, he saw that the restaurant's furniture had been put out on the street and that it must be going out of business. He phoned Javier Plascencia and told him that this was their opportunity to resurrect a piece of the city's history.

Plascencia's family obtained the lease and set about restoring the restaurant—completely refurbishing the once elegant mahogany bar, adding period photographs and antique coffee machines, and creating a menu based on the restaurant's continental past but with a contemporary Baja Med flair mixed in.

The timing couldn't have been better. As Plascencia and his family opened Caesar's and Misión 19, Tijuana was undergoing a huge economic transformation, almost unnoticed by city residents. In the 1970s and 1980s, Tijuana had grown exponentially as hardworking women and men from south and central Mexico moved north looking for opportunities on the border. The children of many of these families had done well, acquiring education and professional success far beyond their parents' dreams, and they began to form an emerging middle class that could afford to invest in leisure and cultural activities.

At first they had crossed the border for entertainment and leisure activities, but increasingly they wanted to enjoy life in their own city, without sitting in a line to enter the country next door. They were ready for their own city to have its own cultural offerings.

Beach resorts in Rosarito and Ensenada, towns just south of the city, and the burgeoning vineyards of the Guadalupe Valley became the first places developed for entertainment, but soon restaurants, cafés, and movie theaters started popping up in Tijuana itself. The group that built the dramatic glass-paneled office tower where Misión 19 is located not only invested nearly $500,000 to bring in Plascencia but also made space for a café, a bar, a wine shop, an art gallery, an event center, and a sky garden. Hovering over the bustling Zona Río, the Leadership in Energy and Environmental Design (LEED)–certified building is as much a symbol of the new Tijuana as the city's star chef.

So too are the city's opera and symphony, both increasingly prominent throughout Mexico and the US Southwest, where they tour periodically. Then there is the Center for the Musical Arts, a graduate university that is training a new generation of musicians. And there is no shortage of art galleries, including El Túnel—the Tunnel—one of the city's most experimental arts venues, whose name speaks to its not-so-distant past as a building that once hid a drug tunnel under the border into the United States.

That, in a nutshell, is the new Tijuana: classy and entrepreneurial, yet edgy and unpredictable. It's a world-class city on the rise but not yet completely beyond its past as a hub for piecework, cheap tourism, and contraband. This combination gives the city a distinct flair—exciting but with an undercurrent of daring.

Twenty years ago, it would have been nearly impossible to imagine the Tijuana of today. When I moved there in 1992, it was still known as the "appliance capital of the world" because of the countless refrigerators, television sets, and dishwashers manufactured in the factory parks that dotted the city.

The factory jobs were often repetitive and low paying, but they provided regular wages and basic benefits, advantages unheard of for many workers elsewhere in Mexico. People from other parts of the country streamed into Tijuana to get work in the factories—and in the construction and consumer industries that grew up around them.

By the mid-1990s, most residents lived in makeshift neighborhoods on the outskirts of town, many without electricity or running water.

I lived in one of these neighborhoods for several years in the 1990s. We were a community of roughly a quarter million people living on the far side of a mountain that separated us from the rest of the city. A single paved street wound its way around the mountain, connecting us to a bumpy, potholed avenue that eventually ambled its way into the main part of the city, often an hour-long journey. During the rainy season, the remaining roads in our neighborhood, all made of compacted dirt, became thick with mud, while in the summer they become slippery with dust.

My neighbors taught me how to connect wires to the power lines overhead to steal electricity for a few light bulbs at night. During the day we burned trash in a pungent haze to make up for the lack of garbage collection. Many of those who moved to Tijuana in the 1970s, 1980s, and 1990s lived in neighborhoods like this one and worked in the low-wage factories that surrounded them.

These factories, known as maquiladoras, were spawned by Mexican legislation in the 1960s that allowed foreign-owned companies to set up shop in the border region to manufacture goods for the US market. They were exempt from import and export tariffs and could hire Mexican workers at a fraction of the cost of US labor. The maquiladora program had been designed to create job growth in the border region after the US government suspended the bracero program, a migrant guest worker program begun during World War II to bring Mexican farmworkers into the United States for short periods. When that program ended in 1964, the flow of Mexicans to the United States continued, but some stayed in border towns and cities to work in the maquiladoras.

By the late 1990s, Tijuana had somewhere between 1.5 million and 2 million residents, making it Mexico's fourth-largest metropolitan area. But by the 2000s the factories could no longer compete based on low wages alone, especially as Mexican salary levels began to increase. Many closed down, and manufacturers moved to countries in Central America, the Caribbean, and Southeast Asia that offered lower-cost labor. Residents of Tijuana worried about the complete collapse of the maquiladora industry, which had been the backbone of the city's economic growth.

Yet as the new millennium dawned, without most people noticing, advanced manufacturing plants, ones that depended on more skilled labor, had begun taking root in Tijuana. Tijuana couldn't compete based on low wages any more, but it had an increasingly educated workforce that attracted companies to put more sophisticated operations there. Many of those companies were either based or had major operations in San Diego, giving the two-city combination a huge comparative advantage. Two industries in particular—medical devices and communications equipment—took off as anchors of Tijuana's new growth, because they were already important industries in San Diego.

Plantronics, one of the largest audio-engineering companies in the world, which supplies headsets for air-traffic controllers, pilots, astronauts, emergency workers, and ordinary consumers, was one of the first communications equipment companies to discover the city. While earlier maquiladoras had used low-skilled workers, Plantronics needed people who could assemble precision equipment. And it also built its own design team of more than a hundred engineers drawn from Tijuana's universities, which were pumping out a new generation of educated professionals. To retain employees, the company invested in a gym, a basketball court, and employee-wellness programs.

As more technologically complex industries have taken root, leadership of the factories has also become increasingly local. In the 1980s and 1990s, foreign managers from the United States, Europe, and Asia typically ran the maquiladoras, overseeing Mexican workers on the assembly lines. Now much, if not most, of the maquiladora management consists of Mexican professionals—people like Alejandro Bustamante, who ran the local Plantronics plant for years and now heads the company's global operations in the United States, Mexico, and China.

Mexican engineers also increasingly staff research and development teams, like the one at Plantronics. And at some factories, like that of nearby Parker, a maker of custom-built packaging with plants on both sides of the border, the R&D team is binational. Engineers in San Diego and Tijuana meet weekly—sometimes several times a week—to design products for the company's plants in each city.

The shift of Tijuana's economy toward advanced manufacturing and engineering has driven the growth of the city's middle class—the people who today eat in Javier Plascencia's restaurants, attend the city's opera performances, and participate in gallery openings at El Túnel. And this new middle class largely consists of the children of men and women who came to Tijuana from the 1970s to the 1990s to work in the city's assembly plants.

Today, even the city's low-income settlements have been transformed. The neighborhood where I once lived is now crisscrossed by paved streets and connected to downtown by a modern highway. Not only do residents have electricity, running water, and regular trash

service, but small stores and quite a few large, modern shopping pla-
zas dot their brightly lit streets. And the neighborhood is bookended
by factory parks with advanced manufacturing plants making medical devices, packaging, and car parts.

On one visit, I spent an hour searching for a friend's home that
I had visited dozens of times before. Finally, I realized that her once
humble wood house on a dirt road had metamorphosed into a giant concrete home with metal gates on a paved street. In the space
of a few years, all my markers had been turned upside down, and
I couldn't get my bearings even in the parts of the neighborhood I'd
known best. Like my friend, most of the neighborhood's residents
have gone from dirt poor to respectably working-class in a generation, with quite a number of educated professionals among them.

And while advanced manufacturing now forms the backbone of
the economy, the city is becoming home to innovative start-ups that
take advantage of proximity to California. One of the more successful
ones, Boxel, is an animation company that contracts with Hollywood
studios, and the city has smaller ventures in everything from video
services to online marketing that seek to tap the big economy to the
north. Tijuana even has its own innovation hub, BITCenter, which has
incubated many of the start-ups.

Javier Plascencia too has taken advantage of the binational market
in new and creative ways. Not only does he draw much of his clientele
for Misión 19 from the other side of the border, but in 2015 he opened
a new, upscale restaurant in San Diego's hip Little Italy neighborhood
near downtown. The restaurant is called Bracero, or "farmworker," in
honor of the low-wage workers who once came to the United States
and the simple food they ate.

But much like his hometown, Plascencia's San Diego eatery shows how something impressive can be built on humble foundations. Zagat named it one of 2015's top restaurant openings in the United States.

As José Galicot prepared for heart surgery in San Diego, he was surprised to learn from his doctor that the heart valve he was about to receive was made in Tijuana, in one of the many medical device plants that now employ around 40,000 city residents. A successful telecommunications entrepreneur in Tijuana, Galicot could afford good medical care, so he had sought out the best doctors he could find in a prestigious hospital in San Diego. But as he prepared for surgery, he found that the critical piece of equipment in the heart valve that would ensure his survival actually came from a factory in his hometown.

As he recovered, Galicot, then in his mid-seventies, began thinking of other things he admired about Tijuana, and he developed the conviction that he should try to help change the image of his city among both its residents and the wider public, including his friends and colleagues in San Diego.

When restored to full health, Galicot, whose passion elicits enthusiasm from those around him, convened several of Tijuana's business and civic leaders and suggested they think of what they could do to promote their town. This sparked the idea for Tijuana Innovadora (Innovative Tijuana), a landmark event highlighting the city's economic, cultural, and civic renaissance.

Galicot, a committed Zionist organizer in his youth, used everything he had learned about mobilizing people to get this project off the ground. He began by signing up the city's business leaders to help, starting with Alejandro Bustamante of Plantronics. Together they went to twenty-five companies and asked them to pay anywhere from $15,000 to $50,000 to display their products at the festival. "I was convincing them to show their booth to a public that didn't need their products," Galicot says, smiling. After all, most of the companies sell their products abroad, not in Tijuana. Yet all of them said yes. The displays may not have won the companies new clients, but they gave residents a stronger sense of the many things made in their city, from sophisticated medical devices to sound systems to drones and robots.

The first citywide event was celebrated in 2010, right as the gang violence was subsiding; it was followed by similar massive events in 2012 and 2014. Galicot coaxed top talent from around the world to participate, including former US vice president Al Gore and Nobel Prize–winning chemist Mario Molina to talk about the environment; Twitter cofounder Biz Stone, Apple cofounder Steve Wozniak, and Mexican billionaire Carlos Slim to discuss innovation; TV and radio host Larry King and political scientist Francis Fukuyama to address politics; and, of course, Javier Plascencia to speak about the city's culinary scene. And the talks were only part of the multiday events: there were food stands showcasing the local Baja Med cuisine, as well as musicians, dancers, and stalls displaying the many goods produced by companies in the city.

Several hundred thousand people participated in the first Tijuana Innovadora festival, and the numbers grew over the next two festivals as word spread about the events. People poured in from neighborhoods throughout the city, including the one I once lived in on the outskirts of town. Most came for the festival's free concerts and cheap food but stayed because they were amazed by what they learned about their city.

Galicot was concerned that the first event drew relatively few Americans across the border. So the next two events, in 2012 and 2014, focused squarely on the relationship between California and Tijuana. In 2012, his staff bused thousands of special guests from downtown San Diego to the festival, whose main theme that year was cross-border linkages. Organizers especially targeted opinion leaders in San Diego—politicians, businesspeople, journalists, and the heads of universities and nonprofit groups—who, he was convinced, would tell others about their experience. In 2014 the event centered on the connection between Mexico and Mexicans living in the United States. As word spread about Tijuana Innovadora, more and more people crossed the border to take part.

Tijuana Innovadora has since inaugurated other projects. One is a cultural center in Tijuana's historically poorest and most violent neighborhood, Camino Verde, now run by the former director of Bellas Artes, Mexico City's equivalent of the Kennedy Center in Washington, DC. The cultural center attracts major cultural figures to this neighborhood, once shunned by outsiders, for presentations and interactive workshops.

Another is a traveling art exhibition that combines famous Mexican painters with budding local talent. The collection began with a gift of paintings from Raúl Anguiano, one of Mexico's most prominent artists, to Tijuana Innovadora. Galicot jokes that it may be "the world's only homeless art museum," since he hasn't found a permanent space for the collection, but as a result, it travels from gallery to gallery around the city and occasionally crosses the border to locations in San Diego. Homeless it may be, but the exhibition is well traveled, highly regarded, and, by now, thoroughly binational.

The genius of Tijuana Innovadora was not inventing a new Tijuana but showing city residents what they already had and connecting different groups that were doing amazing things—from chefs and painters to inventors and entrepreneurs. Says Tonatiuh Guillén, longtime president of the Northern Border College and a frequent participant in Tijuana Innovadora activities, "There are concentric circles around different issues, and the great innovation of Tijuana Innovadora was to connect these together."

Guillén believes that Tijuana has always been much more "horizontal" than other places in Mexico. Tijuana was more like the western United States—a frontier that people moved to in search of opportunities or to escape problems elsewhere—than like the rest of Mexico, which was built on a history of conquest and hierarchical relationships.

Guillén, who grew up on the border as the son of working-class transplants from southern Mexico, is himself a product of this horizontal environment, rising to head the city's most prestigious university by dint of talent rather than connections. So too is Galicot, the son of Sephardic Jewish immigrants from Istanbul, who made his fortune developing telecommunications hardware. And so is Plascencia, the descendant of Italian immigrants whose family built an empire on pizzas and pastas before he helped start a local nouvelle cuisine revolution. In a city of mobility and innovation, Tijuana Innovadora helped connect different people and fields and then present them to the world.

As the violence subsided and Tijuana's economic strength and cultural palette became more visible, not only Tijuana's residents but also their American neighbors in San Diego discovered the city. And

Tijuana Innovadora, by getting people from San Diego to visit, helped build a new perception in the city across the border.

In mid-2012, a poll conducted by the San Diego Foundation showed that only 9 percent of San Diego's residents thought their city's future was closely tied to Tijuana's. The city next door was, at best, an afterthought; at worst, an embarrassment to be avoided. Three years later, a second poll conducted by the University of California, San Diego, found that more than 70 percent of San Diego residents saw Tijuana as a major part of their future. These were different polls that asked questions about Tijuana in slightly different ways— but the shift in attitudes is still remarkable.

Galicot, honoring his heritage, likes to use the Hebrew expression *kollektiviut ra'yonit* to describe the ethos of Tijuana Innovadora. "It means 'a common ideological concept,'" he explains—building a common view of a city on the rise. And that collective vision is no longer limited to Tijuana. People on both sides of the border are now dreaming together about the geographical area they share.

There is perhaps no more important evangelist for the relationship between San Diego and Tijuana than Malin Burnham, San Diego's most successful real estate developer and prominent philanthropist, still every bit the image of a successful businessman at the age of ninety—tall, fit, perpetually well dressed, with a regal shock of white hair. But he worries that the border, as it's now managed, is too inefficient and slow to keep up with the integration going on between the two cities.

"We are doing so many things together culturally and economically," he says. "But we could do it ten times faster." Long border wait times dissuade people from crossing over to the other city just to have dinner, see a concert, or attend a meeting, and wait times essentially operate as a tax on goods produced jointly on both sides of the border in shared manufacturing operations.

In 2007, long before others were paying attention to the city next door, Burnham helped spearhead a new group, the Smart Border Coalition, which brought together business leaders from both cities to press for border procedures that would allow goods and people to move across quickly and efficiently. A prominent Republican whose Rolodex includes billionaires, movie stars, and political leaders, Burnham believes that the real danger at the border stems not from immigrants coming across but from inefficient security measures that damage the economic vitality and natural linkages between the two economies.

Every time a truck idles for three or four hours to cross the border, the cost of whatever it is transporting goes up, he notes. Toyota estimates that each of the cars it produces on the Mexican side of the border, in the neighboring city of Tecate, costs $600 more because of the wait at the border. And businesses such as Parker, where binational teams work together in both cities, must count on hour-long waits each time team members cross the border to meet. No one knows for sure what the overall cost of these delays are, but a few years ago the San Diego Council of Government estimated that they were reducing gross domestic product (GDP) in the region by $6 billion a year—$4 billion of that on the San Diego side—and costing both cities tens of thousands of jobs.

Burnham's Smart Border Coalition has lobbied for more express lanes to allow frequent border crossers—including shipping companies vetted by the Department of Homeland Security—to cross quickly; for a new rail border crossing that would allow cheap and efficient shipment of heavy products like cars and airplane parts; and for the creation of a new truck crossing east of San Diego. The group also helped drive the conversation about—and eventually find common ground on—the bridge to the Tijuana airport, the new symbol of collaboration between the cities.

The board of the Smart Border Coalition has grown into a who's who of business leaders from the two cities, including Tijuana Innovadora founder José Galicot. Every two months they convene a working group of representatives from the major government agencies involved in border facilitation, including local, state, and federal authorities, and once a year they hold an annual event that has become one of San Diego's top gatherings and includes occasional visits by cabinet secretaries from the two countries.

While the Smart Border Coalition is the most prominent cross-border organization, it is hardly the only one. It seems that almost every organization, from museums to business associations to political groups, has gotten on the binational bandwagon. The San Diego Association of Governments (SANDAG), which brings together the municipalities and counties in the San Diego region, now offers an observer seat for the Mexican government and provides office space in its downtown San Diego building for representatives of the Tijuana city government and the Baja California state government to facilitate a constant exchange of information. One of SANDAG's most prominent task forces is the Committee on Binational Regional Opportunities, which meets monthly to tackle shared economic challenges such as border facilitation and workforce planning.

The San Diego Chamber of Commerce, headed by former Republican mayor Jerry Sanders, is also a leading advocate of binational integration. The chamber and its Tijuana counterpart organize a trip each year for business and political leaders from the two cities to both Washington, DC, and Mexico City to lobby authorities in both countries on improving border transportation.

José Galicot also convenes a bimonthly meeting of Tijuana Innovadora in San Diego that is attended by members of the Smart Border Coalition, SANDAG, and the Chamber of Commerce. In the past few years, San Diego's top business, political, and academic leaders have worked within multiple forums to brand their city as part of a large, binational metropolitan region, understanding that this may be their city's comparative advantage.

Not all residents of San Diego share this vision, of course. Plenty of San Diegans have never crossed the border, and some people in Tijuana still don't have a visa that would allow them to do so. And a return of violence in Tijuana or a major terrorist attack in the United States could easily sever the growing integration between the cities. But that hasn't deterred leaders in the two cities from throwing their lots in together.

For more than a decade, Malin Burnham has floated a proposal among civic leaders on both sides of the border that would take the relationship to an entirely different level. "Why not hold a binational Olympics in San Diego and Tijuana?" he asks. South Korea and Japan already hosted a binational World Cup in 2002, but no one has ever attempted to organize the Olympics, the ultimate symbol of global accord, in two bordering countries.

Unlike the 2002 World Cup, where teams had to get on airplanes to fly from country to country, a San Diego/Tijuana Olympics would take place within the same metropolitan region, with short drives between the two countries. The Tijuana/San Diego metropolitan area includes two major aquatic training centers, one on either side of the border, and several stadiums, counting university and professional arenas on both sides.

That dream may still be a distant reality. The two cities did launch a joint exploratory bid to host the Olympics a few years ago, but at the time Olympic Committee rules didn't allow for a two-country event. Eventually, San Diego submitted a proposal to host the 2024 Olympics, prominently noting its complementarities with Tijuana, but without success. With Los Angeles now hosting the 2028 Olympics, a San Diego/Tijuana Olympics may be a long way off, but some events could possibly be held in the binational region.

While people far from the US–Mexican border might think of the region as filled with chaos and calamity, those who live near it increasingly see the connection between the two sides as a competitive advantage. Nowhere is that truer than in San Diego and Tijuana. Tijuana's rebirth as a cultural mecca and a hub for advanced manufacturing has caught the attention of its neighbors to the north, who increasingly see that they are better off thinking in terms of a shared binational region than of two separate cities.

And while people far away from the border argue about how to close it off, residents of San Diego and Tijuana are plotting to build bridges across it—by sharing airports, cultural offerings, businesses, and even sporting events—so that they can accomplish even more together.

2

"North America Has Become a Shared Production Platform"

Trade Transforms the Mexican and American Economies

When Terry Wanzek thinks of Mexico, he thinks about soybeans and pinto beans and occasionally corn and wheat. A successful North Dakota family farmer, he once visited Mexico City, but his real connection to the country is through his crops. Speaking to me from his seeding machine, which buzzes as it adjusts and turns, he says, "Every bit of demand in Mexico helps our price." Roughly 30 percent of the edible beans in North Dakota go to Mexico, he notes, double the amount for the rest of the United States, making Mexico a major market in a state that depends heavily on the success of its farmers.

For American agriculture, Mexico has become a vital export market, the top destination for corn, dry beans, dairy, and chicken and the second market for wheat, soybeans, pork, beef, and many other products. In a decade, from 2005 to 2015, Mexico doubled its imports of American farm products. In return, Americans buy much of their fruits and vegetables, from strawberries to tomatoes, from Mexico.

"We depend on these overseas outlets to keep us out of the red and be profitable," says Wanzek, who sends much of his soybean and pinto bean crop to Mexico each year. And though most of his corn and wheat production is for domestic consumption in the United States, he points out that all farmers who grow these crops depend on demand in Mexico to keep prices up and ensure they can make a living.

But agriculture is only a microcosm of the larger trade relationship between the two countries. Since the North American Free Trade Agreement (NAFTA) went into effect in 1994, trade among the three signatories—the United States, Mexico, and Canada—has quadrupled, and together they constitute the largest trading bloc in the world, outpacing even the European Union.

Over a third of all American exports go to the NAFTA partners, 18.5 percent to Canada and 15.8 percent to Mexico in 2017, making them by far the two largest buyers of American-made products in the world. American producers export more to Mexico alone than to China, Japan, and South Korea—combined. And they send more exports to Mexico than to the United Kingdom, Germany, France, the Netherlands, and Belgium—America's principal European markets—put together.

At least thirty of the fifty US states depend on Mexico as one of their two principal export markets. This is not surprising in the border region—Texas and Arizona send almost half their exports to Mexico—but it's also true for agricultural states like Nebraska, Iowa, Kansas, South Dakota, and North Dakota and for industrial states like

Michigan, Ohio, Pennsylvania, Tennessee, North Carolina, and New Jersey.

The United States imports a great deal from China but exports comparatively little to it. In contrast, Canada and Mexico have surprisingly balanced trade with the United States, both buying and selling goods. The United States has a slight trade deficit on industrial goods with Mexico but usually a surplus on agricultural goods, energy, and services. And not only do we trade goods with each other, but increasingly we build products together to sell to the rest of the world.

No one could have imagined this amount of commercial exchange in 1990, when the three countries first started discussing a free trade agreement. Canada and the United States already had a robust trading relationship and a free trade agreement that went into effect the year before. But Mexico and the United States had only modest economic relations and very limited political engagement. Americans knew little about their neighbor to the south, and Mexicans greatly distrusted their neighbor to the north.

But Mexico's economy had been in a tailspin throughout most of the 1980s as the result of a global debt crisis and the government's own mismanagement, and newly elected president Carlos Salinas (1988–1994) was looking for a way to turn it around. A decade before, American president Ronald Reagan had proposed a trade agreement with Mexico but was rebuffed. Now Salinas proposed the idea to Reagan's successor, President George H. W. Bush.

The timing worked in Mexico's favor. The Berlin Wall had come crashing down just months before, and the Soviet Union was in the process of imploding. Bush was a strong believer in free trade, but he also saw a new world order emerging after the end of the Cold War, and he wanted to ensure a close relationship with America's two closest neighbors. This was an opening with Mexico he didn't want to miss, and the Canadians agreed to join in to create a three-way trade area.

It took two years to negotiate NAFTA, with all three countries bargaining hard for the access they wanted for their products. The final agreement eliminated or phased out tariffs on most goods and services within the trading area, although a few had longer phase-out times than others.

NAFTA was approved quickly by the Canadian parliament and the Mexican Congress but weathered a bruising fight in the US Congress. In fact, it only passed after new president Bill Clinton, who had campaigned against NAFTA, decided to support the agreement and was able to convince the other two countries to sign side agreements on labor and environmental issues, as well as to create a North American Development Bank that would help develop the US-Mexican border region.

NAFTA, one of the first trade agreements in the world that included both highly developed and emerging economies, has remained controversial in all three countries. It was expected to produce benefits that no trade agreement could possibly generate but has also been saddled with the blame for maladies that go far beyond what it could plausibly have caused.

The best available evidence shows that some American low-wage jobs did transition to Mexico, especially in the early years, and some factories moved parts of their operations there, but increased US exports to Mexico more than balanced these losses out. Shared manufacturing across the three countries helped many US industries compete in the global economy in ways they otherwise couldn't have. And for Mexico, NAFTA helped turn around its once struggling economy and, over time, grow its middle class.

After more than two decades, the American economy has become deeply intertwined with the economies of its neighbors, and tearing them apart would be almost impossible—and certainly extremely painful. Millions of American jobs depend on trade with Mexico—on both exports to Mexican consumers and on industries in which the two countries share production seamlessly.

President Donald Trump was elected to office after calling NAFTA "the worst trade agreement ever" and threatening to withdraw, but he soon came face-to-face with the complexities of doing so and the consequences for the United States. At one point, in April 2017, as he approached his first hundred days in office, he appeared poised to withdraw from the trade agreement. According to multiple accounts, Secretary of Agriculture Sonny Purdue managed to pull him back from this decision, in large part by warning of the effect it would have on America's farmers, some of Trump's most loyal supporters.

"A trade war would not help anyone," says Terry Wanzek, who is not only a farmer but also a Republican state senator in North Dakota. "It would be devastating."

Wanzek's district voted overwhelming for Trump. So did America's rural voters overall, who favored him two to one in the 2016 presidential election. This political calculus appears to have helped keep the president from doing something that would have hurt one of his most loyal constituencies.

Today the three countries are renegotiating NAFTA, but most of the focus appears to be on updating it. Even supporters recognize that the agreement is two and a half decades old, drafted at a time before digital commerce existed and before the three countries began to integrate their extremely robust energy markets. There are many parts that could be renewed and expanded. It's possible that a revised NAFTA may actually end up strengthening rather than weakening the ties among the three countries, if only because any other outcome would damage all three economies.

But that outcome is far from certain. There is also a chance that ideology will overpower reason and that President Trump will try to scuttle the deal entirely. That would have an immediate effect on American farmers like Terry Wanzek, and over a longer term it would undermine some of most important industrial sectors in the United States that have become deeply integrated with Mexico and depend on these close ties to compete against foreign companies in the global economy. That's why most observers still expect NAFTA to survive the current negotiations, even if it goes through some modifications along the way.

"North America has become a shared production platform," says Luis de la Calle, one of Mexico's top trade analysts. Today it would be almost impossible to get through a day in the United States—or in Mexico or Canada—without riding in a vehicle jointly assembled in the three countries.

And that's not just true of cars, buses, trains, and airplanes made by American companies. Increasingly, most of the cars sold in the United States—even those made by foreign automakers like Toyota and Volvo—are made within the three NAFTA nations, with parts

sourced across them. And while Mexico and Canada are deeply embedded in these production processes, most assembly still takes place
in the United States.

This success would have been unimaginable only three decades
ago. In the 1980s, Americans worried that imported cars would dis-
place American-made models. Instead, the major American automakers thrived, and foreign auto companies also decided to build plants
within the NAFTA region rather than export to the United States.
And exports of cars from the NAFTA region to the rest of the world
almost tripled.

Most companies only slowly adapted to this new reality after
NAFTA went into effect, gradually developing operations across
all three countries to build cars, trucks, trains, and airplanes. But
one company found itself ahead of the curve: Rassini, a small Mexican mining and investment company that sold most of its holdings in the late 1980s and early 1990s and invested them all in auto
manufacturing.

Though few Americans have ever heard of Rassini, the parts it
makes—brakes and suspension systems—are in most cars sold in
the United States. The Chevy Silverado, one of the toughest trucks on
the road, depends on Rassini brake systems for both its front and rear
brakes. So does the Tesla Model X, one of the most cutting-edge vehicles
on the market today.

"We provide technology for our customers," says Eugenio Madero,
CEO of Rassini, recognizing that his company is as much an engineering company as it is a manufacturer, adapting its offerings to different
kinds of vehicles.

Rassini got its start as an auto manufacturer by signing a contract with Jeep back in the early 1990s. To grab the attention of the

American auto industry, which had never had Mexican counterparts, Rassini started a research and development center in Plymouth, Michigan, in the heart of the American auto industry. "We were looking to be close to the headquarters of a customer base," says Madero.

Soon other contracts followed with Detroit's Big Three: Chrysler, Ford, and General Motors. By the mid- to late 1990s, Rassini had established itself as a major supplier of suspension systems for US automakers and branched out into brake components too. Then the Asian automakers, Nissan and Toyota, followed suit. They had decided to open factories in the United States and Mexico rather than ship everything across the Pacific.

Rassini grew from a small player to become a central link in the automotive supply chain in North America. Today, most cars made in North America—and the majority of pickup trucks built in the United States—have suspension systems made by Rassini, which also supplies more than a quarter of all automotive brakes in the three NAFTA countries.

And while Rassini is still a proud Mexican company, two of its major plants are now in the United States—one in Flint, Michigan, and the other in Montpelier, Ohio—where the company hires American workers to build components for the North American auto industry.

"The automotive industry is superbly integrated," says Madero. His company acquires steel from factories in Wisconsin and Nebraska, manufactures brakes and suspension systems from it—usually in Mexico but now sometimes in Ohio and Michigan—and then sends the finished products on for assembly in automobile plants owned by the major auto companies, mostly in the United States but occasionally in Mexico or Canada. By the time a single car is assembled, its parts have crossed the US-Mexican border several times in both directions and almost certainly ventured into Canada as well.

Today, dozens of Mexican suppliers have become part of the supply chain for cars and trucks. Most are small and medium-sized companies, but a few Mexican companies have become global players. In addition to Rassini, these include Vitro, which makes window glass, and Nemak, which makes engine heads and blocks. The Jeep Cherokee and the Ford Focus, for example, use Nemak's engine heads and blocks.

Nemak also makes some of its products in the United States using American workers at its plants in Kentucky, Alabama, Tennessee, and Wisconsin, where it has made capital investments of more than $300 million over the past eight years. In fact, Nemak is the only independent supplier of engine heads and blocks that manufactures in the United States using American workers, though a few of the major auto companies have their own integrated operations. Mexican companies have discovered that it's useful to have some of their plants close to the assembly factories in the United States to cut down on transportation costs, and they've ended up creating jobs directly in the United States as a result.

Despite fears in the 1970s and 1980s that the American auto industry was at the point of imploding in the face of Asian competition, American production has remained surprisingly robust over the years, increasing from 9.7 million cars a year in 1990 to 12.1 million in 2015 by embracing a shared production chain that includes both Mexico and Canada. And 2 million of these cars are sold abroad because the integrated supply chains across the three countries have kept prices competitive.

Mexico's production of assembled cars has grown even faster than America's, from just under 1 million in 1995 to 3.5 million in

2015, but this still represents only a fraction of those produced in the United States, where most car assembly still takes place. Canada remains a distant third.

Mexico is not really new to auto production, notes Kristen Dziczek of the Center for Automotive Research, since Ford had its first plant there in the 1920s. But she says that the largest expansion has been over the past two decades. "Localizing the supply chain takes time," she says, because companies "need a manufacturing ecosystem to supply several customers." It's taken two decades for Mexican cities, like Puebla and Aguascalientes, to become major manufacturing hubs because they now have strong supply networks around them. But final car assembly is likely to remain mostly in the United States, even if Mexico and Canada play a greater role in the production of auto parts, simply because that's where most of the final consumers are.

And the three countries have become increasingly integrated in other industries too, such as aerospace manufacturing, medical equipment, electronics, and domestic appliances. In some cases, American and Canadian companies have simply added a few manufacturing operations in Mexico, but many of these industries are more and more integrated across North America, with near-seamless supply chains connecting factories in all three countries.

According to Christopher Wilson, a trade scholar at the Woodrow Wilson Center and deputy director of its Mexico Institute, half of what counts as trade between Mexico and the United States actually entails the exchange of intermediate goods, the component parts later assembled into cars, airplanes, refrigerators, smartphones, and other finished goods.

Wilson estimates that anywhere from 15 to 20 percent of the content in Mexican exports to the United States is actually made in

America, a figure that one study places as high as 40 percent for finished goods, such as refrigerators and the cars assembled in Mexico. This contrasts with China, where American content makes up only 4 percent of finished goods exports, and the European Union, where the figure is around 2 percent.

Mexico and Canada stand out as the only large countries where finished goods exported to the United States have significant American-made content, since many of these products are being assembled jointly in all three countries. For Canada the proportion is around 25 percent, a little less than Mexico but still very significant. These figures point to the fundamental nature of the economic relationship among the three NAFTA countries: we no longer have just a trading relationship—as the United States does with Europe or China—but rather a shared production relationship, where we are making goods together.

This makes it particularly difficult to calculate who has won or lost with NAFTA. There's no question that some American jobs have moved to Mexico from US factories and also that Mexican companies, like Rassini and Nemak, have created new jobs in the United States. But NAFTA's larger effect on the United States has been keeping US industries competitive in the global economy at a time when most people predicted a long decline.

But America's success in manufacturing hasn't always translated into jobs. In fact, US manufacturers have shed as much as a quarter of their jobs since 1980 at the same time that actual manufacturing output has more than doubled. Companies made major productivity gains during this period by substituting technology for manpower. While this allowed them to increase efficiency, it ended up reducing the overall industrial workforce. The American car industry, for example, has expanded its production by a quarter since 1990, largely by taking advantage of North American integration, but it has also reduced employment slightly, from 1.05 million to 940,000 jobs, as manufacturing operations have become leaner and more automated.

One study estimates that 85 percent of the job losses in manufacturing stem from automation, with another 13 percent tied to trade and offshoring of production. Other studies see slightly higher losses from trade and offshoring, but they point out that trade with Mexico, unlike with other countries, has a negligible—and very likely a positive—effect on American manufacturing employment because of the integration effects.

Yet there are elements of a NAFTA renegotiation that could strengthen the job-creating effects of integration and mitigate the job-loss effects. One of these would be to ensure that the Mexican government enforces its own labor laws by allowing industrial workers to form independent unions. Currently most foreign investors in Mexico find it easy to avoid unionization or to strike sweetheart deals with complacent, pro-government unions. This has the effect of lowering wages in Mexican manufacturing more than would happen otherwise.

Negotiators could also look at ways of ensuring that North American–produced goods rely even more on components built in the region, since sometimes it's possible to source a significant percentage of inputs from outside the three countries and still qualify for tariff-free trade. But this too would largely be a tweak to the existing system rather than a wholesale shift in the nature of the economic relationship that has tied the three countries tightly together.

Indeed, it would be almost impossible to undo the single, integrated platform for producing manufactured goods that the NAFTA countries have created without doing extensive damage to all three economies. Resurrecting tariffs would dramatically raise the price of finished products from air conditioners and refrigerators to cars and trucks, while also undermining the region's competitiveness in exporting to the rest of the world. One industry estimate suggests that withdrawing from NAFTA could reduce vehicle production in North America by 450,000 units and reduce US employment by 31,000 jobs. The future ultimately lies in deepening and improving economic integration rather than trying to abandon it.

"There is no such thing as an American car, a Mexican car, or a Canadian car," says Christopher Wilson. "The only thing that exists are North American cars." And the same could increasingly be said of many other industrial goods that are produced—more cheaply and better—across the three countries.

A few years ago, as Javier Mesta walked through the small warehouse he'd rented to start his new aerospace business, he couldn't help wondering if he'd made a mistake. Mesta and his family had once run one of Chihuahua's premier clothing factories, Ropa Diamante, employing more than 3,000 people. They'd sold their line of shirts and jeans throughout Mexico and even in the United States, Europe, and Russia. Now he had only seven employees in a single-room workshop. They were sewing the tops of emergency flotation devices for airplanes, the only contract he had in an industry he knew next to nothing about. It was a humbling experience for someone who'd once been one of the city's leading businessmen.

Mesta and his brother had tried everything to save Ropa Diamante, the company their father had started in 1949. In the late 1990s they even moved the operations further south to Veracruz, where wages were lower. But, he admits, "we just couldn't compete with the Chinese." In 2006 he closed down the company and wondered what to do next.

One day a friend in state government called and suggested that Mesta get into the aerospace business. He'd heard a bit about the aerospace factories springing up around Chihuahua—Cessna, Bell Helicopter, Boeing, Embraer, and dozens of others whose names he couldn't remember. But that just wasn't his line of work. "Our experience was in sewing," he says, not airplanes. But his friend insisted that he might want to look at a small contract being tendered for sewing emergency flotation devices.

Despite their doubts, Mesta and his brother put in a bid and won the contract. They rented a small workspace, bought some used machines, and hired the handful of employees they could afford. "We didn't know the industry, the culture," he says. "It's a different language." The biggest hurdle was getting certified to international standards, a contract requirement that took several months to complete.

As it turned out, "once we did that, people in the aerospace industry started taking us seriously." New contracts followed, not just for emergency equipment but also for seat cushions and other parts of aircraft interiors. Soon the Mestas had to rent a much bigger warehouse and hire more workers—more than three hundred of them, all trained to industry standards. Within a couple years, SOISA Aerospace was providing interior parts to all the major airplane and helicopter manufacturers. "Today we are no longer strangers in the industry," he observes with pride.

Once a quiet provincial town filled with small and medium-sized businesses, Chihuahua has become a major hub of the aerospace industry, as has the city of Queretaro further south. The aerospace industry remains far less developed in Mexico than the automobile industry, but it's growing fast. Since 2005, the number of aerospace companies in Mexico has grown from 61 to 330, and employment has been growing at 13 percent a year for the past five years.

NAFTA's impact has undoubtedly been greatest in Mexico, which has the smallest economy of the three signatories and was the least open to trade beforehand. With Mexico's increasing economic openings—it joined the Global Agreement on Tariffs and Trade, the predecessor of the World Trade Organization, in 1985 and later hitched its economy to the two other larger economies in North America—its economy underwent a rapid transformation. Foreign investment flowed in, spurring growth after a decade of stagnation, but much of it was for heavy manufacturing that required fewer, more qualified workers rather than the labor-intensive operations, like textiles, common in the country before. Many companies, like the sewing plant that the Mestas ran, simply couldn't compete with cheaper Asian producers who were part of the global trading system. Starting in the 1990s, many Mexicans during this period of change chose to migrate north to the United States to look for work there.

But over time, Mexico's economy began to develop new, high-wage jobs in export manufacturing sectors, and some entrepreneurs who had done well in the old, more closed economy, like the Mestas, actually found ways to tie into the new export-led economy. SOISA Aerospace is now one of the most trusted suppliers in the global aerospace industry, much like Rassini and Nemak have become in the automobile industry.

Today almost a third of Mexico's workforce is in export manufacturing, where wages are higher and jobs more secure than in other areas of the economy. These industries have also helped spur the growth of Mexico's middle class, a somewhat nebulous group that makes up probably somewhere around 40 to 45 percent of the population, according to Mexico's census agency. First-time visitors to Mexico's biggest cities, where middle-class residents often comprise a majority, are sometimes surprised by how modern it all seems, so far from the image of the traditional Mexico they expected to find.

But defining the middle class isn't easy, and thoughtful people differ on exactly who makes up this group. Members of the middle class usually own their own homes, have a car, and even have some savings, and they generally have enough money left over each month, after covering their necessities, to spend on leisure activities, including travel.

But many in this group still live precariously—a single major illness or economic downturn might push them back into poverty. They have access to goods and experiences never available to them before, but they also worry—with good reason—about losing what they have. In some ways they are a lot like the American middle class of the 1950s, whose members often enjoyed a level of consumption and leisure beyond the reach of their parents. Today, of course, some in the American middle class are living on the edge of an economic cliff not so different from that on which Mexico's emerging middle class is perched.

The signs of Mexico's growing middle class are everywhere. The number of cars on the street has almost quadrupled over the past two decades. Movie theaters too have expanded from only 500 in 2006 to over 6,000 in 2016. Home mortgages have tripled in coverage since the late 1990s, allowing more Mexicans to purchase homes. And credit access overall has more than doubled since the turn of the century, rising from 15.5 percent of all Mexicans in 2000 to 33 percent in 2015.

But while the growth of the middle class may be good for Mexico overall, it's had a limited effect on the almost half of the population that continues to live in poverty. To be sure, there is far less extreme poverty—hunger and serious deprivation—today than before, but somewhere between 40 and 50 percent of Mexicans remain poor, according to a variety of different measures. Gerardo Esquivel, one of Mexico's leading economists, says, "Ten percent of Mexicans have between fifty and sixty percent of the income." He notes that the disparity is probably even greater if you look at assets rather than income, though no reliable data currently allow us to calculate asset inequality in Mexico.

Of course, inequality is something that Mexicans and Americans share—both are among the most unequal countries in the world. But while income inequality has dropped slightly in Mexico as educational attainment has increased and the middle class has expanded, it has grown significantly in the United States over the past two decades.

Inequality is due in part to fiscal policy, which penalizes smaller businesses and lower middle-income earners, says Esquivel. But it also has to do with the vast differences between the globally integrated sectors of the economy and the more inwardly focused ones. One study by the McKinsey Global Institute found that the productivity of large Mexican businesses with over a hundred employees had increased by an impressive 5.6 percent a year in the decade from 1999 to 2009, but small businesses with fewer than ten employees had actually lost productivity at the rate of 6.5 percent a year. Medium enterprises with more than ten but fewer than a hundred employees grew at an anemic 1 percent a year.

Inequality also persists because most smaller Mexican businesses, including family businesses, remain firmly anchored in the
informal economy, where they are not registered and don't pay taxes
but also have no access to credit or long-term security. Over half of
Mexico's nonagricultural workers are in the informal sector, largely
because it's simply too complicated and expensive to register a small
business legally. In a country where average wages are a quarter of
those in the United States, it actually costs around five times more to
register a small business. As a result, most small businesses simply
stay under the radar, avoiding taxes and labor laws but also unable
to apply for loans or government contracts that would allow them to
expand.

Despite these limitations, overall Mexicans are more prosperous
today than at any time in the country's history. On average gross national income per capita—people's average share of the country's
wealth—grew around a third in real terms over twenty years and is
closer today to that of Russia, Romania, and Bulgaria than to other
developing countries.

And today average educational attainment is around nine years,
up from an average of six years only two decades ago, and almost
three times as many students attend college. Over the same period life
expectancy has also risen from seventy-three to seventy-seven, only
two years less than in the United States, as health care has improved.

Mexico's dual-speed economy is hardly the perfect recipe for the
future, but there's no question that the country has moved ahead
economically and now has a large and increasingly confident middle
class. Mexico's transition to an open economy undoubtedly played a
major role in this shift. As discussed elsewhere in this book, there are
also other reasons for these improvements, including investments by

expatriate Mexicans in their home communities and Mexico's still relatively new insertion into the innovation economy. But greater integration with the two larger economies to the north played a crucial role, and the most dynamic sectors of the economy remain linked to North American trade.

And perhaps as a hallmark of the changes afoot, Mexico, which has always had the smallest economy of the three—about a fifteenth of the size of the American economy and about 25 percent smaller than Canada's—is slated to surpass Canada by 2050 and become one of the top ten economies of the world.

At the Mariposa border crossing in Nogales, Arizona, it's hard to miss the signs that something different is going on. When trucks headed north from Mexico to the United States pull up to the border crossing point, both Mexican and American customs agents inspect them together at the same crossing point.

It used to be that trucks first had to go through Mexican customs to check their outbound paperwork and then pull into American customs to get their import paperwork inspected. But Mariposa is one of several places along the border where American and Mexican customs inspectors are actually housed together in a single facility, working side by side. This "unified cargo processing" is designed to speed up border-crossing times and help improve the economic integration between the two countries, while making the border even safer. Both the export companies and the trucking companies are also subjected to extensive background security checks as part of the deal to participate in the single inspection process.

Doug Ducey, the Republican governor of Arizona, says, "What the program demonstrates is that safety, security and efficiency can all exist together." And he adds, "In fact, it has enhanced security efforts by allowing [US Customs and Border Protection (CBP)] and Mexican customs to focus on high-risk shippers while also facilitating trade and commerce." And he touts the way that the program has brought down crossing times from over three hours to less than an hour, on average.

Something similar—but even more dramatic—is happening in Tijuana, where a large nondescript warehouse about a half mile south of the border has been turned into a preinspection station for trucks filled with strawberries, tomatoes, and other produce headed north. Here US and Mexican customs inspectors not only work side by side but do so inside Mexico, inspecting the trucks before they even reach the border.

Once approved for export and import by customs inspectors from the two countries, the trucks then follow a dedicated road to the border, where a US inspector does a cursory check of their paperwork and waves them through. The American and Mexican customs officials inside Mexico share a single building and a small laboratory for testing.

A similar experiment is underway at the Laredo, Texas, airport, this time with Mexican inspectors inside the United States. They inspect machine parts being sent through air cargo to factories inside Mexico. Here the agents from the two countries work side by side inside a hangar at the Texas airport, about nine miles north of the border. The Americans approve goods for export, and the Mexicans review them for import.

These joint inspections—both at the border and inside the two countries—are part of an effort by the two governments to improve economic competitiveness by speeding up border crossings while making the border more secure.

Governor Ducey, a conservative Republican and strong supporter of President Trump, might seem like an unusual promoter of cross-border trade, but he has made clear that his state's future depends on its relationship with Mexico. "Mexico is Arizona's largest trading partner times four," he says. "It's not even close." Trying to improve the speed of trade is simply good business for his state.

This is a very different vision of how to make the border secure than the one that often emanates from Washington, DC. National politicians often think that the border will become more secure if it is thicker—with more agents and more fencing. But at the state and local levels, most politicians—not to mention most communities—want to make it smarter instead. And federal officials have increasingly gotten on board with this too.

Alan Bersin, a former CBP commissioner and later assistant secretary of homeland security for policy during the Barack Obama administration, says the goal of these efforts is to have "both security and trade facilitation," which are two sides of the same coin. A brilliant bureaucratic entrepreneur and a hard-driving former prosecutor, Bersin played a critical role in promoting many of these efforts that have gotten the two countries to manage the border together using risk-management strategies and information sharing. He says that the key is to focus on the flows across the border, not the border itself. And flows can be inspected and prioritized in different ways to make the country more secure while making the border less of a barrier to the legitimate movements of people and goods that keep the economy afloat.

"There are three ways to look for a needle in a haystack," says Bersin, explaining how border management has shifted in recent years—and what might be possible in the future. "One is to look at every piece of straw." That was the old way of doing things: stopping every vehicle and every pedestrian for an equal inspection. But as the volume of cross-border activity has increased, this has become impracticable and inefficient.

"The second way," Bersin says, "is to use intelligence that allows you to reach into the haystack and pluck out the needle because you know where it is." This requires not just having good intelligence in US agencies but creating channels of communication to share information on potential threats with Mexican counterparts. That's been fairly effective and is reason for physically locating agents next to each other. Today, even at traditional border crossings, where several hundred feet might separate the American and Mexican agents, CBP has made sure that its agents meet frequently with counterparts on the Mexican side and have ways of contacting counterparts in real time.

But it's impossible to anticipate all potential threats, Bersin says, so "the third way [to look for the needle] is to make the haystack smaller." He adds, "You do that by separating the flows of low-risk trade and travel so that you can concentrate on the flows that pose a higher risk or about which you lack sufficient information so that you can make a judgment about the degree of risk they do present." In practice, this means segmenting the flow of people and goods into those you know something about and those you don't and expediting the border crossing of the low-risk group.

And this is the second part of how these new joint inspections work. Truck companies—and in many cases the farmers and factories that produce the goods—undergo an extensive background check to be part of the trusted traveler program, known as the Customs Trade Partnership Against Terrorism (CTPAT). As part of the program, they must follow strict security protocols for packaging and shipping their goods. In return, they get access to a much quicker route to transport their goods across the border, with less probability of inspection.

Trusted traveler programs have existed at both the Mexican and Canadian borders for well over a decade now, allowing frequent border crossers and vetted shippers to use special fast-access lanes to get across the border in return for extensive background checks. What's new is how fast and how far these programs have expanded as trade has exploded among the three countries—well over half of all cargo shipments from Mexico and Canada now go through CTPAT, according to CBP statistics—as well as the new emphasis on agents from different countries working side by side and increasingly in each other's territories.

Rassini CEO Eugenio Madero, who depends on the border to import US steel into Mexico and then export brakes to the United States, says, "For us it's seamless.... It works perfectly." For companies that depend on just-in-time manufacturing, the movement of goods across the border has become increasingly fluid and efficient.

And, Bersin notes, one revolutionary idea has been to not "funnel everything through the bottleneck at the border." That's the logic behind moving inspections into airport hangars and inspection stations inside the countries. In Canada, many inspections of shipments coming into the United States also take place before trucks reach the border. Passengers flying from most major Canadian cities to the United

States go through immigration and customs before getting on the plane as opposed to after landing. Something similar may eventually happen in Cancun and Los Cabos in Mexico too, and maybe one day in Mexico City, though working the details out is taking a while.

Politicians may be talking about whether to build a wall on the border, but frontline officials of both governments—working with state officials, the business community, and local stakeholders in border cities and towns—have been moving the other direction, trying to make the border far more fluid and intelligent.

The border isn't disappearing, but it's becoming much more sophisticated. It's the kind of border that three integrated economies need to trade and produce goods together without adding unnecessary bureaucratic costs. It's also the kind of border needed to prevent twenty-first-century threats.

This is one of the least heralded and most important achievements of the NAFTA period. Not only can the countries exchange goods with no additional tariffs, but they can also move people and goods back and forth efficiently, making joint production processes possible.

"Mexico is our partner," says Governor Ducey of Arizona. "It's even more than that—it's our neighbor." It's one whose economy is intimately tied to Arizona's—and to that of the United States as a whole. Ducey adds wryly, "We're more than neighbors. Neighbors can move—we can't."

3

"Production Has Gone Up, Employment Has Gone Up, Investment Has Gone Up"

Mexican Companies Invest in American Growth

When Raúl Gutiérrez, chairman and CEO of the Mexican steel giant DeAcero, first visited the nail factory he had just acquired in Poplar Bluff, Missouri, in 2013, the reception was anything but welcoming.

Mid-Continent Nails was the last large nail factory in the United States, and the workers suspected that their days in the industry were numbered. After all, Chinese companies could produce nails more cheaply than American companies could, thanks to the extensive production of low-cost steel in China. No one expected Mid-Continent, tucked away in the Ozarks in the southeast corner of Missouri near Arkansas, to survive much longer. Imported nails from foreign-owned companies already made up 85 percent of the American market for nails, and of the remaining 15 percent, Mid-Continent had half the American production, and that was shrinking.

Gutiérrez, a tall, plain-spoken Mexican business executive in his mid-fifties, was used to more receptive crowds than the workers at the Mid-Continent plant who had assembled to meet him. Mostly white, male, and muscular, they were an intimidating audience for a Mexican businessman who, they suspected, planned to pink-slip them. They waited in silence, anger brewing beneath the surface, many with their arms crossed, defiant of the fate that awaited them.

To their surprise, Gutiérrez had come not to close the plant but to revive it. He promised that he would keep the factory open and add new jobs and new investment. He calmly explained that with the steel from the company's plants in northern Mexico, they could create an integrated production chain that would make Mid-Continent competitive again as an American company.

Many of the Mid-Continent workers didn't believe what they were hearing. After all, another factory that made air conditioners—in the very same industrial park—was already closing and moving its production to Saltillo, Mexico, an hour away from Gutiérrez's corporate office. Most of the workers were still convinced that they'd be next.

Poplar Bluff had once been a prosperous industrial hub on the rail line between St. Louis, Missouri, and Little Rock, Arkansas, known as the place where some of America's earliest calculators had been produced. But by the time Gutiérrez arrived to speak with the workers at the Mid-Continent plant, the city was a shell of its former self, beset with unemployment, lost hope, and heroin addiction.

More than three miles of still resplendent brick streets, built in the early twentieth century at the height of the city's glory, led into a downtown that was largely boarded up and abandoned except for the county and city government buildings, the library, and a couple small diners. Even the city's beautiful art deco movie theater remained closed and crumbling in the heart of what was once the downtown business district. Workers at the Mid-Continent Nails plant had no reason to believe that things would get any better.

But by the end of his opening speech, Gutiérrez had convinced some of the workers that he might be serious, and he finished off by promising that at the annual company picnic "we are going to have tacos!" That got a round of applause and some laughter from the still skeptical workers.

Four years later, Gutiérrez gets a very different reception when he visits Mid-Continent. By 2017, the plant had grown from just under four hundred to around six hundred factory jobs, and it had added a third factory building to the two that already existed. Today it produces over 450 tons of nails a day, up from 250 tons in 2013. These nails literally help build the infrastructure of America's cities and towns, reaching all fifty states. And Mid-Continent has held its own against imported nails, keeping costs down by using steel wire from DeAcero's Mexican plants and maintaining its market share by emphasizing a degree of reliability, flexibility, and speed that foreign producers can't match.

DeAcero's investment in Mid-Continent quite literally saved the American nail industry at a time when cheaper imports were on the verge of wiping it out entirely. "Production has gone up, employment has gone up, investment has gone up," said one of the workers enthusiastically when I asked him about what had changed since DeAcero bought the company.

And at the first annual picnic after the acquisition, there were tacos, alongside the usual hot dogs, hamburgers, and pork barbecue.

DeAcero is only one of several Mexican companies that have invested heavily in the United States in recent years. Since 2005,

Mexican foreign direct investment in the United States has quadrupled, reaching $17 billion in 2016. This is more than investment from all the oil-rich Persian Gulf countries and Israel put together. And surprisingly, Mexicans actually hold more portfolio investment in the United States than Americans do in Mexico, $157 billion versus $143 billion in 2016, much of it in long-term debt like bonds and US Treasury bills.

Much of the political rhetoric around the North American Free Trade Agreement (NAFTA) in the United States has focused on the fear of American jobs going to Mexico—much like the air conditioning plant in Poplar Bluff, which ceased operations and shifted production south. But over the past decade, investment has been flowing north too, often saving or expanding American companies. While some jobs have been lost, many others have been created or preserved by cross-border investment.

Mexican companies have become industry leaders in a range of sectors. These include cement, where Monterrey-based CEMEX has become one of the two largest cement companies in the United States and in the world. Mexico's largest glassmaker, Vitro, owns Pittsburgh Glass Works, while Mexico's largest aluminum company, Cuprum, owns Louisville Ladders, among the best-selling in the United States. Two Mexican chemical companies, Mexichem and Alpek, are among America's top producers of plastics, pipes, and the petrochemicals needed to make them.

And, of course, Mexican companies are everywhere in the food industry—as we know from the presence of the bread, tortilla, and potato chip factories in and around Hazleton. And Mexican companies own some of America's most storied brands of milk, hot dogs, and lunch meats as well.

In the telecommunications and financial sectors, Mexican companies have found important niches, primarily serving low-income customers. America Móvil, started by Carlos Slim, owns both Tracfone and Straight Talk, which dominate the pay-as-you-go cell phone market in the United States, where users purchase the airtime they need rather than sign a monthly contract. This model is particularly popular in Mexico, and Slim's businesses originally targeted Mexican immigrants, but then the services caught on with younger cell phone users who didn't want to be tied to a monthly plan.

Mexico's Grupo Electra owns Advance America, the leading check-cashing and payday-loan service in the United States, also serving lower-income Americans who rely on small loans to get them from paycheck to paycheck. By sheer coincidence, Advance America has one of its paycheck offices in Poplar Bluff, Missouri, right next to one of the city's six or seven Mexican restaurants and not far from the Mid-Continent Nails factory.

No one truly foresaw this outcome when NAFTA was first negotiated. Everyone expected investment to flow into Mexico, which hadn't seen any economic growth for a decade. And at first, that's exactly what happened. American companies, like General Electric, Walmart, and Ford Motor Company, set up operations—a mix of low-cost manufacturing and retail sales—around Mexico. And some of these foreign companies put Mexican enterprises out of business.

Rossana Fuentes-Berain, one of Mexico's most respected journalists, reflects on how closed the Mexican market had been before the economic opening in the mid-1980s and early 1990s. "When I grew up, there was only one political party, one church, and one brand of detergent," she quips, referring to the lack of choices in all aspects of Mexican life.

Many Mexican companies had been protected from outside competition by tough restrictions on foreign investment, and quite a few had government-protected monopolies. The opening of Mexico to trade, first through the Global Agreement on Tariffs and Trade and then more deeply through NAFTA, changed this. "They were forced to compete," says Fuentes-Berain about Mexico's large companies, and "many Mexican companies didn't survive."

But others held their own, maintaining and growing their share in the Mexican market, exporting to the United States, or becoming successful suppliers to US and other foreign manufacturers who had set up shop in Mexico. And a few of those that flourished in this new competitive environment began to think that perhaps they could compete outside Mexico.

Not until the late 1990s did a few Mexican companies begin to invest north of the border, and by the early 2000s several more were poised to try. Most that have done so have flourished—and helped American communities along the way.

Fernando Villanueva, who runs DeAcero's US operations from Houston and once lived in southeastern Missouri overseeing the Poplar Bluff plant directly, has come to have a great appreciation for the professionalism of American workers. "There is a work culture here that is very deeply ingrained."

He loved his time in Missouri and came to respect the American colleagues he worked with day in and day out. But he also notes that in many ways, American industry seems to have become a bit complacent in the face of foreign competition. He believes that DeAcero brought from Mexico not only capital to invest and the ability to integrate operations across the border but also the drive to innovate and succeed in the global marketplace.

"You put together the work ethic of American workers with the drive for change that we bring," he says, "and you have an ideal mix for success."

In 2008 Daniel Servitje, chairman and CEO of Bimbo, the large Mexican bread maker, faced the most difficult decision of his career. George Weston, the bakery conglomerate that included Orowheat, Thomas' English Muffins, Boboli Pizza Crust, Arnold, Freihofer's, and Stroehmann's, as well as many regional brands, had decided to sell its holdings. Bimbo already had a relationship with George Weston, having acquired some of its products in the western United States a few years earlier, so Servitje knew that Bimbo would be a logical buyer for the rest of the company.

"It was a very risky move," Servitje confesses, his normally controlled voice breaking for a moment. The United States was in the middle of a recession, the consumer market was contracting, and Bimbo had few good options for putting together the financing. But Servitje worried that if he didn't make the acquisition, someone else would, and Bimbo would lose the opportunity to become a major bakery in the United States. "Getting left out was more dangerous than jumping in," he says. But not everyone in the company agreed.

Twelve years earlier, at the age of thirty-eight, Servitje had taken over leadership of the company that his father, Lorenzo, had founded in 1945 as a single bakery in Mexico City and gradually turned into Mexico's largest supplier of packaged bread, pastries, and other baked goods. By the time Servitje became CEO, Bimbo's products were on the dinner table of almost every Mexican family, and the company's logo, a small white bear with a baker's hat, was almost as familiar to Mexicans as the national flag.

Despite the company's extraordinary growth, his father, a devout Catholic, had made sure that Bimbo's corporate environment retained the ethos of a small, family-friendly company. Visitors to the corporate headquarters were always amazed by the welcoming environment where everyone from guards and secretaries to senior executives greeted you in the hallway, something almost unheard of in Mexico's usually hierarchical corporate environment. Bimbo was also one of the first companies in Mexico to have embedded philanthropy in its operations, and the elder Servitje had poured much of his time and profits into supporting the rural communities that produced the grains for Bimbo's products.

Now Daniel Servitje, his son, wanted to make a risky bet that, even if it succeeded, would transform the company beyond recognition, turning the very Mexican, family-oriented business into a global behemoth.

After considerable negotiations both inside and outside the company, Servitje put together the deal and won approval from his board to proceed. "It doubled our size," he says. Overnight Bimbo became not only the largest baker in Mexico but one of the largest in the United States.

Servitje elected to keep the existing brand names that already had a reputation north of the border, so little changed for American consumers familiar with these products. But inside the company, corporate culture began to shift dramatically. For the first time, most of the company's profits were no longer generated in Mexico, and the executive team became highly international, a far cry from the close-knit family feel of before.

Shortly afterward, Sara Lee, another venerable American brand, came up for sale, and Servitje made a deal to buy it. That deal added brands in Spain and Portugal too. Previously Bimbo had acquired brands in China, and Brazil, so by 2011, when the Sara Lee deal closed, Bimbo became the largest baked goods company in the world. While Bimbo remains a household name in Mexico, few Americans have ever heard of the company that sells more than a quarter of the fresh bread and a fifth of all bakery goods—including hot dog and hamburger buns, packaged donuts, cupcakes and brownies, fresh rolls, buns, and croissants—that we consume each year.

For the workers, little changed either, at least in their day-to-day routines. They continued to report to the same managers, who in turn reported to the head of Bimbo Bakeries, the company's subsidiary in the United States. A longtime senior executive at George Weston, he is based just outside Philadelphia in Horsham, Pennsylvania, where Bimbo Bakeries has its headquarters.

The acquisition of Sara Lee required some consolidation of redundant operations—mostly distribution routes—but it also stabilized a company that had passed from hand to hand, in the control of different private equity investors for years, and put it firmly inside a global bakery company. Today Bimbo has more than sixty plants around the United States, employing 21,000 American workers, with 11,000 distribution routes that reach every state in the country.

Bimbo is no longer the relatively small, fully Mexican company it once was. Although the board and top leadership remain Mexican, many other senior executives are drawn from the company's operations in the United States, Canada, Europe, Latin America, Africa, and Asia, often working remotely from their countries of origin. Servitje notes that though the company has lost some of its intimate feeling, it's also gained a lot. "When we acquire a company, it's not just the assets but the people," he says, "and this human capital...enriches and feeds the company a great deal." He notes that this growth has generated new approaches to doing business too, like emphasizing safety and a commitment to the environment, new focuses derived from incorporating practices from other businesses.

And Bimbo has shown how a major company, firmly rooted in Mexico, can compete on a global scale, holding its own against once larger competitors. "Still a decade ago," says Servitje, "there was a lot of incredulity, a lot of surprise" whenever people in the corporate and financial world realized that they were dealing with a global Mexican company. But a lot has changed in a few years, with Mexican multinationals increasingly showing that they can compete internationally. Now, he says, "there is a greater openness in the world to Mexican companies," and no one seems to be surprised any more—even if most Americans, outside boardrooms, haven't heard of these companies yet.

When Eduardo Tricio was going to college, he used to fly to the livestock auctions in Wisconsin, Minnesota, Ontario, and Quebec on the weekends to scope out the best dairy cows and heifers for farmers in his hometown of Torreón, in the La Laguna region of Mexico's center-north. He made a fair income for a college student by doing this. "I used my weekends well," he says, smiling.

It was an enterprising start for a college student who would later show his potential on the global stage. "Our blood is white," he jokes, referring to his family's obsession with milk. "I'm a rancher," he adds. "It's what I was and what I continue to be."

Tricio's father had a more difficult start. An immigrant from Spain, he worked initially as a manager on a small farm until he could get a loan of $2,000 to buy a few cows. Over time, he bought a ranch also.

In 1949, several ranchers in La Laguna banded together and started their own milk pasteurization and bottling facility. They called the brand Lala, short for "La Laguna," in homage to the region where they lived.

In the 1970s and 1980s, what had started out as a regional brand of milk began to grow. "It took us until 2000 to be in all of Mexico," says Tricio. As his family's ranch continued to prosper, Tricio was elected to the board of Lala, a business controlled by the dairy farmers themselves. And in 2000, when the board asked him to become the company's chairman, he was determined to figure out how to expand the brand globally. Within a few years he had succeeded, first making Lala the leading dairy brand in Mexico and then in 2006 starting a co-packaging alliance with a small yogurt factory in California.

His idea for the United States was to market to Hispanics, especially Mexican immigrants, who already knew the Lala brand. The company soon acquired a dairy factory in Omaha, Nebraska, with the same idea. But along the way, they discovered that if you could market to Mexican immigrants north of the border, you could market to other Americans as well. The two markets were surprisingly intertwined.

In 2008, Eduardo Tricio decided that Lala was ready to go further. Dairy Farmers of America, one of the largest producers of milk products in the United States, wanted to sell its processing facilities,

National Dairy, which included Borden Milk, Velda Farms, Dairy Fresh, and other brands. With the purchase, Lala acquired twenty factories for processing milk, cheese, and yogurt, stretching from Texas and Alabama to the Carolinas, Kentucky, Ohio, and Colorado. Soon after that, Tricio and Lala acquired three more brands: Promised Land in Texas, Skim Plus in New York, and Nordica in Colorado. Lala had now become one of the largest dairy producers in America, distributing its products under these national brands as well as a variety of regional brands. Over time, it had also become the top producer of drinkable yogurt in the United States, with the Frusion and Lala brands.

The hardest part of moving into the American market, says Tricio, is how regulated it is compared to the Mexican market. "It's a very competitive market; it's regulated much more than the Mexican market...with many archaic laws." But once they figured out the rules, it became easier to keep expanding.

Like Lala, many Mexican companies have moved into the US market thinking at first that they would appeal to Mexican immigrants and perhaps Latino consumers primarily, only to discover that they could widen their nets. Daniel Servitje made a similar discovery with Bimbo's investments in the United States. "Because of migration," says Servitje, "there was a market" north of the border among Mexican migrants who remembered the food they had grown up with. "That's how our expansion started...to satisfy that nostalgia." After becoming conversant in the American market through its first ventures serving Spanish-language consumers, Bimbo began to venture further, gradually acquiring well-known American brands like Entenmann's and Sara Lee and adding new plants to serve a broad swath of American consumers.

Sigma Foods, owned by Mexico's Grupo Alfa, followed a similar path, first trying to appeal to Latino consumers with its low-cost hotdogs and lunch meats. But once in the US market, the company very soon discovered that segmenting off Latino consumers was hard. It could just as easily market to a broader swath of Americans. It now sells its Bar-S brand of hotdogs, the leading bargain brand, in Walmart and Costco, as well as in local stores.

Gruma, Mexico's largest maker of tortillas and tortilla flour, also started in the American market, back in 1977, with the idea of selling these staples to Mexican immigrants. But by the 2000s American tastes were evolving, and many non-Mexicans were beginning to eat tortillas. The US tortilla market jumped from only $3 billion in sales in 1999 to $14 billion in 2015, an almost fivefold increase, buoying Gruma's sales north of the border. The health-conscious trend to substitute wraps for sandwiches gave a particularly strong boost to wheat tortillas, which now sell evenly with corn tortillas in the United States. Even more surprisingly, tortillas have actually outsold white sandwich bread in the United States since 2010. Gruma, which sells tortillas under the Mission and Guerrero brands, now has its largest tortilla factory—in fact, the largest tortilla factory in the world—in California, producing as many as 25 million tortillas a day. And it has another twenty-one plants around the country, all employing American workers, including the Mission Foods plant right next to Hazleton, Pennsylvania.

This outreach to Mexican-origin consumers in the United States helped Mexican companies expand north of the border, but so did a key generational transition in Mexico's business community that took place in the late 1990s and early 2000s. Several of the country's largest corporations turned leadership over to a new generation of executives who were then in their late thirties and early forties. These new executives had either been educated abroad, like Daniel Servitje of Bimbo, or, like Eduardo Tricio of Lala, at Monterrey Tec, Mexico's largest private and most globally minded university. Raúl Gutiérrez of DeAcero did both, studying at Monterrey Tec as an undergraduate and at Purdue as a graduate.

It turns out that twenty of the CEOs in Mexico's Fortune 100 companies, and probably a majority of those who led expansions in the United States, studied at the "Tec," as Monterrey Tec is commonly known. José Antonio Fernández, who chairs the board of the Tec, says that the university was largely modeled on the Massachusetts Institute of Technology (MIT), where Tec founder Eugenio Garza Sada, then also chairman and CEO of Femsa, the bottler of Tecate and Dos Equis beer, had studied in the early 1900s. Like MIT, the Tec had a global orientation from the beginning.

José Antonio Fernández, the current chair of the Tec and also chairman of Femsa, is himself part of this new generation of business executives who took their companies global. A graduate of Monterrey Tec, he took over as CEO of Femsa in 1995, when he was only forty-one, and then as chair in 2001, when he was forty-seven. Under his leadership, Femsa has become the largest bottler of Coca-Cola in Latin America, with operations from Mexico to Argentina, and a recent expansion into the Philippines. He also made Oxxo, a Femsa subsidiary, the largest chain of convenience stores in Latin America, with more than 16,000 stores, and it recently has expanded into Colombia, Chile, and even the United States, with a few stores in Texas. To the surprise of some, he also made an ambitious deal by exchanging all of the Mexican brewery operations owned by Femsa for a 20 percent ownership stake in Heineken worldwide. Fernández now serves as

Heineken's vice chair and has positioned Femsa well as a major shareholder in one of the world's largest beer companies at a time when the brewery market has been consolidating. Femsa shares have soared and the company has become a true global player in all three of its business areas.

Fernández notes that when his predecessor, Eugenio Garza Sada, founded Monterrey Tec in 1943, his goal was to give students south of the border the same kind of first-class education he had received at MIT. While the Tec became world famous for its specialties in engineering and business administration, it also built partnerships early on with several top American and European universities so that its students could study abroad. Nowadays, a full 60 percent of all students graduate with either an educational exchange or work experience in another country, often but not exclusively in the United States. And roughly a quarter go on to work abroad. Today Monterrey Tec has formal partnerships with around 559 universities around the world, including many in the United States. The relationship with MIT is, not surprisingly, particularly close.

Fernández says that Monterrey Tec's philosophy has been "not to produce people who consume jobs but those who create them." In other words, it has focused on teaching entrepreneurship as well as professional skills. Almost a quarter of graduates go on to run their own company—often small start-ups—within the first year of graduating, and over two-thirds do so within twenty-five years of graduating.

Fernández has also noticed a recent trend at the Tec, where students from other countries, including the United States, are choosing to enroll there rather than attend US universities. "A year at MIT costs the same as the whole course of study at Monterrey Tec," he notes.

And Monterrey Tec has succeeded in establishing its global reputation, with at least two of its degree programs—including business administration—placing in the top fifty worldwide in the QS World University Rankings.

Monterrey Tec appears to have played an outsized role in creating the new generation of business executives who had the knowledge and confidence to take their companies global. This generation was comfortable in international boardrooms and thinking through the complexities of structuring a global company. Today many other universities are also expanding their international offerings, aware that Mexico's future lies in large part in its relationship with the United States and other countries around the world.

Of course, as Mexican companies expand, they also change and become multinational firms. For Lala, the dairy company that started out as a small cooperative venture in Mexico's La Laguna region, that transformation has been quite dramatic. In the space of a generation, Lala—now known as Borden in the United States—has grown from a small local enterprise into one of the world's top dairy producers and the second biggest in the United States.

Eduardo Tricio, who still uses metaphors from his days as a rancher, says that Lala today is "a cross-pollination of cultures, practices, and processes," a company still rooted in its rural origins but now modern enough to compete with the largest dairy companies in the world.

It's hard to know how many jobs Mexican companies that have invested in the United States have created. Together they employ at least 123,000 Americans directly, according to a study by the Woodrow Wilson Center's Christopher Wilson. If you include distributors and contractors, who depend specifically on these Mexican-owned businesses, the number is probably several times larger; including indirect spillovers into construction and services would increase it even more.

In small cities like Hazleton, Pennsylvania, and Poplar Bluff, Missouri, there is, as yet, little awareness that Mexican capital helps sustain the local economy. Members of the local chambers of commerce certainly know this, as do the employees of the specific Mexican-owned plants, but few average citizens do. Since these companies generally manufacture under American brand names, there is little reason for people to have any idea that the owners are Mexican.

What distinguishes investment by Mexican companies in the United States from other foreign direct investment is their close ties to production operations next door. The American nail industry continues to exist, thanks to investment from a Mexican steel company, precisely because DeAcero could integrate its steel supply a thousand miles away with the nail production in southeastern Missouri. The same is, of course, true of the auto-part companies that make brakes in Flint, Michigan, engine blocks in Dickson, Tennessee, or windshields in Pittsburgh, Pennsylvania.

In other cases, Mexican companies have found niches that complement business lines they know well. Lala is one of America's top dairy companies overall, but it dominates the American market in drinkable yogurt. This is not surprising, since drinkable yogurt is much more common south of the border.

Similarly, America Móvil took its model of pay-as-you-go cell plans across the border, introducing an economical approach to

American consumers used to monthly cell plans. Gruma helped mass-market tortillas, Mexico's national food, to an American market increasingly looking for healthy alternatives to bread.

But there is no question that while Mexican companies pump capital into the American economy, some American companies have also taken some of their production facilities to Mexico. Poplar Bluff has seen both. Just as DeAcero purchased and expanded the Mid-Continent Nails plant, the local refrigerator factory owned by Nortec moved most of its production to Mexico, keeping only 150 out of 500 jobs in Poplar Bluff.

But it turns out that cases like the Nortec plant, where the jobs simply leave—much like the Carrier plant in Indiana that President Donald Trump criticized at the beginning of his administration—are the exception. For the most part US companies invest in Mexico not at the expense of American workers but to the advantage of workers in both countries.

Theodore Moran and Lindsay Oldenski, two American economists, have found that from 1990 to 2009, whenever a US company increased its investment in Mexico by generating ten new jobs, this led, on average, to an increase of 1.3 percent in the size of its US workforce, a 1.7 percent increase in its exports from the United States, and a 4.1 percent increase in its research and design spending in the United States. This may seem counterintuitive, except that the production chains are so linked between the two countries that investment from one country in the other is usually part of an overall expansion, not just a shifting of resources from one side of the border to the other. As in the case of DeAcero, precisely the closeness between the operations in the two countries allows them to be competitive in the global market.

Without question, a few companies do move plants from one country to the other, but most investment today by American companies in Mexico is part of an expansion in operations that also includes American workers. And Mexican companies investing in the United States have been expanding their overall operations in Mexico too.

Contrary to popular myths and political invective, investment in North America is rarely zero-sum among the three countries. That doesn't mean it affects everyone equally or that there are no upheavals in some firms, but trade and investment across the border has been, on average, creating jobs for workers in both countries.

And sometimes, as in the case of Mid-Continent Nails, investment flowing across the border can even save an entire American industry.

4

"Creating Innovative Technology That Solves Real Problems"

- -

Innovation Networks Expand Across the Border

When the eight Americans had finally driven away, Blanca Treviño's two colleagues just stared at her. They didn't have to say anything. They all knew that their company, Softtek, probably wouldn't be winning a contract from one of the world's largest multinational companies, a contract that could have made them a major player in the United States and around the world.

Treviño had gained a reputation as the best salesperson among the original partners who had started Softtek in the early 1980s. She'd been key to the company's expansion throughout Mexico and South America in the 1990s. But now Treviño had gone wildly off script. In Softtek's spartan conference room, when the lead executive from the multinational company had asked her why they should consider using a Mexican company for IT services, she abandoned her carefully prepared charts and graphs and simply turned the question around: Why *wouldn't* they use a Mexican company? There was an awkward pause during which no one spoke. "I think I sounded arrogant," Treviño admits.

In 1997, the need for technology services was exploding in the United States. But US companies wanted to sign new IT contracts in India, not Mexico. "Mexico wasn't perceived to be in the IT field," Treviño says, "just in manufacturing."

After that awkward pause, she explained that Mexican companies could provide service in real time because they operate in the same times zones as US companies and that Softtek's Monterrey headquarters was only a couple hours' flight from any of the multinational's major offices in the United States. Outsourcing to Indian companies required sending instructions to be executed overnight. "Nearshoring"— a term Treviño and her colleagues at Softtek had coined to explain Mexico's next-door advantage—didn't. Her software developers could work in real time with the multinational's teams. "The relationship between provider and user could be much tighter," says Treviño.

The Americans had seemed unconvinced.

Then they'd asked for a tour. Treviño showed them half-finished facilities and at least one entirely empty floor that hadn't even been furnished yet. Softtek may have been the biggest provider of IT services in Latin America, but from the look of its office space, it had a long way to go before it became a global player.

Yet a couple days later the executives from the company called again to set up another meeting. Within a few months Treviño managed to secure a contract. And within a few years Softtek handled most of the company's IT needs in Latin America—and then in the United States as well.

Today Softtek generates half of its income north of the border and serves twelve Fortune Fifty companies in the United States. It has since opened centers of its own in India, China, and Silicon Valley, as a way of servicing its clients in the location most convenient to them.

Since Softtek broke into the US market by selling its proximity to the United States as a strategic advantage, many of the world's largest software companies have discovered the advantages of nearshoring and opened their own offices in Mexico. These include companies such as Cisco, IBM, Hewlett-Packard (HP), Intel and, increasingly, Indian companies such as Tata Consulting Services and Infosys.

Guadalajara, capital of the state of Jalisco, once known mainly for its mariachis, tequila, and folkloric dancing, has captured enough foreign IT investment to be referred to as Mexico's Silicon Valley. Since the mid-1990s, the city and state governments have attracted IT businesses by offering tax incentives, encouraging local universities to establish programs in information technology, and setting up an incubator for new tech start-ups.

Mexico City, the country's financial and political capital, also has a thriving technology industry. And incipient tech clusters are forming in several other cities, including Tijuana, Aguascalientes, and Puebla.

In Monterrey, where Softtek is based, most of the energy to jump-start the technology industry has come from entrepreneurs like Blanca Treviño, but it's been complimented by efforts from the state government and local universities to build public-private partnerships. One of the most visible of these in Monterrey is the Technological Innovation and Research Park (PITT), where university-based researchers and corporate research and development (R&D) departments share space on a single large campus in order to create links across different sectors. Framed by a giant metal arch, the facility now houses researchers from several Mexican universities, the University of Texas, and companies as diverse as Motorola, PepsiCo, and various auto-part companies.

Researchers located there work on the practical application of innovation to the different industries in and around Monterrey.

One of my favorite initiatives at the PITT research campus has brought the Plastics Institute, which looks at new-generation technology around plastics, together with Reynera, a hundred-year-old broom and household goods company. It's the ultimate pairing of high and low tech to innovate in making the most basic of all household instruments. Jorge Treviño, owner of Reynera and no relation to Blanca Treviño, wanted to automate the factory floor of the venerable company, located about a half hour out of Monterrey in the city of Cadereyta, so they could respond quickly to changing trends in household goods and ensure that their products appealed to Walmart and other leading American retailers.

Relying on the Plastics Institute at the PITT, Reynera figured out how to build its own molds to make the key broom components, something that once had to be done by hand using decades-old machines. Jorge Treviño calls Ricardo Corona, head of the Plastics Institute at the PITT, the "mental force" that helps get the most out of his workforce. And since Reynera's sales have skyrocketed with its ability to respond quickly to new orders, he's been adding workers while simultaneously automating the company. "Now we sweat less and plan more," says Treviño about the power of innovation even in one of Mexico's most traditional industries.

Few people initially associated Mexico with high-tech innovation, but increasingly its principal cities are becoming seedbeds of creativity both for new ways of getting the most out of traditional industries, like broom making, and for creating cutting-edge technology that services the needs of the digital economy, as Softtek has done.

Manufacturing may have jump-started Mexico's economy over the past two decades, but technology is certain to play a role in where it heads over the next two decades. "If there is an industry that could represent an opportunity for Mexico," says Blanca Treviño, "it's technology."

In 2009, as the economy of Silicon Valley started to recover from the financial crisis, Bismarck Lepe, a successful tech entrepreneur with a Stanford degree, began to look for ways of sourcing talent for his growing company, Ooyala, which provides online video solutions for business. He knew that the venture capital companies would be ready to open the tap again after the economic slowdown, and Ooyala was ripe for a big expansion.

Lepe also knew he would need to increase the company's workforce dramatically, but Silicon Valley was becoming way too expensive to handle the kind of talent expansion he had in mind. He gave his friend Mark Ellis, whom he had met while both worked at Google, the job of conducting a global study of where they might place the operations of the growing company.

Lepe was a bit surprised when Ellis came back with the proposal to expand the company in Guadalajara, Mexico's second-largest city. "I was originally a little hesitant," admits Lepe, "given that my parents had left Mexico."

Bismarck Lepe's parents had been migrant farmworkers from a small town not far from Guadalajara, and Lepe had never seen Mexico as a land of opportunity, much less a place to invest. Some of his earliest memories were of going back and forth from California to his parents' small village until they finally settled permanently in Oxnard, California, when he was five years old.

But Ellis insisted, telling him that Guadalajara had a strong talent pool with lots of young programmers and engineers. Its technology ecosystem was not as mature as those in other cities around the world—including several in India—but it was developing quickly.

Starting in the 1960s and through the 1980s, a number of foreign companies, including Kodak, Motorola, IBM, Hewlett-Packard, and Siemens, placed some of their manufacturing operations in Guadalajara. Local factories made semiconductors, printers, and photo equipment, among other basic components for the tech industry. "All the directors of the plants were American," remembers Jaime Reyes, who joined HP's Guadalajara operation in the 1980s.

But Reyes remembers that this began to change in the 1990s, and he himself became HP's first Mexican manager in 1994. By the end of the decade, most of the managers were Mexican, and Mexican engineers, programmers, and designers were working at the plants, even though they still mostly specialized in basic tech manufacturing.

Over this period, corporations worked closely with local universities to expand their tech-related courses, and the collaboration paid off in generating local talent. It looked like a highly successful model through which Guadalajara would eventually move up the value chain.

Then it all came crashing down.

The entry of China into the World Trade Organization devastated Guadalajara's tech industry, and many of the factory jobs moved to Asia. At the end of the decade, the industry seemed to be vanishing, unable to compete with even lower wages for assembly work in China.

But Guadalajara reinvented itself within a few years as a major center for research and development, programming, design, and other high-skilled tech occupations, building on the foundation laid years earlier. Reyes remembers the moment in the early 2000s when HP's Guadalajara operation produced the first printer designed entirely in the company's Guadalajara offices. "We inverted the model to become the designers—and Taiwan the manufacturer," he recalls.

Today Oracle, Intel, HP, and IBM all have major R&D and programming facilities in Guadalajara. Continental Tires, a German company, produces around twenty patents a year from its local research facility. The city still does some low-wage component manufacturing and assembly but is now known primarily for its engineering talent and creativity.

Bismarck Lepe eventually came around to the idea that Guadalajara could be the right place to base most of Ooyala's operations. Along the way he had asked Adal Flores, a young, aspiring entrepreneur from Guadalajara, to work for him for a couple years to launch Ooyala's Guadalajara operations. Flores really wanted to start his own company, but Lepe convinced him that it was worth his while to learn the ropes in a more established start-up.

Lepe's bet on Guadalajara paid off. The company became immensely successful, and he eventually sold it in 2014 to the Australian telecom giant Telstra for $410 million. The buyout came about in large part because of the strength of Ooyala's Guadalajara operations. And by then Adal Flores had already gone on to start his own company with support from Lepe and other Silicon Valley investors.

But a year later, Bismarck Lepe was back in Guadalajara with his latest start-up, Wizeline, a business solutions company that specializes in integrating databases. Today Wizeline has over 300 employees in Guadalajara with plans to expand to 1,200 in 2018. Meanwhile, the San Francisco head office remains lean with around twenty-five to thirty staff.

Lepe has become an evangelist for the benefits that Guadalajara offers for America's tech industry. "You're starting to get the second or third generation of technologists who have experience build[ing] scalable products," he says. "And it's not only the talented people that are there but the ones we can attract to live there," he adds, noting that Wizeline has employees from Egypt, France, Ecuador, Colombia, China, New Zealand, and, of course, the United States working at its Guadalajara offices. Getting them work visas is easy, something that is becoming harder north of the border, and they love the quality of life in a city that is far less expensive than Silicon Valley but still has great cultural and recreational options.

Lepe is so convinced by Guadalajara that he started a nonprofit, Startup GDL, to promote the city as a tech hub to other Silicon Valley start-ups. It currently has a long pipeline of US-based small and medium-sized tech companies looking at putting part or all of their operations in Guadalajara.

Bismarck Lepe has no illusions that everything in Mexico is perfect. He knows that corruption and the lack of upward mobility, some of the issues that drove his parents to leave, are still a major problem. But he's also become convinced that Mexico increasingly has spaces where creativity and innovation can thrive, and he's willing to bet on these, especially in Guadalajara. "This is definitely not my parents' Mexico," he says.

When Adal Flores left Ooyala, after almost three years working for Bismarck Lepe, he knew what he wanted to do. He had used his time at Ooyala to learn the ins and outs of running a start-up business, and he'd connected with people in Silicon Valley who could mentor and support him—from a top technology lawyer to venture capitalists to one of the most successful serial entrepreneurs in world.

By the time Flores launched Kueski, a company that gives small online loans, he was positioned for success. Between 2012 and 2016, he raised over $37 million in venture capital. The company now employs eighty-five people, and it has become an online alternative to loan sharks and small, informal community savings networks.

"The problem in Mexico," says Flores, "is that the majority of people don't have traditional banking credit." Banks won't lend to them, which means that they can't access funds to deal with medical emergencies, school payments, or major purchases. Kueski uses everything from neighborhood data to behavioral analytics to determine the creditworthiness of clients and then makes small online loans that range from 1,000 to 9,000 pesos (roughly $55 to $500). Most customers repay the loans within twenty-two days, and there is only a 12 percent default rate—most of which can be easily rescheduled for payment over a slightly longer period.

"We want an experience where people can [access funds] quickly, simply, conveniently, transparently," says Flores, and "in which the client is treated with respect." It's a sharp contrast to the way that payday-loan services and pawnshops work in Mexico. Surprisingly, he's found that almost a quarter of the applications come from small-business owners who need a loan to pay their employees on time.

Technology innovation in Guadalajara was once mostly the province of large foreign-owned corporations, but today a growing number of Mexican-owned tech start-ups are taking hold. Jaime Reyes, the former HP general manager who now serves as the first secretary for innovation, science, and technology in the state of Jalisco, where Guadalajara is located, says that Mexican-owned companies now make up close to 40 percent of all tech companies, up from only 15 percent ten years ago.

Many of the Mexican start-ups, like Kueski, address problems specific to Mexico but perhaps common to other emerging economies, like the lack of credit access. They are looking at practical solutions to real problems in Mexico, but they may be scalable to fit other similar markets around the world.

Unima, a company started by four PhDs in chemistry, fits this mold. The founders developed an online diagnostic test that rural clinics with no doctor present can use to diagnose a range of diseases. An app reads the patient's blood sample, analyzes it, and shares it with a doctor at a remote location, who can provide a diagnosis.

"We were the first Mexican start-up accepted in Y-Combinator," Silicon Valley's most prestigious technology accelerator, says José Luis Nuño, one of the company's founders. That experience helped put them in touch with venture capitalists willing to back them. Now, with several millions of dollars in investment from the Gates Foundation and US and Mexican venture capital funds, Unima is about ready to initiate production of the diagnostic test in its own plant in Guadalajara. It hopes eventually to distribute the tests not just in Mexico but around the world, especially in parts of Africa where access to medical care is even more limited than in rural Mexico. "Our goal," says Nuño "is to empower the patient," to enable people to get real-time medical care no matter where in the world they are.

Conekta, another successful start-up—this one in Mexico City rather than Guadalajara—is trying to solve the problem of connecting people who don't have credit cards with access to online shopping and bill-paying platforms. The start-up has teamed up with Oxxo, the largest chain of convenience stores, to provide a system for consumers to pay for online purchases. Users go online to buy an item—or pay their property taxes or car registration fees—and then go to the nearest Oxxo to pay in cash.

Back in Guadalajara, two car enthusiasts started Rigs, an online platform for ordering auto parts. In Mexico it's almost impossible to get spare parts for older cars outside major cities. Rigs taps a network of auto-part suppliers in both Mexico and the United States to identify the part that's wanted and deliver it to the consumer for a small fee. To the founders' surprise, around one in nine of their customers actually lives in the United States, and they're almost always Mexican immigrants who just enjoy the convenience of the online, Spanish-language website as an alternative to stopping at the local auto parts store.

Still another Guadalajara-based company, Sunu, makes a wristband for the visually impaired that helps its wearer navigate throughout the day by sensing objects nearby. It's essentially a digital complement to walking canes, using ultrasound to send signals to the user about obstacles in the environment that go beyond what a cane can detect. It's young founder, Marco Trujillo, got the idea while doing community service at a school for the blind in Guadalajara. His big break came when Sunu was admitted into MassChallenge, Boston's equivalent of Y-Combinator, which has strong links to health-care technology. This experience opened up investment from US as well as Mexican-based venture funds. Most of Sunu's sales are in the United States, though the technology was developed in Mexico.

This is just a sampling of the many start-ups taking hold in Mexico. Whereas Guadalajara was once a manufacturing hub for technology components, it's now becoming a seedbed of innovation for new technologies that can improve everyday life in Mexico—and sometimes in other countries as well.

Every July, 25,000 Mexican young people gather in Guadalajara at the Campus Party, the largest technology innovation meet-up in the country, addressing everything from drones and 3-D printing to gaming, medical technology, and financing for start-ups. Pressed into a large convention center, the enthusiastic participants—almost all under the age of thirty—come from all over Mexico in hopes of learning and making connections. Computer screens are everywhere, as are comfortable cushions and couches to lie down or work on your laptop for a bit.

The keynote speakers are tech innovators from Silicon Valley, Mexico City, Scandinavia, Germany, and East Asia. There are almost no politicians, media stars, or CEOs of big multinational corporations anywhere to be found. Instead the roster of headliners includes names familiar to any aspiring entrepreneur around the world but almost unknown to the general public, much less to politicians. And other than Jaime Reyes's Secretariat of Innovation, which helps support the event, there are few signs of any government presence at all.

Ruy Cervantes, a local scholar who once worked as the director of knowledge management in Jaime Reyes's Secretariat of Innovation, has written extensively about the emerging innovation culture in Guadalajara. "It's a culture that's inspired by, not copied from, Silicon Valley," he says. But like in Silicon Valley, it's about horizontal relationships based not on kinship but on talent, mutual sharing of ideas, and risk taking. Those business practices are not common in most Mexican companies—or even many American companies—and they are nurtured by constant conversations among innovation entrepreneurs about their efforts. Many entrepreneurs in the field are driven not solely to make their businesses succeed but also to "transform the community of people who work here, [so] they get a new mind-set," he says.

And there is no shortage of groups in Guadalajara and throughout Mexico helping to promote an exchange of ideas about innovation. One of the most active groups in Guadalajara, Hackers & Founders, the local affiliate of the world's largest technology entrepreneurs' network, hosts a monthly meet-up under the stars for potential entrepreneurs to get to know each other and swap tips on building a technology company from scratch.

Mak Gutiérrez, who runs Hackers / Founders in the city, says that it promotes "cross-pollination among young people," as well as provides practical support to help them get their companies going. Hackers / Founders also has its own cooperative, which allows a handful of start-ups to share space under the same roof, get ongoing advice and contacts for their businesses, and develop relationships with potential venture capital funds. The start-ups give up a small percentage of their future profits to the cooperative in return for the services they receive.

"It's a collaborative form of capitalism," says Jonathan Nelson, a former nurse turned serial tech entrepreneur who founded the original Hackers / Founders chapter in Silicon Valley. He took the model of a start-up accelerator, where a single corporate entity nurtures seedling businesses, and gave it a slightly more collective touch to appeal to the unique innovation culture. He notes that Guadalajara's chapter of Hackers / Founders has become the most active one outside the original chapter in Silicon Valley, a testament to the rising potential of Guadalajara's innovation potential.

Nothing highlights the different approach to innovation culture more than a visit to Kueski's offices in Guadalajara, a buzzing beehive of activity filled with staff who are almost all under the age of thirty. Sitting inconspicuously at a computer terminal among the crowd of millennials is Adal Flores, one of the few in the large, shared space who is already in his thirties, the owner and the elder statesman of the group. When it's time for a meeting, he plops down at the large wooden table in the center of the room, which doubles as the only meeting space in the wide-open office filled with computer screens.

"Our unofficial motto," Flores says, "is to fight against verticalism." He expects everyone working at the company to have opinions about how to run it better and to run his or her part of the business.

It's no different halfway across the city at Wizeline, Bismarck Lepe's company, where the general manager, Vidal González, sits anonymously among the other computer programmers. An open-air café, built on the remains of an old shipping dock, doubles as the company's meeting space.

"We are bringing the Silicon Valley culture [here]," González explains. "It's about openness and sharing knowledge." He adds, "We're trying to flip the pyramid," a particularly revolutionary endeavor in Mexico, where corporate culture has always been quite hierarchical.

But González, who started his first business with Adal Flores years before, says that "Guadalajara has the same heritage as Silicon Valley." It started with the big technology companies and their alliances with local universities, and now it's morphing into a city full of small innovative start-ups.

Adal Flores too sees the similarities, and he thinks that Guadalajara is only at the beginning of its rise as a hub for technology innovation. "We're going to see more and more start-ups," he says, but "the challenge will be for start-ups to have exits," either through public offerings in the stock market or acquisition by larger companies, as generally happens in Silicon Valley. Flores knows that those paths forward haven't yet been built, but he hopes to be one of the trailblazers.

Sitting at the large wooden table, I ask Flores if any of young people at his company will one day start their own tech enterprises. He breaks into a big smile and looks around the room before responding, "At least five or six." He recognizes that it will be his job to mentor them and invest in their efforts in the way that Bismarck Lepe once did with him. "There's a resurgence of Mexican entrepreneurship," he adds. And it's just the beginning.

When Lynne Bairstow, a former Wall Street investor, decided to move to Punta Mita, an upscale resort community on a beautiful stretch of the Pacific in the Mexican state of Nayarit, she had no idea that she would start one of the first binational venture capital funds to invest in Mexico's growing technology industry. And when she first started to raise money for the fund, much of it from Americans in Silicon Valley, she encountered more than a few skeptics. Venture capitalists had started to expand their focus beyond the Bay Area toward India, Israel, England, and several other cities in the United States, like Boston and Austin, but Mexico was nowhere on their radar screen.

"Mexico was a great manufacturer of technology," she says, "but not an innovator." Yet she could see that this was changing and that a new innovation ecosystem was emerging. She wanted to be there at the beginning. "What an ecosystem needs is funding," she says. So in 2011 she started hosting the first of what has now become an annual event, the MITA TechTalks, which brings investors and innovators from both sides of the border together. And in 2012 she made it her role to convince others from the United States to take a chance on some of the start-ups in Mexico by raising her first MITA Ventures fund.

She is drawn to Mexico in part because she lives there for much of the year but also because it just makes good economic sense. An industry was developing that needed investment, and she could be there at the takeoff. Says Bairstow, "I see them creating innovative technology that solves real problems," just like how things started in the early years of Silicon Valley. She has invested in Sunu, the company that makes wristbands for the blind, as well as other companies that harness solar power and develop security solutions.

While Bairstow was creating a private venture capital fund, Adriana Tortajada was working inside the Mexican government to build programs to invest in start-ups. In 2003, Tortajada and her small team created the first Mexican public investment fund for tech and science start-ups inside the National Development Bank (Nafinsa) with resources from the National Council of Science and Technology (Conacyt). At the time, they didn't know they were helping create the first chapter of the entrepreneurship and innovation ecosystem in Mexico, providing seed funding to many of the country's first start-ups.

After ten years, Tortajada moved on to help found the National Entrepreneurship Institute (INADEM), a new government agency created to support small and medium-sized businesses. INADEM now has a public budget of over $200 million a year for innovation, of which 40 percent goes to strengthen private venture capital funds, another 20 percent gets invested directly in start-ups that are trying to scale up their operations, and the balance goes to efforts to build the larger innovation ecosystem. At INADEM Tortajada created special grants for high-impact entrepreneurs, helping, among others, both Kueski, the online credit business, and Unima, the medical testing company, to get off the ground.

Recently she's moved on to start up a public/private program called Mexico Ventures, which she codirects with a senior manager at SunCapital in the United States. In this role, she and her colleague oversee five separate funds that are together capitalized at around $250 million with both public and private funding and dedicated to investing in innovation start-ups. Unlike her earlier efforts within the Mexican government, Mexico Ventures operates far more like a private investment fund but with public backing. Mexico Ventures, in turn, is part of a larger system called Fund of Funds that pairs private and public capital for strategic sectors of the economy, including not only technology innovation but also energy and infrastructure. It's the Mexican government's most audacious move so far to support the country's innovation ecosystem by pairing its resources with those of private investors.

Tortajada points out that the number of venture capital funds in Mexico has exploded in recent years. At the turn of the century only one fund invested in innovation start-ups; in 2008 there were still only seven, with a capitalization of around $10 million. In contrast, today there are more than fifty private venture capital funds in Mexico, focused on different areas and stages of start-up growth, capitalized with over $50 million.

Legal changes played a role in this growth, notes Tortajada, as Mexican law began to allow minority investors to have voting rights on company boards, something which had not previously been a practice in Mexico. But the biggest shift has been the awareness among investors of the money to be made by investing in start-ups—and that it can have a positive economic and social impact too.

A legal change in 2009 also allowed Mexico's private pension funds to invest a small percentage of their holdings in higher-risk investments, which has provided a new, though still incipient, source of funding for the venture capital funds. An even more significant funding flow has come from banks, which have also begun investing heavily in start-ups, realizing that much of the innovation in financial technology—fintech, as it's often called—may help them reach potential customers among the majority of Mexicans who currently lack a bank account. Most of Mexico's major banks have some investment in venture capital funds and often host their own innovation labs where aspiring innovators can work.

A visit to the headquarters of BanRegio, a midsized bank in Monterrey known for its loans to small and medium-sized businesses, feels like a field trip to a hip coworking space in Silicon Valley. The entire first floor, dedicated to developing innovative technology, is filled with young people in T-shirts and jeans working quietly on their computers, a few of them sprawled out on couches. In an adjacent room a couple of them play Ping-Pong while working out the solution to a problem.

Demetrio Strimpopulos, one of the bank's founders and now the director of BanRegioLabs, its innovation area, oversees the creative hub. The grandson of a Greek immigrant to Mexico, Strimpopulos, also in jeans, touts the need for the bank to learn to be agile and creative, the way it was when founded a little over twenty years ago. "We wanted it to be an experimental lab, not another department of the bank," so that we could influence all areas of the bank's culture, he says. The lab develops new technologies to help clients manage their money more responsibly, in hopes of providing solutions to improve customers' lives.

BanRegio also invests in four venture capital funds that support start-ups in fintech. They hope to learn from others in the innovation ecosystem by participating actively in it. By engaging with start-ups through the funds, he says, "we started to learn what people were thinking in the ecosystem of fintech."

He recognizes that traditional banks have only been able to get so far in reaching potential customers in Mexico. "The start-ups are appropriating the last mile" of financial access, he says. "Banks can learn from them and partner with them to build innovative tools that will help potential clients prepare for their financial futures."

Although Mexican venture capital is expanding, Silicon Valley funding remains the holy grail for most Mexican start-ups. It provides not only larger investments but also prestige and connections that can help them scale up their businesses over time. Most of Mexico's successful start-ups, like Kueski, Sunu, and Conekta, have benefited enormously from US investment during their period of greatest growth. "All of the Mexican start-ups want a foothold in Silicon Valley," says Lynne Bairstow. It raises their profile and provides access to many more investment options for different stages of growth.

But there is no question that Mexican funds are growing in importance too, and most of the successful start-ups have benefited at some point from Mexican venture capital, even if the biggest investments still come from north of the border.

And Mexican investors are learning to balance their risk too. Most Mexican investors who have started or joined venture capital funds balance their investments in Mexican start-ups—still a new and risky venture—with investments in more established Silicon Valley companies. They do this in part in hopes of getting more secure returns on investment but also because they want to learn what works. It's as much about being an active part of both ecosystems, north and south of the border, as it is about balancing risk.

As it turns out, like most investment generally, venture capital flows in both directions, north and south, between the two countries.

Bairstow admits that her attempts to raise her first venture capital fund to support start-ups in Mexico raised a lot of eyebrows, since most American investors had never looked south of the border before. But now, as she is raising her second fund, the landscape has changed dramatically. Over the past five years, Mexican start-ups have really taken off, and investors in the United States have taken notice.

"No one questions it anymore," says Bairstow.

5

"We Can't Talk About US Energy Independence, but We Can Talk About Energy Independence in North America"

- -

Finding a Common Future in Energy

Armando Garza surveyed the drilling rigs extending across the horizon. On them, he knew, Mexican and American workers toiled together. He was proud of these workers, proud to be the CEO of the first private Mexican company involved in extracting shale oil and natural gas from the earth, an activity forbidden by the Mexican constitution for decades. And his gamble on getting into oil and gas had paid off handsomely for his company, Grupo Alfa, one of Mexico's most successful and diversified business groups. The extraction operation was now generating many times Alfa's original investment.

But something was eating at him. Garza had always wanted to invest in Mexican energy, but the rigs he was looking at—his rigs—were not in Mexico but in South Texas, in the deep, rich deposits of the Eagle Ford shale formation. And most of the jobs and royalties were staying on the US side of the border.

This hadn't been the plan. In 2001 newly elected president Vicente Fox, the first opposition candidate elected president in Mexico after seventy-one years of one-party rule by the Institutional Revolutionary Party (PRI), had promised an energy reform that would allow private investment in oil exploration in Mexico. Garza wanted in.

Two years later Roger Wallace, a friend and a senior vice president at Texas-based Pioneer Natural Resources, approached him and suggested a partnership with Alfa, a conglomerate whose business lines included foodstuffs, auto parts, and telecommunications as well as petrochemicals. Pioneer would pair its know-how in the energy business with Alfa's Mexican connections and knowledge of the local terrain. "In 2003, still in the time of Fox, there were hopes that soon there would be changes in Mexico's legislation," remembers Garza.

But Fox was never able to get his reform through a Congress controlled by the PRI. Neither could his successor, Felipe Calderón, who was also from Fox's party and shared his commitment to energy reform.

So in 2006 Alfa and Pioneer decided to invest in Texas instead, originally in an area called Edwards Play, where Pioneer was already invested, and later in Eagle Ford. They figured it would be a good way to try out the partnership and give Alfa some direct experience in the extraction business. "We started on this side of the border," says Wallace, "but we had thought it would be on the other side." And for Alfa, the venture promised to help provide the low-cost natural gas needed to power its industrial plants that produced parts for the car industry.

The venture turned out to be profitable well beyond expectations, striking both oil and gas in enormously rich deposits. "Just remember the oil business isn't always like this," Wallace remembers telling Garza about their unanticipated success.

Allowing private investment in energy has long been an emotional issue for Mexicans, who remember the nationalization of the industry in 1938, when President Lázaro Cárdenas (1934–1940) wrested control from the international oil companies that had profited for decades while paying next to nothing to the Mexican government in royalties. Cárdenas created the national energy company Petróleos Mexicanos, known by its short name, Pemex, which over the next few decades generated profits that helped finance roads, hospitals, and schools throughout the country. In the early 2000s, even as Fox and Calderón pledged to open the industry up to competition, public sentiment ran strongly against allowing private investment back in.

But Pemex had become a fountain of corruption and an example of immense inefficiency. It employed almost twice as many workers as Brazil's state-owned oil company, Petrobras, even though it produced roughly the same amount of oil. And Mexico's oil production had been dropping, from a high of 3.4 million barrels a day in 2004 to only 2.55 million a day in 2012. Old oil fields were drying up, and Pemex had neither the technical knowledge nor the investment capacity to go after new deposits in the deep waters of the Gulf of Mexico or the shale formations in the north of the country. Mexicans still loved their national oil company, but it was a shadow of its former self.

By 2013 recently elected president Enrique Peña Nieto had looked at the country's finances and decided something had to be done about dwindling oil production. Revenues from Pemex made up a third of the federal budget, and they were declining rapidly. In August he too proposed a constitutional amendment to allow private investment in

Mexico's energy sector. This time, before the year was even up, it went through.

"They had the leadership to do it," explains Wallace. As a member of the PRI, which had carried out the oil expropriation decades before, Peña Nieto simply had more political capital than his predecessors to carry out reform. Plus he had a majority in Congress and in the state governments, which also ratified the constitutional change almost as soon as it passed the federal legislature.

Since then, dozens of companies—Mexican, American, Canadian, European, and Chinese—have bid on new contracts for oil exploration in Mexico. Alfa, armed with its oil and gas experience in Texas, won bids for exploration areas in the second round of the oil auctions through its subsidiary Newpek.

Because Mexico has long been the third or fourth supplier of oil to the United States after Canada, Saudi Arabia, and sometimes Venezuela, Mexican energy reform has prompted huge expectations north of the border. "We can't talk about US energy independence," says Wallace, "but we can talk about energy independence in North America."

One report predicts that if Mexico's energy reform generates the kind of investment that's expected over the next few years, the three countries of North America could be close to energy security by 2020. Others put that date a few years further out. But almost all analysts agree that Mexico, the United States, and Canada will soon reach the point at which their combined energy resources meet and even exceed their needs.

The reform process has already led to new collaborations between Mexico and the United States—and between Mexico and the rest of the world. Surprisingly, probably the biggest change since the reform has been to open the tap of natural gas flowing to Mexico. Today half of America's gas exports are to Mexico, helping lower Mexico's electricity prices, once among the highest in the world. This will almost certainly continue to grow as the two countries finish building pipelines across the border to shepherd gas from one side to the other.

Renewable energy has also taken off, with US and other foreign companies working alongside Mexican companies to tap the sun, wind, and plants as new sources of energy for the future. And increasingly the two countries are looking at ways to connect their electrical grids—as Canada and the United States already do—so that excess electricity production on one side of the border can make up for shortfalls on the other side.

Armando Garza is convinced that Mexico's energy reform will spur economic growth nationally. "I do believe that Mexico will generate a much bigger rhythm of growth over the long term," he says, thanks to the new dynamism of the energy industry. And as oil prices recover, the rate of investment—which is already quite significant—will continue to increase.

Roger Wallace believes the effects will go well beyond Mexico, making the entire North American region—and perhaps the whole world—far less vulnerable to supply shocks from crises in any specific country. "Mexico's energy reform could help create a powerful new North American shock absorber," he says, one "that would enhance energy security and diminish energy volatility in the years to come."

Few sights are more awe-inspiring than the transformation of scrap metal into steel. Bits and pieces of desks, chairs, signs, and leftover car bodies are poured into a 150-ton metal cauldron and heated to 1,600 degrees Celsius. After a few minutes the bubbling contents pour out in a red-hot river of iron, ready to be mixed with additives in another bubbling cauldron a few feet away. The contents are then poured into molds and forged into long, steaming steel bars that can be made into I-beams, rebar, wire rod, and other usable steel products.

DeAcero, the company that operates America's last big nail plant in Poplar Bluff, Missouri, has three steel plants in Mexico, two of them in the northern state of Coahuila and one a bit further south in Guanajuato. These plants supply the wire that makes Mid-Continent's nails, but they also produce many of the other steel products used in Mexico. The process of forging steel from scrap metal requires heavy machinery, precision, and workers strong enough to haul machine parts and smart enough to direct the chemistry behind the processes. The largest cost in making steel is the labor, as the workers are highly skilled and well trained.

But the second biggest cost, not far behind the labor, is the energy. Heating and mixing metal to unbelievably hot temperatures requires a constant flow of electricity. In fact, almost all major manufacturing industries—from steel to auto parts to airplane parts—require huge inputs of energy. But until recently, Mexico had some of the costliest electricity in the world.

Traditionally, Mexico's national power company, the Federal Electricity Commission (CFE) generated the country's electricity, primarily by converting oil into power. Oil is hardly the most efficient—or cleanest—way to make electricity, but Mexico had it in abundance, and natural gas, which had to be imported by ship, was expensive.

As a result, Mexico's electricity prices were considerably higher than those in the United States, a huge burden both for manufacturing industries and for average citizens.

But the most surprising change in Mexico's energy sector over the past few years has been the rise in imports of cheap natural gas from the United States by pipeline, which has dramatically reduced electricity costs for Mexico's industrial plants. Residential consumers, whose electricity costs are already subsidized, haven't felt this change yet to the same degree, but that's not far behind.

This has also been a boon for American gas producers, who have found a natural market in the country next door, one reachable by pipeline rather than tanker. Today around half of American gas exports go to Mexico, roughly 4 percent of all American natural gas production.

This shift got underway even before Mexico's energy reform, as the Mexican and US governments agreed to allow pipeline construction across the border, and the CFE gradually began to transition some of its older power plants from oil to natural gas. But the energy reform gave a huge boost to these efforts because it provided security to investors that the gas in the pipelines would find a market on the Mexican side of the border. Today, CFE still buys most of the natural gas coming across the border, but private companies in Mexico can also buy gas directly from American producers, and that's likely to become a bigger part of the electricity market in the future.

The capacity of natural gas pipelines crossing the border nearly doubled from 2011 to 2016, and experts expect it will double again by 2018. Sixteen pipelines currently cross the border, another four pipeline projects are under construction, and two more are in the planning stages for a total of 3,300 new miles of pipeline between the two countries expected by 2020.

In 2016, America exported roughly $3.5 billion of natural gas to Mexico, which made up 1.3 percent of all US exports to the country next door. For the first time, the United States has a substantial trade surplus with Mexico in energy, which makes up around 9 percent of all American exports once refined oil is added in. All signs point to the volume of exports increasing substantially over the coming years. In fact, if President Donald Trump hopes to balance America's trade deficit with Mexico—a dubious goal, perhaps, but one he's argued for repeatedly—trade in energy is likely to do much of the work in narrowing the gap.

Today most of the cheap natural gas arrives in northern Mexico, but the CFE is working on increasing Mexico's existing pipeline structure by 75 percent compared to 2012, building sixteen new pipelines so that imported gas can reach generators further south. IEnova, a public company owned by San Diego–based Sempra, and the Canadian oil and gas company TransCanada are also working on a gigantic underwater pipeline that will pipe gas from Brownsville, Texas, all the way to the port of Tuxpan in Veracruz on Mexico's Caribbean coast, which will allow the gas to get to central Mexico quicker.

Duncan Wood, a leading expert on North American energy and director of the Woodrow Wilson Center's Mexico Institute, notes that the advent of trade in natural gas has been a huge boon to both countries. For Mexico, he says, it's helped improve the competitiveness of manufacturing industries. "From the point of view of the United States," he adds, "it helps maintain jobs in the old fields, and it helps stabilize gas prices." Gas prices otherwise might drop even further and make further gas exploration impossible.

When the Mexican government passed the energy reform in 2013, it hoped to spur oil production and exports from Mexico, but the most important result, at least in the short-term, has been to unleash the potential of low-cost natural gas imports. So for Mexican manufacturers, the most tangible change associated with the reform so far has been the drop in what they pay for electricity each month. And at the DeAcero steel plants, as at most of Mexico's manufacturing plants, the effect has been to reduce input costs and boost competitiveness. Cheap gas is helping power up those giant bubbling cauldrons to ensure that steel can still be made at reasonable prices.

La Rumorosa, a stunning rock formation along the US-Mexican border between Tijuana and Mexicali, seems like an unusual place for experimentation in renewable energy. It's a series of mountains made of large boulders, jumbled together, one on top of the other, looking like the leftovers of a rock fight between mythical giants. The wind whips inhospitably through the rocks, as a single road plies its curvy way through the mountains to connect the two cities. I've long been fascinated with this place. It looks and feels like the ends of the earth, even though it's only a couple hours away from San Diego and Tijuana.

Today dozens of wind turbines stand at the top of some of the mountain peaks, harnessing the unstoppable currents of wind to make electricity. It was a gargantuan project to put them there, rooting the giant turbines in the rocks against the constant gusts and then running the transmission lines back to the city.

Even more interestingly, these wind turbines actually supply renewable energy primarily to California, taking advantage of a cross-border transmission line that runs from Tecate, near Tijuana, to Imperial Valley, just east of San Diego. The entire project was put together by Sempra though its Mexican subsidiary IEnova. Sempra also owns San Diego Gas and Electric, the local power supplier in Southern California. The project was a way of meeting new California state requirements mandating that electricity be generated partly from renewable sources.

IEnova already had a long presence in the Mexican state of Baja California, which includes Tijuana and La Rumorosa. Since 2008 the company has operated a gas terminal just south of Tijuana that supplies pipelines along the California border. It also has a thermoelectric plant near Mexicali, the state capital.

Even more importantly, according to Tania Ortiz Mena, IEnova's chief development officer, "Baja California was integrated to the California [energy] market, not that of the rest of the country." California and Baja California had been sharing energy across the border for quite some time. As a peninsula, Baja California wasn't connected to mainland Mexican pipeline networks. Instead it developed an interconnected energy infrastructure with California, starting with a pipeline to Mexicali in 1997.

Planning for the wind turbines in La Rumorosa that supply electricity to San Diego actually began before the energy reform in Mexico—although they didn't come online until 2014. But the energy reform has since spurred even greater interest in renewable energy. Duncan Wood notes, "Mexico has become the place in the world to invest in renewable energy...and it caught everybody by surprise."

Mexico had started down this path a few years earlier as part of its commitment to the Paris Accords on Climate Change. President Felipe Calderón was personally quite interested in renewables, and he made climate change a major anchor of Mexican foreign policy, even hosting one of the global climate summits in Cancun in 2010. As part of Mexico's effort to meet its climate goals, the CFE had opened up wind and solar plants even before the energy reform and offered Mexican private businesses the opportunity to invest in return for a guarantee of long-term lower-cost supplies of energy. In 2016, over 15 percent of electricity in Mexico came from renewable energy sources other than hydropower, and that proportion may be inching up closer to one-fifth today.

With the energy reform, Mexico's commitment to renewable energy went global, and the government opened up a bidding process, as it did for oil and gas exploration, for domestic and foreign companies to build new renewable energy plants. Over two rounds of auctions, thirty-two companies were chosen through an open bidding process to build wind, solar, and bioenergy plants. The winners included companies from Mexico, Spain, China, Canada, and, of course, the United States that are now building plants around the country. In return, CFE is committed to buying the power these plants generate.

In addition, the energy reform opened up the possibility for the first time that private electricity-generating companies, including those in the renewable industry, could sell power directly to high-volume users, primarily industrial plants like DeAcero's steel factories in Coahuila, which have already made a commitment to buy solar energy from a nearby producer.

Among the largest projects underway is a giant solar facility in Villanueva, Coahuila, taking advantage of the semidesert conditions of the area. The Villanueva plant is the largest photovoltaic plant under construction in the Western Hemisphere, and the project is being carried out by Enel, the Italian power company. It consists of two plants being built simultaneously and is expected to begin functioning in 2018, generating more than 1,700 gigawatt hours per year and powering over 1.3 million households.

Wood notes that although much of the early interest in Mexico was in wind, with areas of the southern state of Oaxaca and Baja California seen as key places to put wind turbines, solar is now edging ahead. "Solar has actually replaced wind because costs have declined," he says.

"Mexico has implemented a very pragmatic approach to its clean energy strategy," says Tania Ortiz Mena of IEnova. "It is benefiting from low-cost natural gas imported from the US and at the same time promoting the development of very competitive renewable energy."

The country's targets for clean energy generation are 25 percent by 2018, 30 percent by 2021, and all the way up to 35 percent by 2024. With the two auctions already completed, Ortiz Mena says, Mexico should be on target to meet its obligations. Some delays in actual implementation could affect the timing but probably not the outcome.

The simple demand for new sources of energy for electricity, combined with the dropping costs of renewable energy generation, are driving investment in solar, wind, and bioenergy power generation in Mexico to an extent no one could have imagined a few years ago. And this will not only drive prices for electricity down and save the country's oil for other uses but also help Mexico meet its targets under the

Paris Climate Change Accords and ensure that the country remains a leader in green technology among emerging economies.

When Hunter Hunt, president and co-CEO at Hunt Consolidated Energy, decided in the late 1990s to develop a new electric utility in South Texas, near the city of Mission, he wasn't thinking about the possibility that one day that utility would turn into an important cog in the integration of the cross-border electricity markets between Texas and Mexico. His goal was more pragmatic. He and his siblings, who started Sharyland Utilities, simply wanted to increase the reliability of electricity generation in a region that had traditionally suffered from underinvestment on both sides of the border. Tying the electrical grids on both sides of the border together was just a practical measure to make sure that when there was a lack of electricity supply on one side of the border, they could pull on electricity from the other side.

The idea was not completely new. The CFE had finalized a cross-border planning study that identified at least half a dozen points at which the grids could be integrated, and there were already several older "synchronous ties" between electrical grids in Mexico and the United States, but these were mostly used for emergency purposes. When demand on one side of the border outstripped supply, the strained electric system could call on that of the other country to alleviate the emergency condition. Thus, these facilities were considered emergency ties and not counted as firm assets for planning purposes. In contrast, the Sharyland Railroad DC Tie, as it is known in the electricity world, would be the first interconnection along the

US-Mexican border that could both support the reliability of the grids and enable commercial trade in electricity.

This is already common practice at the northern US border. Over a century ago, Canadian and American power companies had the same idea and built the first tie between Ontario and New York State. Since then, Canada and the United States have built thirty-five ties between the electrical grids in the two countries, along the entire extension of the border, and there is a thriving shared market in electricity in both directions as demand ebbs and flows on each side.

The two countries—Canada and the United States—trade roughly seventy-seven terawatt hours of electricity a year, more than enough to power all of Austria and almost enough to power Venezuela for a year. Canada supplies most of that, more than sixty-eight terawatt hours, largely drawn from hydropower, while the US grid sends nine terawatt hours north. Canadian power provides 16 percent of New England's electricity, 13 percent of New York's, 12 percent each of Minnesota's and North Dakota's, 6 percent of Michigan's, and 2 percent each of California's and Washington state's. And all of those states also send excess power northward from time to time. Indeed, the grids between Canada and the United States are just as closely tied as those between regions within the United States.

In contrast, the conditions of the Texas and northern Mexico grids and the regulatory frameworks were still a work in progress. When the Sharyland Railroad DC Tie went into operation in 2007, it was possible to transfer electricity to the grid run by the CFE and to receive excess electricity from the Mexican side, but it took at least eighteen months for the Electric Reliability Council of Texas (ERCOT), the Texas regulator, and CFE to agree on protocols and procedures that would enable the DC tie for this purpose.

The tie has proved particularly useful to consumers on both sides of the border. "When Texas was short of power such as in the winter of 2011, when a severe weather event affected the power plants in the state, CFE stepped in and supplied critical support to the South Texas grid," says Enrique Marroquín, who leads the development of the cross-border infrastructure projects at Hunt. "A couple of days later the storm system that hit Texas moved south to Mexico, and Texas stepped in and helped support the northeastern grid, which was also severely strained at the moment."

Despite the success of the Sharyland tie and a handful of others on the border, electricity trade between Mexico and the United States remains severely underdeveloped, with roughly eight terawatt hours coming from Mexico to the United States and under one terawatt hour going the other direction—only a fraction of the trade with Canada—but this seems likely to change in the future.

Today, Hunt is working on a new electricity tie to interconnect Nogales, Arizona, with Nogales, Sonora. The nearby Palo Verde hub in Arizona is one of the largest electricity trading hubs in the United States, with thermal, nuclear, hydro, and renewable generation in its mix. When finished, the Nogales interconnection would allow Mexico to import some of the excess power available on any given day in Palo Verde, which should be reflected in lower power prices in Mexico. At the same time, this DC tie will also increase the reliability of the southern Arizona grid, which would benefit from having a second supply source from south of the border. According to Marroquín, "The role that Hunt is playing is to assist in the strengthening of the cross-border grids while facilitating the integration of the markets" on both sides of the border.

We are a long way away from the day when the United States will have the same degree of electricity integration with Mexico as it has with Canada—after all, that took a century to achieve—but we seem to be at the beginning of a process to integrate the grids of the two countries, which will help ensure reliable power for states on both sides of the border.

In 1961, Rudesindo Cantarell, a poor fisherman in the state of Veracruz, was out fishing when he discovered what looked and smelled like oil. He kept his discovery to himself for a few years, but he kept going back to the spot and wondering if it might be important.

It took him a few years to get up the courage to pass on the information to people he knew in a nearby town who worked with Pemex, and it would take another three years before anyone at Pemex got around to following up on the tip. When the national oil company finally sent a few engineers to check out the information in 1971, a full decade after Cantarell's original discovery, Mexico's relationship with oil was transformed. The field turned out to be the second largest in the world, and it would drive Mexico's oil production for the coming decades.

By the time the oil wells were up and running, at the end of the 1970s, Rudesindo Cantarell had become a Mexican hero. The field was named Cantarell in his honor, and he received accolades and awards for his discovery. Pemex even named him an "honorary worker" for his find. Well into his sixties by then and a grandfather, he basked in the glory of his sudden national fame, which lasted until his death in 1997 at the age of eighty-five.

But Cantarell never missed the irony that his discovery, which helped make the country wealthier, never brought him any benefit as far as his own personal wealth was concerned. He died in the same small fisherman's home he had lived in when he first made the discovery decades earlier, still a humble fisherman, though one whose name was known to almost all Mexicans.

Other discoveries followed Cantarell's, though none quite as large. Throughout the 1980s and 1990s, Mexico's oil production skyrocketed, leading to a sense that it was the gift that would never stop giving.

But there were ominous signs. Although production continued to grow, investment in exploration stalled, and discoveries of new oil wells were few and far between. The country's known reserves began to dwindle, and production declined. The United States had 2,366 oil platforms in the Gulf of Mexico in 2017, while Mexico only had 46, even though there's no reason to believe that the oil deposits magically disappear as you cross the invisible border in the sea. After 2004, Mexico's oil production declined precipitously, dropping from 3.8 million barrels per day in 2004 to 2.1 million barrels in 2017, as legacy basins no longer produced as much as they used to and new exploration has been limited.

To make matters worse, the Mexican government has squandered some of its most productive years of oil production. As one Mexican politician told me in confidence, Pemex, the national oil company, became the government's "petty cash," used to fund pet projects and line the pockets of politicians. To be sure, some profits from oil were funneled into infrastructure and productive investments, but most went to covering recurring expenditures—at one point oil revenues made up 40 percent of the federal budget—and far too much ended up in private hands as the result of government corruption. And some oil was stolen directly from pipelines by organized crime groups and resold to gas stations on the black market.

President Lázaro Cárdenas's nationalized oil industry probably benefitted all Mexicans in the short-term, but in the long-term, without sufficient investment or accountability, it may have ended up fueling private avarice as much as public development.

The bet on turning around Mexico's lagging oil production through private investment is now a long-term gamble, and a five- to ten-year time frame seems most likely before production begins to turn around. Most people involved seem to agree that the Mexican government has done an admirable job of guaranteeing transparency in the bidding process for oil exploration—which has not always been the case with bidding processes for procurement in Mexico. Duncan Wood notes that the first round suffered from technical problems that reduced investor interest, but the government adjusted the process quickly and has had several successful rounds since. Despite a sudden drop in oil prices right as the bidding process began, there has been considerable interest from around the world.

Contrary to fears that American companies would take over Mexico's oil industry, Asia-Pacific-based companies have actually won over a third of the early bids, and European companies have garnered another third. US and Mexican companies have taken 13 and 12 percent, respectively. As of early 2017, there were commitments of $38 billion in investments for exploration and extraction. The strong showing of Mexican companies, like Alfa and several newer entities created by existing Mexican conglomerates, has been one of the many positive outcomes of the bidding process.

In July 2017 two consortia exploring in shallow waters announced major oil discoveries, the first major finds since the bidding began two years earlier. One, composed of Premier Oil of Britain, Talos Energy from Texas, Sierra Oil and Gas from Mexico, and Riverstone Holdings, announced it had found an oil field containing over a billion barrels, the largest discovery in years. A second consortium, led by the Italian energy company Eni, announced that it had also found much more oil than expected while drilling one of its wells in shallow water.

For Mexico, regaining growth in oil production is a question of national development. Although Mexicans differ in opinion as to whether allowing private investment was right, all agree that oil is part of the answer to the riddle of the country's development and that it's crucial to turn around low production.

For the United States, enhanced oil production in Mexico also matters. Mexico once supplied up to 13 percent of American oil imports, but that's fallen to only 9 percent today, still a substantial percentage but continuing to drop. Robust Mexican oil production in the future would help all three countries of North America—the United States, Canada, and Mexico—guarantee energy independence by providing a hedge against shocks and crises in other parts of the world.

When Secretary of Energy Rick Perry met with his Mexican counterpart Pedro Joaquín Coldwell in July 2017 to discuss bilateral cooperation, they concluded by calling for an energy partnership that would strengthen both countries. While Coldwell pointed out the still budding nature of the energy trade between the two countries, Perry called for securing a joint energy strategy. The countries might well be feuding over migration and trade, but both could agree on the shared importance of energy.

Energy trade between the two countries has a long history, but the old taboos have been lifted only recently, and this is likely to generate even closer cooperation on energy for the foreseeable future. Some Americans want to limit trade with Mexico, and some

Mexicans remain skeptical about the constitutional reform to open the energy industry to private investment. But it seems highly unlikely that anyone, on either side of the border, could walk back the steps already taken to modernize Mexico's energy sector.

"They can't unmake that," says Duncan Wood about the constitutional reform, noting that it would be almost impossible politically in Mexico to reverse the decisions made so far, even though a future government could slow down future bids for oil exploration.

And it seems equally unlikely that any American government—no matter its stance on trade—will want to slow down the burgeoning trade in natural gas, oil, renewable energy, and electricity that has taken off between the two countries and is crucial for North America's future energy independence.

6

"We've Got a Huge Problem Here"

- -

Learning to Cooperate on Security Issues

Stephen Kelly wasn't sure whom to call first. For a moment, he could only stand there, in the middle of a busy street in Mexico City. It was Monday, September 5, 2005, a week after Hurricane Katrina had left hundreds of people dead, tens of thousands stranded, and more than a million displaced across Mississippi, Louisiana, and Texas. Kelly, second in command at the US embassy in Mexico City, had just gotten off the phone with his Mexican colleague Bosco Martí. Mexico wanted to help. President Vicente Fox could send two hundred soldiers commanded by a four-star general. They had forty-five vehicles, two portable water-treatment units, and a mobile kitchen that could feed 7,000 people a day. Kelly had thanked Martí for the kind offer—and then told him that the US government couldn't accept it without following a complicated permission procedure. His country had already turned back a German plane carrying fifteen tons of food intended for storm survivors because it hadn't been properly authorized.

Martí paused. Actually, the troops were already on their way. They would be at the border within forty-eight hours. If Kelly didn't do something, they too would be turned away. And that couldn't happen.

The Mexican Army had long been deeply suspicious of the United States. It believed that US drug-enforcement policies threatened Mexican sovereignty. It resented the obsolete, hand-me-down equipment it received from the US government. A century and a half after the war in which Mexico lost almost half its territory to the United States, the military was still training regularly to repulse a new invasion from the north. Security cooperation between the two nations had been limited and almost always fraught with tension and misunderstanding.

Yet now the Mexican Army was offering to help. "The last thing we wanted," Kelly says, "was to ruin the Kodak moment" by turning a genuine opportunity for collaboration into yet another source of conflict.

Kelly walked back to the embassy and started working the phones, reaching out to every Washington official he could. Martí called his own contacts in the State Department and Homeland Security. Both kept calling until late Wednesday night, when Joint Task Force Katrina finally agreed to accept the Mexican assistance. Contacts between the militaries on the two sides of the border also helped push this through.

The next morning, in Laredo, Texas, the Mexican Army set foot on US soil for the first time since the Mexican-American War ended in 1848. Images of the troops crossing the border were splashed across front pages throughout Mexico. As the soldiers made their way to San Antonio and served more than 170,000 meals to those displaced by the hurricane over the next three weeks, they made headlines across the United States too.

This simple act of kindness—accepted with good grace—had a transformative effect on the US-Mexican security relationship. "It became much more fluid," says Martí, head of North American affairs in the Mexican foreign ministry. "They stopped seeing us just as people who just lived nearby but rather also as partners who were willing to help out."

The goodwill built by the cooperation after Katrina would become particularly important in the coming years, because the challenges were about to get much bigger and would require a shift in thinking on both sides of the border.

A few years before Katrina, Adela Navarro, a young reporter, was studying English in the archives room of *Zeta*, the weekly newspaper of Tijuana, right across the border from San Diego. Suddenly a frantic call came in. "We've been shot! We've been shot!" It was her boss, Jesús Blancornelas, a founder of the paper, desperately radioing from a few blocks away.

Blancornelas had been ambushed on his way to work. His driver was dead. So was one of the ten attacking gunmen, killed by a bullet that ricocheted off his SUV. Blancornelas was wounded; bullet fragments were lodged in his stomach and intestines and near his spine. By the time Navarro got to the crime scene a few minutes later, Blancornelas was unconscious. As paramedics put him on a stretcher and wheeled him into an ambulance, they handed Navarro his bloody clothes.

Navarro and another colleague, Francisco Ortiz Franco, assumed command of *Zeta*. Navarro, then twenty-nine, had joined the paper right out of college after hearing Blancornelas speak at her school. She had been impressed by the way he'd challenged the city's corrupt legal system. "The police forces, prosecutors, and judges were all bought off," she says. "And Blancornelas had been the only one investigating them."

It was Thursday, November 27, 1997—a deadline day. With another issue of *Zeta* due out the next morning, Navarro and Ortiz Franco started on the story that mattered most: the shooting of their boss. The entire editorial team worked late into the night until it had enough evidence to conclude that the assassination attempt was the work of the Tijuana drug cartel run by the Arellano Félix family. In the following weeks, the journalists exposed bit by bit the details of the plot to kill Blancornelas—and named powerful people in the city behind the cartel.

Blancornelas survived and returned to run the paper. But in 2006 he succumbed to cancer, leaving Navarro, then only thirty-eight, to oversee *Zeta* once more—this time without Ortiz Franco, who'd been gunned down by cartel hit men two years before. Navarro, now traveling with bodyguards, vowed to continue the paper's fearless coverage of government and business complicity with the Arellano Félix family.

"We can't think of fear," she says, remembering that moment as her dark eyes narrow with intensity. "I just have to concentrate on the information. If I can confirm it, I'll publish it."

In the 1980s, Mexican traffickers like the Arellano Félix family, once small-time marijuana traffickers, started cornering the far more lucrative cocaine market, offering a new route to Colombian traffickers whose Caribbean routes American authorities had shut down. Within a few years, a handful of small Mexican trafficking groups—most of them with roots in the state of Sinaloa, south of Tijuana—dominated the cocaine business. And soon they began adding methamphetamine and heroin trafficking to their business model.

As the Mexican trafficking organizations grew in size, they often took control of local police forces and bought off local—and some-times even national—politicians, police chiefs, and prosecutors. And they also began to fight among themselves over smuggling routes, especially seaports, where they could import cocaine, and swaths of the border, which they needed to transport drugs into the United States. Most of the hard drugs—cocaine, heroin, and meth—crossed the border hidden in cars and trucks, while marijuana, a bulkier and cheaper product, often made its way through the desert. And some of the trafficking groups, including the Arellano Félix family, would eventually learn how to tunnel under the border too.

The first big mafia war took place in the late 1990s between the Arellano Félix family, who ran the Tijuana Cartel, and Joaquín Guzmán Loera, leader of the Sinaloa Cartel, better known as "Chapo" Guzmán. Blancornelas almost lost his life for reporting on the conflict between these competing groups, which included rival strategies for co-opting different law enforcement agencies into their service and frequent shoot-outs in the streets.

But this was only a prelude to the carnage to come. By the early 2000s there were four major crime groups—the Tijuana Cartel, the Sinaloa Cartel, the Juárez Cartel, and the Gulf Cartel—and a few smaller local ones. Both the Tijuana and Juárez cartels were essentially splinter groups that had broken away from the Sinaloa Cartel in the late 1980s and early 1990s. The Sinaloa Cartel, Mexico's largest crime group, divided again in 2008, giving birth to the ruthless Beltrán Leyva Organization.

Meanwhile, the Gulf Cartel, which had its own separate history in northeastern Mexico, just south of Texas, would eventually split too, giving birth to the Zetas, perhaps Mexico's most bloodthirsty crime group, whose name is ironically the same as that of the courageous Tijuana newspaper. The Zetas, in turn, would create a small but equally vicious cartel in southern Mexico called the Michoacán Family.

As these groups began to fight over territory, Mexico went through a spiral of violence. From 2007 to 2011, the nation's homicide rate tripled, from a modest 8 per 100,000—not far above the US homicide rate at the time—to more than 24 per 100,000, among the highest in the world. More than 45,000 Mexicans died in organized crime violence in those five years, with some cities, including Tijuana and Ciudad Juárez, outpacing some of the war-torn cities in Afghanistan and Iraq in the sheer number of deaths each day. Ciudad Juárez was, for three years, the world's most violent city, and Tijuana was not far behind.

Journalists in the cities where violence skyrocketed often played major roles in keeping citizens aware of what was going on in their hometowns—and they often paid a high price for this. More than a hundred reporters lost their lives between 2000 and 2015, according to the attorney general's office. While it's impossible to know how many of these deaths were linked directly to organized crime coverage, most probably were. Even today, Mexico still rivals several Middle Eastern countries as the most dangerous place to be a journalist.

In Tijuana, things worked out somewhat better than in other places. To implement the federal government's security strategy in

Tijuana, Mexican president Felipe Calderón assigned an army commander, General Alfonso Duarte, who built close ties both with civilian authorities and with the press. Rather than working around the local authorities, as often happens, he housed the police chief and state prosecutors on the military base, the only safe place in town to operate at the time, and backed the city government as it rebuilt the local police force from the bottom up. Adela Navarro gives General Duarte considerable credit for anchoring the security strategy and helping make the city safe.

Meanwhile, citizens—armed with knowledge they gained each week from reading *Zeta*—demonstrated in the streets against corrupt officials and businesses, shaming them and forcing authorities to arrest dozens of the cartels' accomplices. Small businesspeople and average citizens put together civic groups that pressured the government to improve policing and reform the judicial system, effecting massive changes in both the police and the courts. The courage of *Zeta*'s reporters, according to many of those involved, laid the foundations for these efforts.

After 2010, homicides began declining quickly in Tijuana, dropping by more than half. Public violence—bodies hung from bridges, shootouts in the streets, executions on main roads—disappeared almost entirely, although smaller crime groups continued to skirmish on the outskirts of town.

There has been an uptick of violence in Tijuana again since 2016, but this time the criminal groups have mostly fought with each other out of public view. Mexico hasn't stamped out organized crime or violence among groups, but in some cities, like Tijuana, criminals are no longer able to co-opt and coerce the authorities into working with them quite as easily as they were before.

Today Adela Navarro is cautiously optimistic about Tijuana. She has seen her city bounce back from its worst period of violence and emerge with more dynamism than ever. Yet she remembers a story she wrote a few years ago revealing that one of Tijuana's most prominent accountants worked closely with one of the kidnapping rings. His job was to help the kidnappers determine how much victims were worth so that they could ask for the right ransom amount. This side business helping kidnappers made the accountant a rich man, one of the many average citizens who became complicit in the city's horrors during its worst years. Navarro and her husband still bump into him from time to time. He serves as a reminder of the impunity enjoyed, even today, by some who collaborated with the crime rings.

It's hard to miss that Tijuana has shown exceptional resilience, thanks to average citizens and courageous journalists who tackled the violence head on. But Navarro knows that some are still willing to collude with the traffickers, and the city could slip back into chaos without the vigilance that journalists and civic groups exercise day to day. To that end, she keeps a large picture of Jesús Blancornelas at the entrance to *Zeta*'s offices, a vivid, daily reminder both of what journalists willing to risk their lives for the truth can achieve—and also of how much they have to lose.

Right as Adela Navarro was first taking Tijuana's *Zeta* newspaper over from Jesús Blancornelas, Arturo Sarukhan was arriving in Washington, DC, to attend a meeting on security cooperation between Mexico and the United States. It was October 2006, and Sarukhan had been the foreign policy advisor to a presidential candidate, Felipe Calderón, who almost no one had expected to do well in Mexico's elections that year. But Calderón had run a strong campaign and pulled out a razor-thin majority in the July elections. Now Sarukhan, a career diplomat who had taken leave from the foreign service to venture into presidential politics, was coordinating the foreign policy operations of the transition team.

As he listened to one of the speakers, a representative of the US Bureau of Alcohol, Tobacco, Firearms, and Explosives (ATF), promise that the agency would soon translate eTrace, its database, into Spanish, Sarukhan realized that things weren't going well. Sarukhan had been stationed in Washington in the 1990s as a young aide to the Mexican ambassador, and he had heard exactly the same speech and the same promise—eight years before. "When I left the embassy in 1998, we discovered we had a big problem with eTrace," says Sarukhan. "The [Mexican] agents in the field couldn't fill out the forms in English," which made it impossible to track weapons used in crimes in Mexico and then check if they had been sold in the United States. The US and Mexican governments had agreed to produce a version in Spanish that would allow the two countries to work together. But eight years later, they were no closer to actually producing the Spanish-language version of the software.

"We've got a huge problem here," he thought as he flew back to Mexico. "The counternarcotics cooperation of the bilateral relationship is on autopilot." Nothing much had changed for almost a decade, and he was about to have to deal with the consequences of that inertia. The experience of mobilizing the Mexican military to help in Katrina a year before might have helped break the ice between the two governments, but that wasn't enough to deal with the unprecedented violence that transnational crime groups were just starting to unleash on Mexico.

While Sarukhan was in Washington taking stock of the cooperation between the two countries, President-elect Felipe Calderón was back home in Mexico City getting reports from the outgoing government about the ways in which these crime groups had begun to take control over large swaths of Mexican territory. "It was very clear that the issue of organized crime was out of control," Sarukhan remembers, "and it had to do with the penetration at the state level."

What had already happened in Tijuana almost a decade earlier was now starting to happen all over the country. A few weeks earlier, right as the transition team had started its work, this had come vividly to the incoming administration's attention. A new organized crime group, the Michoacán Family, threw five severed heads into the middle of a dance floor in Uruapán, Michoacán, not far from where Calderón had grown up. This crime group, unlike most others, mixed a dose of religious fervor—a bizarre combination of Catholicism and Calvinism—with bloodthirsty criminal activity. Most crime groups existed only to make money, but the Michoacán Family had its own book of religious sayings and strange cultlike rituals, a frightening metamorphosis of an already deadly phenomenon.

Calderón, who barely mentioned public security issues during his presidential campaign, had begun to realize that they would have to be a priority for his administration when he took office in December. He would later consider the incident of the severed heads his wake-up moment. "If there was any event or trigger, that was it," Calderón told the *Wall Street Journal* four years later.

Calderón likened his realization to a surgeon's opening a patient, expecting appendicitis and instead finding a spreading cancer.

For the next six years, nothing would occupy him nearly as much as tackling organized crime. What at first promised to be a quick, clinical procedure would turn into a series of complex operations to manage a disease with no known cure. And this issue would dominate US-Mexican relations like few others.

Sarukhan, after his visit to Washington, realized the other part of the equation: there was little to no real strategic cooperation across the border to deal with organized crime groups that moved back and forth between the United States and Mexico. These groups lived primarily from the sales of illegal narcotics to American consumers, and the money and arms they obtained in the United States fueled the violence in Mexico. But Mexico's weak rule of law had also allowed them to gain a foothold in Mexico, using the country as a transshipment point for cocaine, and as a producer of marijuana, heroin, and methamphetamine. Tackling these groups without the assistance of the neighbor to the north would be impossible.

Calderón wasn't a natural fan of greater collaboration with the US government—he was a nationalist with a deep suspicion of the United States—but he agreed that Mexico needed help in confronting this growing threat. He and Sarukhan began to figure out how they could broach this with the American government.

"The only way we're going to get the Americans to have skin in the game is if it costs them," Sarukhan remembers he told Calderón. The Mexican government would have to ask the Americans to put money into attacking the organized crime groups, although the larger objective would be to get them involved in sharing intelligence and know-how in tackling the criminal networks. "It was one of the best ways to start fostering this relationship of co-responsibility."

On November 9, President-elect Calderón and President George W. Bush met for the first time at the White House, and Calderón raised the issue. Senior aides from both sides remember that Bush and Calderón met alone for a long time in the Oval Office, and when they emerged, maybe thirty or forty minutes later, Bush told his team that they would be working on security cooperation closely with the Mexican government. During the private meeting, Calderón had already floated a round number he wanted to request in security aid: $1 billion over three years. When Bush had asked him what he needed in terms of equipment, a straight-faced Calderón had responded, "If Jack Bauer's got it, I need it."

Bush had been well briefed about the growing violence in Mexico long before the meeting, and he longed to do something that would allow him to show solidarity with the country next door. As a former Texas governor, he knew Mexico better than any other country, and he wanted to create a meaningful bilateral agenda.

"This was an opportunity for real broadening and deepening of the cooperation," recalls Tony Garza, the US ambassador to Mexico at the time, a longtime confidant of President Bush and his close ally in Texas politics. Plus, adds Garza, "it was a natural extension of our counterterrorism efforts," which had already involved close collaboration since 9/11 between Mexican and American authorities to keep terrorists out of the hemisphere. But Bush also knew that funding for the Mexican government might meet with resistance in a US Congress already weary from the Afghanistan and Iraq wars.

Between January and March, the Mexican government began to put together the outlines of a request to the US government as it prepared for a summit meeting with Bush and Calderón, their first official meeting as heads of state, at a beautiful colonial hacienda near Merida, Yucatán. Sarukhan knew that what Mexico was about to request bore similarities to what the Colombian government had asked for in the 1990s to address drug trafficking gangs in that country. But unlike with Plan Colombia, a security cooperation package that involved US military collaboration and cash transfers, Sarukhan wanted to make sure there were no US boots on the ground in Mexico—a sensitive subject in a country that had lost so much territory to the United States in the 1848 war. And he knew that the Americans would want to make sure no actual money was transferred—an equally sensitive subject in the US Congress because of worries about corruption in Mexico.

Sarukhan, who had since been named Mexico's ambassador in Washington, had an even broader agenda behind pushing for the accord. "What NAFTA did for the economy, this would do for the geopolitical, geostrategic, intelligence side," he says, "which in a post-9/11 world was critically important." Americans were focused on security because of the 9/11 attacks, while Mexicans were becoming increasingly terrified of the reach of organized crime groups. Security would therefore be the logical anchor for the next round of cooperation between the two countries, much as trade had been in the 1990s.

In March, the long-awaited summit near Merida, Yucatán, produced the outline of an accord, called the Merida Initiative, with the US providing helicopters, airplanes, scanners, and software systems to Mexico, along with civilian training to improve rule of law. The package would not include any direct cash transfers or American boots on the ground, recognizing each side's particular sensitivities.

Many Mexicans applauded the deal, wanting the United States to step up and address an illegal trade driven by American consumption of narcotics, but some Mexicans also worried about opening the door to American interference in internal security affairs. On the other side of the border, reactions were similarly mixed. Most members of the US Congress applauded the chance to tackle the problem together with Mexico, but some worried about engaging with a country that still had serious problems with corruption and weak rule of law.

But the agreement between the two heads of state in Merida was really just the beginning. The Mexican government now had to come up with a coherent proposal that would make a difference in the government's ability to address organized crime and pass muster with the US Congress. Ambassador Garza remembers that the Bush administration decided that it was up to the Mexican side to come up with the first draft of a proposal. "We essentially handed Mexico the pencil and said how far can you go?"

Sarukhan acknowledges that the process wasn't easy. "What we did between March and June was a very painful process of getting all the requests lined up." It involved not only getting the Mexican security agencies—the army, navy, federal police, attorney general's office, intelligence service, customs, and migration service—to think about what they needed but figuring out how each agency's particular priorities added up to a coherent whole. The US government has a tradition of figuring out strategic priorities through interagency meetings convened by the National Security Council, but the Mexican government lacked an equivalent strategic process.

What eventually emerged was a $1.4 billion request spread out over three years, with $400 million in the first year, which included a mixture of hardware, software, and training. Not until October 2007, almost a year after the first meeting between Bush and Calderón, did the two presidents announce the final agreement on the Merida

Initiative. It marked the beginning of a new era of recognition that the two countries needed to tackle transnational crime groups together.

But a few bumps in the road would have to be navigated before these efforts could get off the ground.

"The goal in Washington," says Dan Fisk, who served as senior national security advisor to President Bush for Western Hemisphere affairs, "is to match ambitions with budgets." Fisk had been with President Bush during President Calderón's first visit to the Oval Office and later at the Merida meeting, and he understood Bush's desire to get something done with Mexico on security cooperation. But as a veteran of congressional and presidential policymaking, Fisk also understood that presidential will was only the beginning. Now came the fight in Congress.

Congress was initially skeptical about security cooperation with Mexico. The wars in Iraq and Afghanistan had strained budgets and pitted Democrats against President Bush. And immigration reform legislation, which Bush had supported strongly in both 2006 and 2007, had many Republicans at loggerheads with the White House—another issue they associated with Mexico.

Throughout the rest of 2007 and most of 2008, the Merida Initiative would languish on the Hill with little action. Meanwhile, violence in Mexico was starting to make headlines as the trafficking organizations started a series of new mafia wars against each other. This left Fisk and his colleagues in the administration "looking at things we could front-load through existing money."

The best way to get the Merida Initiative to a congressional vote appeared to be to attach it to an omnibus bill that included funding for the troops in Afghanistan and Iraq. "That was the vehicle that was moving the earliest," recalls Fisk. But many of Bush's cabinet members—and the powerful Office of Management and Budget—wanted to keep competing issues off the bill to fund the troops.

It took some inside lobbying from Fisk and then a last-minute call from Ambassador Tony Garza to the president's office to make the case for adding the Merida Initiative into the funding bill. They argued that the Mexicans simply couldn't wait any longer for the Bush administration to come through on its pledge of support. Garza made a trip to the White House to see Bush too, and after they talked, the president picked up the phone and called both Steven Hadley, his national security advisor, and Condoleezza Rice, the secretary of state, to make sure they knew he wanted the Merida Initiative within the funding bill.

So in fall 2008, the Congress approved the first tranche of Merida aid, $400 million worth of helicopters, airplanes, and scanners for border crossings. It was a huge step forward, but there was still a long way to go. American aid is subject to extensive procurement rules that can often delay equipment, especially larger items, for a year or two.

Sigrid Arzt, Calderón's national security advisor, remembers the consternation on the other side of the border as even more months passed without the expected equipment arriving. A young national security specialist who had befriended Calderón when he was president of his political party, Arzt found herself in the uncomfortable position of trying to explain America's slow-moving political process at a cabinet meeting as tempers exploded around her. One cabinet secretary wondered about the promised delivery of planes, another about helicopters, and third about other equipment. Some of the cabinet officials suspected that the Americans were toying with them, promising things that they couldn't deliver while Mexico burned.

And Mexican officials remembered a recent case, from 1999, when they had to return seventy-three surplus helicopters bought from the US government because they were barely serviceable. The experience had left a deep impression, especially in the Mexican military, which already distrusted American offers of assistance.

"There were a lot of stereotypes," remembers Arzt, but some of it was based on very real differences too. "In this we are oil and water," she says. Mexico's bureaucracy might not always work perfectly, but if the president wanted something done, government officials would cut through red tape with a knife to make it happen. In contrast, the American president had his hands tied not just by Congress but also by complex procurement rules designed to ensure careful vetting of foreign aid and fair competition in the bidding process to produce equipment that would be sent abroad.

Not until 2010, well into the Barack Obama administration, did Mexico finally begin to receive shipments of the promised helicopters and airplanes. But by then some of the training programs and software systems and a few smaller pieces of equipment had already begun to arrive, thanks to Bush administration officials who found ways of moving these less expensive parts of the agreement quickly.

The new president Obama and his secretary of state Hillary Clinton had made high-profile visits to Mexico shortly after Obama's inauguration—in March for Clinton and April for Obama, among their first trips abroad—during which they spoke about the need for "shared responsibility" in dealing with organized crime. Obama went to great lengths to point out that Americans' demand for illegal narcotics was driving the violence in Mexico and that money earned through drug sales in the United States and arms purchased in American gun stores were fanning the flames.

While Mexicans greatly appreciated this rhetorical acknowledgment of America's role in the violence, the two governments by then were already far down the path of collaborating in other, more tangible ways. Before Katrina, the relationship between security agencies on both sides of the border—both military and civilian—had been limited and fraught with tensions. The cooperation during Katrina had opened a window of opportunity to reassess this. Now the agreement on the Merida Initiative had gotten security agencies on both sides of the border talking to each other in new ways.

As we'll see in the next chapter, this cooperation would eventually extend quite deep into the agencies of both countries, allowing them to work together in unprecedented ways. This would help them take down some of Mexico's most feared organized crime groups over the next few years, often in jointly supported operations. But even as they reduced violence in some parts of the country— returning cities like Tijuana and Ciudad Juárez to some degree of normality—criminal violence would appear in other parts of the country, as circumstances on the ground in Mexico and American demand for illegal narcotics changed over time.

Between 2008 and 2017 the Merida Initiative provided over $2.7 billion in support for Mexico's efforts to deal with organized crime violence, helping its government acquire equipment and know-how to tackle some of the world's best-armed criminal organizations. By 2015 most of these organizations would be on the defensive, splintering into smaller crime groups with much-reduced reach. And Mexico's homicide rate had dropped significantly by then as well.

Later Mexico's homicide rate would rise again, as heroin use in the United States, but this period of intense cooperation showed what was possible. Perhaps the clearest effect of the Merida Initiative is that the two countries learned they could tackle a particularly difficult shared problem without excessive finger-pointing or ceding of sovereignty.

Today policymakers in the two countries address these issues less publicly than previously, but the cooperation is actually far more robust than anyone could have imagined in 2006, when the two governments first started fumbling their way toward greater cooperation in dealing with organized crime, or in 2005, when Katrina created the first opening for the security agencies of the two countries to engage with each other by breaking some of the taboos of the past.

According to Arturo Sarukhan, the former Mexican ambassador who helped negotiate the Merida Initiative, "It has slowly started to modify the way agencies on the two sides of the border relate to each other. We are nowhere near an ideal point…but we are miles from where we were."

7

"Turning the Cosa Nostra into the Sopranos"

Americans and Mexicans Confront Organized Crime Together

A s Eric Drickersen, a career agent in the Federal Bureau of Investigation (FBI), stared through his binoculars into Mexico from the US side of the border, he knew that things could go horribly wrong. On one cellphone he had members of the young man's family, guiding them through what they should tell the kidnappers who'd taken their son from their home near Los Angeles the day before; on another he had the Tijuana police, coordinating the joint rescue effort they were about to carry out. Positioned on a hill above the border, Drickersen caught sight of two kidnappers in the house on the other side of the fence. He could just make them out through the windows. He was pleased to have got there quickly, even ahead of the Tijuana police, who were also on their way.

He'd instructed the young man's family to keep communication open with the kidnappers and to offer to bring a ransom. The kidnappers had relayed the spot for the drop to the family, who then called Drickersen with the information. Drickersen passed it along to his contacts in the Tijuana police, who could then identify the location. Fortunately, it was just across the border fence in clear view from the US side.

As Drickersen had driven there from his downtown San Diego office, he had coordinated the mission with the Tijuana officers. Upon reaching the hill, he'd passed on specifics about the house—the location of the front door, which room the young man was in, where the kidnappers were standing, everything he could see from his vantage point. He knew the Mexican officers had a lot of experience with kidnappings—far more than any US agency would—but he also knew that a lot could go horribly wrong in a rescue attempt. Now all he could do was wait.

Drickersen, the FBI's border-liaison officer responsible for coordinating with Mexican police forces on everything from car theft to drug trafficking, had been offered the job in 2007, right as "things started to explode," he says. "Before, most of the violence had been infighting" among the cartels, "but then the business model changed.... They found new areas for revenue, like kidnapping for ransom and debt collection."

For Drickersen, who had grown up in Fairbanks, Alaska, and then spent most of his teens in his mother's hometown of Mexico City— once working as a balloon pilot so he could see the country from the air—the border-liaison job was a dream come true. After more than fifteen years serving as an FBI agent around the United States, he was finally working the border between the two countries he had called home as he was growing up.

He spent much of his time trying to break up drug-trafficking rings, but the cases that kept him awake at night were the kidnappings, when organized crime groups grabbed a victim in one country and ferried him or her across the border. Here a single misstep—or a cop on the take—could end someone's life.

"You find the people that you connect with, and you work with them," Drickersen explains. Official procedures through diplomatic channels could take days to work their way through the system, bouncing from the border to various offices in Washington and Mexico City and then eventually back again. When someone's life is at stake and you have to act quickly, it's all about the people you know and can depend on. "There is no law to compel Mexicans to enforce US laws," Drickersen says. "You're literally calling your friend to do the right thing." He adds, "The ability to get things done is based on personal relationships and the ability to call someone, have them answer, and put a plan in action"—just as he had done with this kidnapping.

In this case, everything went according to plan. The Tijuana police surprised and neutralized the kidnappers before they could fire a shot, secured the victim, and hustled him into a waiting vehicle. Drickersen picked up one of his phones and told the family their son was safe, then picked up the other and thanked the Mexican police commander who'd overseen the operation. Later that afternoon, he'd have to do the paperwork to justify the mission, get the kidnap victim back across the border to his family, and eventually extradite the kidnappers to the United States to stand trial. But for now, he could rest easy.

Things didn't always work out this well. Drickersen had already had to reckon with the ways corruption eroded trust in dealings across the border when one of his closest contacts in Mexico had been arrested for colluding with an organized crime group in 2010. He had worked a number of cases with this particular counterpart, a high-level state official, and considered him a law enforcement ally—that is, until the day he was listening to a wiretap of a particularly violent group, an offshoot of the Tijuana Cartel, and heard his counterpart speak on the other end. "He had a very distinct voice," he remembers. "I was in shock—I felt sad and betrayed."

After that, Drickersen learned to watch out for the warning signs that things were not as they seemed. While he continues to value his close working relationships with trusted colleagues, he is aware that sometimes "there is a gradual erosion of principles" among police officers who live surrounded by criminal groups and are subject to constant pressure to give in to them.

Still, he remains convinced that most of the officers he deals with in Mexico are not on the take. Like other US law enforcement officers, Drickersen has come to depend on his Mexican colleagues and calls them "the hardest-working cops I've ever worked with."

One of the least-known aspects of security cooperation between the United States and Mexico is the extent to which frontline officers now work together day to day, sharing investigations and intelligence. Most Mexicans know that Drug Enforcement Agency (DEA) agents collaborate in their country—news reports have associated them with the takedowns of many major drug lords in recent years. But most Mexicans—as well as most Americans—would be surprised by the actual depth of cooperation on both sides of the border and the personal bonds that drive this engagement. And they would be surprised to know that Mexican law enforcement officers are stationed inside the United States, much in the same way as American officers are in Mexico.

The border is, without a doubt, a unique place, where multiple law enforcement agencies stare at one another across a fence and have to develop mechanisms of trust to get things done on the other side. "The structure becomes personal at the border," says Drickersen.

But deeper inside both countries, many of the same dynamics are at play. Collaboration has grown closer over the past decade, as officers in key security and law enforcement agencies in the two governments have formed bonds of trust while trying to tackle the organized crime groups that move illegal drugs, money, and weapons between the two countries.

Cooperation efforts have focused not only on taking down criminal groups that prey on citizens on both sides of the border but also on investing in building institutions that make it hard for them to operate with impunity, such as courts, police, and prosecutors, as well as securing the border and strengthening communities' resilience in the face of violence. Civic organizations and individual activists for change in both countries have played a huge role in these efforts too, building a bridge between citizens and government. And they often push governments to enact needed changes and hold them accountable for their actions.

On the ground, the story of the past decade has been one of intense and often unseen cooperation across the border. It's showed that even on the most difficult and sensitive of issues, Americans and Mexicans have been able to find common ground and develop close forms of cooperation that go far beyond the preconceptions that they once had of each other.

But politicians haven't always risen to the occasion. After a period of intense focus on security cooperation, political leaders in both countries have started to pay less attention to the serious issues that organized crime represents for the two countries and have given far less guidance on priorities for security cooperation.

This has done little to lessen the extent of day-to-day engagement between agencies and civic groups in the two countries, but it's left the broader strategy for dealing with organized crime adrift at a time when the criminal groups are mutating in new and dangerous ways, in large part as a result of the heroin epidemic in the United States.

Still, even without high-level attention, the day-to-day inter-actions between agencies and individuals remain the backbone of US-Mexican efforts to stymie and stop drug traffickers, money laun-derers, arms dealers, kidnappers, and other criminals who use the border to their advantage. "Cop to cop, it's always been a good rela-tionship," Drickersen says. "There may be leadership guidance that changes. But on the ground, guys work together."

Shortly before Eric Drickersen arrived at the border, Roberto Hernández, a young Mexican lawyer, was starting to spend time in the archives of a Mexican courthouse, and he was horrified by what he learned. In 2002, Hernández was conducting a survey-research project to understand the disparities in sentences handed down by judges, but every time he wandered into the archives, he felt he should photograph the scene. The shelves, overflowing with files haphazardly thrown on top of each other—often with key evidence missing—seemed a perfect metaphor for Mexico's broken judicial system.

Thumbing through some of the files, he came across cases that ranged from bizarre to simply baffling. One man had been jailed for stealing a plastic mango, another for pilfering an old belt, yet another for swiping a crushed Twinkie from its rightful owner. In many other cases the infractions were much more serious, but the evidence was often flimsy, and it was sometimes hard to tell if the suspect convicted of the crime had anything to do with it at all.

Hernández, then in his late twenties, knew the Mexican judicial system was corrupt. All Mexicans knew that. But he started to realize that the problem was also one of structure. Even without corruption, the courts were set up to fail. They lacked even the most basic procedures to ensure a fair trial. Entering the justice system was "a kind of lottery," he recalls.

Most Mexicans had seen *Law and Order* and *CSI*, prime-time programs broadcast on Mexican television, and they thought their police and court systems were similar to those in the United States, just less effective and more corrupt. They didn't realize that Mexico had no courtrooms and that almost no one gathered forensic evidence—or much evidence at all.

Instead, prosecutors presented confessions, circumstantial evidence, and often questionable eyewitness testimony in written briefs to a judge, who presided over what accounted for a trial in his or her office. Defendants could offer written rebuttals that would be added to the file for the judge to review. On rare occasions defendants were allowed to respond verbally to accusations in the judge's office—but only while locked in a contraption that looked like a giant metal cage. In reality most defendants never even saw a judge during their trials, much less had a chance to confront their accusers, since judges rarely showed up, leaving court clerks to take testimony and pore over the written evidence in the judge's chamber.

Hernández was at a loss for what to do until one day he walked into a judge's office and saw a scene every bit as shocking as the disorderly archives. In the midst of a trial, the judge had stopped the proceedings to celebrate a birthday. The judge, prosecutor, and defense attorney were all drinking, eating cake, and laughing loudly together in the magistrate's small chamber while the defendant sat in the giant metal cage in the corner.

"You wouldn't recognize this as a courtroom," Hernández thought, but "surveys just aren't going to pick up any of this." He realized that he would have to film what the judicial system actually looked like and show it to the Mexican people.

Hernández convinced a highly respected corporate lawyer, Ernesto Canales, who shared his passion for judicial reform, to help finance a low-budget documentary about the courts. He pieced together small grants from the US embassy and the California-based Hewlett Foundation to make ends meet.

It took him a year to produce a simple documentary, *The Tunnel*. Through a series of interviews, it provides dramatic evidence of the egregious inefficiency and ineffectiveness of the Mexican judicial system. Hernández even filmed the judge who had presided over the unseemly birthday party in his chambers. Then he and Canales spent several months showing the film to lawmakers in the Mexican Congress, who were looking at ways to change the country's criminal code.

The film was far from polished, but for the first time it offered people outside the court system a firsthand look at how haphazardly the judicial system operated. Even lawmakers found the gap between reality and their expectations shocking. Hernández and Canales also convinced Televisa, the country's leading television network, to broadcast the film one evening, providing a vivid and embarrassing contrast to the usual fare of *CSI* and *Law and Order*.

The Tunnel played a sizable role in pushing the Mexican Congress to approve a far-reaching judicial reform in July 2008, right as violence was on the rise across the country and Mexico and the United States were trying to come to terms on the Merida Initiative.

The reform—drafted largely by the Network for Oral Trials, a small group of lawyers, journalists, and activists that Ernesto Canales had helped start—enshrined in the constitution the presumption of innocence, limited the use of confessions, and required that all evidence be presented in open court, where family members, friends, and the press could be present. It also allowed for plea bargaining and alternative sentences for minor crimes, imposed clearer procedures for interrogations, and mandated strict regulations for keeping records of trials. It was a sweeping change to a system that had been largely ignored for decades.

Though few realized it at the time, the Network for Oral Trials, the eclectic group of lawyers pushing for the reform, had received most of its support through a grant from the US Agency for International Development (USAID) via the American embassy. The US government was working quietly to assist Mexican organizations that were trying to strengthen rule of law, even while Congress was still debating the Merida Initiative.

But Roberto Hernández knew that Mexico's courts had eight years to implement the reform—an eternity in bureaucratic terms—and there was a good chance that the changes might never get put into practice. Before long, he and his wife, Layda Negrete, also an attorney, hit upon what they would do next to make sure the reform actually garnered public support.

The family of Toño Zúñiga, a young man imprisoned for murder, approached them and begged them to take his case. After some thought, they agreed and succeeded in getting a retrial. They also decided to film the upcoming court case—something never before done in Mexico.

The movie that emerged from that effort, *Presumed Guilty*, is a masterpiece of documentary filmmaking and tells a gripping story—so much so that it won an Emmy in the United States when shown on PBS, and 1.7 Mexicans paid to see the film in theaters, making it the third most popular Mexican movie of the year. USAID quietly helped fund the movie, along with the Hewlett Foundation and, of course, Ernesto Canales, the corporate attorney who had invested in Hernández's first film.

Presumed Guilty covers the retrial of its protagonist, Toño, a well-spoken computer programmer, rapper, and break dancer from a working-class neighborhood who is accused of murder. During the retrial, Toño's lawyer—a top criminal attorney recruited by Hernández and Negrete—manages to take apart all the prosecution's evidence and get the only witness to recant his testimony. Despite that, the judge, relying only on the written evidence, again convicts Toño of murder and sentences him to another twenty years in jail.

But the story doesn't end there. In a twist worthy of a Hollywood blockbuster, an appeals court, on viewing video of the retrial, which Hernández and his wife have filmed, overturns Toño's conviction and sets him free. As the movie ends, Toño, who married his longtime girlfriend while in jail, is released just in time to hold his newborn son. Audiences routinely finish watching the film in tears.

Presumed Guilty played a huge role in educating the Mexican public about the way the court system actually worked, and it helped place judicial reform at the top of the public agenda in Mexico and ensure implementation of the reform. Today courts that have done so—now a majority in the country—have more structure and coherence. Trials are filmed, and judges have to show up. Defendants can question their accusers and any witnesses. And minor crimes can now be dealt with through alternative sentencing that focuses on restitution rather than jail time.

Hernández, who has been studying the implementation, believes that the rate of wrongful convictions has gone down noticeably under the new rules. That's good for innocent defendants, but it also places greater responsibility on police to catch the right person at the outset, thus reducing impunity. He knows that these changes are not enough—there are still too many wrongful convictions in the country—but it's a step in the right direction.

Roberto Hernández is only one of Mexico's many social reformers who have been tackling the country's weak rule of law with creativity and determination. In the northern city of Monterrey, Miguel Treviño de Hoyos, another member of the Network for Oral Trials, and his colleagues decided to take on the issue of public corruption by staging a public bus tour of corruption sites around their city.

"We wanted to do something simple and playful," says Treviño de Hoyos, "something that was didactic and understandable." The result was the "Corruptour," which looked like one of those bus tours that ferries tourists around town but instead aimed to show locals places where government authorities had engaged in malfeasance or conspired with organized crime groups. Stops on the tour included, among many others, city hall, the state congress, the former home of a major drug lord who had lived in plain sight, and a burned-down casino extorted by an organized crime group in league with city officials.

The Corruptour was so effective in putting corruption on the public agenda that in 2015, when the state of Nuevo León—where

Monterrey is located—held elections, the only candidate who had campaigned on rooting out corruption won. In one of his first moves, the new governor created the country's first Prosecutor's Office for Corruption, giving the new office wide-ranging authority to pursue allegations of public corruption. And the governor named Ernesto Canales, the corporate lawyer who had funded Roberto Hernández's films and helped start the Network for Oral Trials, as the first person to serve in that role. Canales, now in his seventies, left his lucrative law practice to take the job.

Canales, in his role as the anticorruption prosecutor, has since filed charges against one former governor, three mayors, and dozens of other public officials for malfeasance, stripping them of the impunity they once enjoyed. Most of the cases continue to work their way through the courts, and their outcome will eventually tell us a lot about whether the Mexican courts are up to the challenge of dealing with high-profile corruption cases.

Ernesto Canales knows that Mexico has a long road ahead to eradicate corruption and build rule of law, but he believes that at least in his home state they've made a start. "A state government official will think twice today before stealing," he says, because for the first time graft may have consequences.

When I asked him what Mexico needs to tackle corruption nationwide, he didn't miss a beat in answering. "We need another *Presumed Guilty*, but this one about corruption."

Lupita Dávila remembers when her teenage son Rodrigo started to practice football—American football, as it's known in Mexico, to differentiate it from soccer, which is also called football. It gave him a sense of focus and purpose, and he came home and told his parents the key lesson he'd learned from his coach about moving the ball down the field: "Don't stop moving your legs." He knew it was a life lesson as well as a football strategy.

But on January 30, 2010, while Rodrigo and a group of his friends were celebrating a birthday party at the house of one of his teammates in Villas de Salvárcar, a neighborhood on the south side of Ciudad Juárez, just across the border from El Paso, Texas, they were suddenly surrounded by members of the Barrio Azteca, a gang allied with the Juárez Cartel. The gang members ordered the girls to leave the party and then started shooting all the boys. Rodrigo and eleven others died in the house, along with three adults from the neighborhood who tried to stop the shooting.

The gang members had apparently heard that some of the kids at the party belonged to the Artistas Asesinos (Killer Artists), a rival gang, usually just called the "Double A," that worked for the rival Sinaloa Cartel. It was a tragic mix-up: most of the partygoers were football players, but a few played baseball in the local youth AA league, also called the "Double A." The killers had mistaken one "Double A" for the other.

Lupita Dávila says that part of her died that day, and on some days—even years later—she still finds it hard to go on when she thinks about Rodrigo. "It hasn't been easy at all," she admits. But she had other children to raise and protect, and she began to look for a way to honor Rodrigo's legacy. Later that year, she helped start Jaguares Jóvenes de Bien (Young Jaguars for Good), a program to keep young people out of trouble in Ciudad Juárez through after-school activities that teach self-respect and discipline. "I was trying to make sense out of

Rodrigo's death," she says. "I know he would do the same things for his fellow comrades."

Starting in January 2008, Ciudad Juárez had become the world's most violent city, with an average of more than eight killings a day in a metropolis with a little over 1 million inhabitants. The violence had started when "Chapo" Guzmán's Sinaloa Cartel decided to wrest control of drug-trafficking operations in the city from the local Juárez Cartel. Both sides recruited local enforcers and street gangs as allies and allowed their supporters to moonlight in other criminal enterprises like extortion and kidnapping. Ciudad Juárez erupted into an inferno of violence worse than anything Mexico had seen before, outpacing even the carnage in Tijuana.

Mexico had been through so many massacres in the previous few years that people had become inured to gruesome killings, but the Villas de Salvárcar massacre shook Mexicans out of their collective state of resignation. It was partly the image of the teenagers as victims that did it—but it was also the parents' response. The parents, including Lupita Dávila, refused to remain silent, and several of them confronted President Felipe Calderón on his next visit to the city about how he planned to change things.

Their courage galvanized other citizens' groups in Ciudad Juárez to spring to action, and President Calderón left having promised not just to send more police but also to invest money in the youth of the city.

Carlos Pascual, who had become President Barack Obama's first ambassador to Mexico only four months earlier, also saw an opportunity in this shift. "What struck me," he remembers, "was that the whole focus of what we were doing was going after bad guys," trying to break apart the crime groups by arresting their leaders. That was important, but it wasn't enough or even a coherent strategy to address transnational crime groups that had taken over cities and towns across Mexico and had tentacles reaching into American communities too. Pascual wanted to do something that would empower communities to fight back.

Working with Calderón's new national security advisor, Jorge Tello, Pascual sketched a four-pillar approach to the security relationship that would combine going after the crime groups (pillar one) with investments in rule of law (pillar two), a new way of managing the border collaboratively (pillar three), and support for community efforts to tackle crime and violence (pillar four).

In the wake of the Villas de Salvárcar massacre, President Calderón created Todos Somos Juárez (We Are All Juárez), an ambitious program to invest in the city through job training, creation of new public spaces, and support for local youth groups. Pascual saw an opening for the US government to work closely on this too. " 'Todos Somos Juárez' took pillar four and put its arms around it and said let's do this in a big way," he says. The US government pledged millions of dollars in matching funds to back citizens' efforts to tackle crime.

Lupita Dávila remembers this as the period when people in Ciudad Juárez began to take their city back. "We achieved a change," she remembers. "Civil society took over the streets"—and took them away from the crime groups that had kept everyone cowering in their homes. And she remembers that a good part of the assistance for building programs around the city came through collaborative efforts with the local consulate. "There was a very good connection" with the US consulate, she remembers. "They built ties with society." And for the first time the Mexican government—federal, state, and local—began to sit down with civil society groups in Ciudad Juárez to plan a strategy for the city's future.

"Organized crime took away my son from me, but today I'm taking young people away from the organized crime groups," Dávila says proudly about her work to give teenagers alternatives to crime. Today thousands of children and youths go through the programs that she and her colleagues run, which address bullying, domestic violence, addiction, and life skills.

Ambassador Pascual and Jorge Tello, the national security advisor, also knew they had to improve rule of law to change the equation in Ciudad Juárez. Together they pulled off a secret binational meeting at a US Army base in El Paso, Texas, to develop a strategy for improving policing in the city. Drawing on the expertise of people from around the world who had dealt with similar conflicts, they came up with a blueprint that included community policing, a rapid-response system for reporting crime, partnerships with civil society groups for monitoring communities, and the use of data-driven policing, much of it implemented over the ensuing months. The two governments also launched a massive campaign to take apart the cartels and their enforcers.

After three years as the most violent city in the world, from 2008 to 2010, Ciudad Juárez actually began to experience a decline in homicides, from around ten a day in 2010 to only two a day in 2012 and then dropping further through 2015. While drug-trafficking groups still ship narcotics through the city—and the Sinaloa Cartel clearly won its fight against the Juárez Cartel—there is nothing today quite like the mafia control of the city that once existed. At night, people are out on the streets again. Today it's sometimes hard to remember that this city, which seems so normal, was once one of the most violent places on earth.

Carlos Pascual's tenure as American ambassador in Mexico lasted only two years, but he left a mark with the idea of a four-pillar strategy that goes beyond law enforcement responses to organized crime to include investments in institution building and civic infrastructure, critical building blocks for strengthening rule of law.

In Villas de Salvárcar a modern athletic complex now stands where empty fields once provided the only green space among the crowded row houses. A small monument bears the names of the twelve teenagers and three adults who died in the massacre. It's an eerie reminder that the city's resurgence is the result of their unwitting sacrifice and their families' willingness to fight for their memory.

And Lupita Dávila, when she feels she can't go on any more, remembers what her son used to say—"Don't stop moving your legs"— and she keeps on with her efforts to make sure her city doesn't slide back into chaos.

When a plane carrying personnel from Mexico's key security agencies returned from Kabul, Afghanistan, in 2010, Guillermo Valdés, head of Mexico's intelligence service, knew he had won the battle to set up Mexico's first international fusion center, a place where agencies from the US and Mexican governments would work together under the same roof. The secret trip had given key members of the security agencies an opportunity to see how an international fusion center operates.

President Calderón had appointed Valdés to head the Center for Research on National Security (CISEN), Mexico's equivalent of the Central Intelligence Agency (CIA), because Valdés was a longtime confidante whom he trusted to guide the government's security strategy. And he wanted Valdés to help manage the growing relationship with the US government, as the Merida Initiative talks were moving forward.

Mexico already had one domestic fusion center at CISEN's headquarters, but it followed a far different model. The original fusion center at CISEN, set up in 2007, was designed to bring the key security agencies of the Mexican government together. It had played a critical role in mapping the seven major crime groups that had terrorized the country, but it operated only occasionally—and the agencies involved often showed significant distrust toward each other.

In contrast, the new fusion center, which opened later in 2010 in the northern city of Monterrey, had representatives not only from different agencies but from both sides of the border living and working together in close quarters. In fact, they were required to live together for six months at a time without going out of the compound to protect them from outside threats. The United States had personnel from multiple agencies, including the Defense Intelligence Agency, CIA, Immigration and Customs Enforcement (ICE), and DEA, colocated with their Mexican counterparts, CISEN, the Federal Police, and the Mexican Army and Navy. At Mexico's request, all the US personnel were civilians, given sensitivities about having US military personnel in operational roles inside the country.

While Mexico was integrating US agencies into its new fusion center in Monterrey, several Mexican agencies were already operating north of the border in US installations at the express invitation of American authorities. The US Northern Command, for example, had invited the Mexican Army and Navy to station officers with them at the North American Aerospace Defense Command (NORAD), the ultrasecret facility that also houses part of the US missile defense network high in the Colorado mountains. And the DEA, which oversees the El Paso Intelligence Center (EPIC), a major fusion center in El Paso, Texas, that looks at drug trafficking, invited agents from the Mexican Federal Police and CISEN to join them. And from time to time, US drug-trafficking task forces focused on specific cases have invited Mexican participation, often from the Federal Police.

Only a couple years earlier, the notion of Mexican troops coming to the aid of Katrina flood victims had been a novelty. Now personnel from each country's top security agencies were embedded with their counterparts from the other side of the border in some of the most sensitive locations each government operated. Valdés was proud of these advances.

The Monterrey fusion center had a narrow but very important mission: to track and destroy the Zetas, the most violent organized crime group operating between the two countries. Unlike other crime groups, which mostly lived off trafficking in illegal narcotics distributed to willing consumers in the United States, the Zetas' business model involved taking over—and starting—a range of illegal activities in the territory they controlled. Other cartels could often operate in swaths of Mexican territory almost unnoticed, since they primarily moved drugs. At most they needed the protection of local police or mayors, but they rarely had an interest in preying openly on local communities.

The Zetas were different. They not only moved drugs but kidnapped for ransom, extorted local businesses, stole gasoline from oil pipelines, and engaged in smaller business ventures, like controlling the local sale of pirated CDs and DVDs. Over time the Zetas would exert a powerful influence over some of the other crime groups, leading them into increasingly predatory behavior. And the Zetas not only preyed on local communities but seemed intent on spreading their model across the country. Originally the enforcement arm of the Gulf Cartel, they had broken away from that group violently in early 2010 and then started a separate mafia war with the Sinaloa Cartel.

Then the San Fernando massacre happened.

For three days straight in March 2011, local Zetas pulled over every bus coming through San Fernando, a small town in the northeastern state of Tamaulipas, and slaughtered the passengers. Some they shot outright; others they tortured; still others they forced to fight each other to the death in gladiator-style matches. By the time the killers had finished, almost two hundred bodies lay buried in mass graves on a ranch just outside town, where investigators discovered them a few weeks later.

No one really knows why the local Zetas went on this brutal killing spree against civilians who appear to have been mostly Mexican migrants heading from the state of Michoacán to the US border, but the gang members probably mistook the travelers for reinforcements on their way to support a rival cartel.

And this wasn't even the first massacre in San Fernando. A few months earlier, the same group of Zetas had slaughtered seventy-three Central and South American migrants passing through on their way to the border. This small town in northern Mexico had become the focus of some of the country's worst violence, and the government hadn't been able to come up with a response. When Guillermo Valdés heard about the second set of killings by the Zetas, he knew that quick action was required to ensure that the killers didn't get away.

Fortunately, with the fusion center in place, the Mexican and US governments had a far more detailed mapping of the structure and operations of the Zetas than ever before. They were able to go after the perpetrators immediately. "Of all those who were involved in the San Fernando massacre," says Valdés, "we grabbed them within three weeks." Only the top leader escaped, and he was eventually captured five months later. There would be no more massacres in San Fernando.

In the rest of the northeast, the battle against the Zetas took longer. "It's like putting together a puzzle," Valdés recalls, "where the last two pieces are the hardest, but they depend on the information you gathered earlier." Through 2011 and 2012 the Mexican government, supported by US intelligence, took apart most of the Zetas' organizational structure cell by cell until only the last two puzzle pieces remained: the two most visible leaders of the organization, Heriberto Lazcano (known as Z-3) and Miguel Treviño (Z-40).

The Mexican Navy played the lead role in going after the Zetas. It has several elite units largely trained abroad in Spain, Israel, and the United States; they are similar to Navy SEALs in the United States—mobile and extremely precise. American intelligence agencies had developed an especially close relationship with these units—and the Mexican Navy overall—noting that they had become quite sophisticated in their operations and careful in their use of intelligence.

"The navy was a virgin organization," says Raúl Benítez, a security scholar at Mexico's National Autonomous University, because it had never been involved in internal security operations before and didn't have the same problems with corruption that parts of the Mexican Army did. In the campaign against the Zetas, the navy would take the intelligence developed by the fusion center and the specific agencies and go after the Zetas' operations piece by piece.

In October 2012, a Mexican Navy unit flushed Lazcano, Z-3, out of hiding and killed him in a shootout. Valdés had left the government by then and was busy writing a book in Spain, but he celebrated when he heard the news.

Then, in July 2013, now well into the Enrique Peña Nieto administration, the Mexican Navy arrested Treviño, the Zetas' most bloodthirsty leader, as he visited family members only a few miles from the US border.

Today the Zetas, once the most feared crime group in Mexico, are a shadow of their former selves, a collection of isolated, small, but sometimes still very violent groups, spread across the eastern coast of Mexico. While many Zetas cells still continue to plague specific towns and regions in Mexico, they appear neither to have any central coordination nor to operate in many areas they once controlled.

Mexico's once most feared organized crime group, it turned out, couldn't withstand a joint effort by the Mexican and US governments. But bringing about this end required that the two governments learn to share information first and transform it into intelligence.

In June 2012, as the Mexican Navy was going after the Zetas in the north of Mexico, dozens of FBI agents, supported by helicopters, converged on a large ranch in Oklahoma. The quarter horses raised there were among the best in the American Southwest, winning races in New Mexico, California, and Texas. The owner was one of the most prolific and sought-after buyers of racehorses in the country.

But as it turned out, the owner was also the brother of Miguel Treviño, the Zetas leader known as Z-40, who had provided the funds for the ranch and the horses as a way of laundering money for the cartel.

The arrest generated more than its share of news—after all, laundering drug money for Mexico's most ruthless cartel through a high-profile horse ranch in Oklahoma was pretty brazen—but it also stood out as one of the few major operations against the support structures of the cartels in the United States.

There is no shortage of small-time drug dealers in American jails—over half of all US arrests are for drug-related offenses—but there have been relatively few high-profile arrests of major facilitators of the drug business in the United States. In fact, we know surprisingly little about how the business operates once the cartels cross the border. "We are lacking strategic intelligence" inside the United States, Guillermo Valdés notes. "We really need to know what is the business and market of the drug trade," including how the groups move billions of dollars in drug profits back to Mexico from the United States each year. We lack this information partly because most of the violence has occurred on the Mexican side of the border, leading to greater attention there, and partly because US agencies that follow domestic crime, such as the FBI and the DEA, do so largely on a law enforcement model, building cases, rather than on an intelligence model that tries to understand the way criminal groups operate broadly.

Throughout 2011, as the FBI was zeroing in on Treviño's Oklahoma horse ranch and the Monterrey fusion center was mapping the Zetas' structure in northeastern Mexico, Valdés worked closely with John Brennan, then the White House's chief counterterrorism advisor (and later CIA director), on a project to map the structure and networks of the organized crime groups on both sides of the border. The secret effort was designed to produce a joint assessment of how these groups operated and the ways that they moved both drugs and money. Ultimately there was too much disagreement among agencies on some of the specifics, and the assessment never saw the light of day.

Despite frequent statements about "shared responsibility" during both the George W. Bush and Barack Obama administrations and pledges by both to address the demand for illegal narcotics, money laundering, and arms smuggling, very little headway has been made on any of these aspects of the drug trade in the United States compared to what the countries do together south of the border.

The one notable exception has been some success in getting American banks to comply with anti-money-laundering statutes, including the levying of gigantic fines against HSBC and Wachovia (now part of Wells Fargo) for violations. But we know relatively little about how the illegal narcotics business operates in the United States, other than that it is highly decentralized, with Mexican organized crime groups partnering with a myriad of smaller US-based gangs, motorcycle clubs, and other local distributors.

In contrast, the two countries have worked together quite successfully inside Mexico to decimate the large criminal organizations that traffic drugs. Alan Bersin, former assistant secretary for policy at the Department of Homeland Security, calls this "turning the Cosa Nostra into the Sopranos": taking giant organized crime groups and turning them into small, less threatening ones.

Today, little remains of six of the seven large crime groups that once controlled large swaths of territory in Mexico: the Zetas, the Tijuana Cartel, the Juárez Cartel, the Gulf Cartel, the Beltrán Leyva Organization, and the Michoacán Family. Only the Sinaloa Cartel, the country's largest crime group, appears to have survived intact, but even it appears to be dividing after the arrest of its leader, "Chapo"

Guzmán, and his extradition to the United States in early 2017. Another medium-sized crime group—the Jalisco New Generation Cartel—has arisen out of parts of the Sinaloa Cartel and may become more threatening over time, but it doesn't appear to have the size of some of the earlier groups that once controlled large pieces of Mexican territory.

Efforts to strengthen rule of law and build resilient communities have also helped reduce the size of the organized crime groups. The greater effectiveness of courts, police, and prosecutors' offices—while still far from perfect—means that it's harder for crime groups to operate openly in many parts of Mexico today, including in those cities like Ciudad Juárez and Tijuana where citizens organized to push for institutional changes and hold their leaders accountable. For the first time, organized crime groups actually have an incentive to operate in the shadows—and in far more decentralized ways, much like they do in the United States—at least in some of the most developed parts of the country.

Homicide rates dropped steadily, by about a third, from 2011 to 2015. And several of the cities that once were the sites of the worst violence—Ciudad Juárez, Tijuana, and Monterrey, among them—have become much safer places to live.

But as things improved, the US and Mexican governments paid less high-level attention to security cooperation as a major issue in the bilateral relationship. Enrique Peña Nieto, who took over as Mexico's president from Calderón in late 2012, was particularly skeptical about high-level cooperation efforts with the US government, although his administration largely left in place the day-to-day efforts between agencies on both sides of the border. Donald Trump, inaugurated in early 2017, was even more skeptical about cooperation with Mexico, although several members of his cabinet have tried to engage pro-actively with their Mexican counterparts. Ultimately, although op-erational cooperation between agencies on both sides of the border continued, there was far less policy attention, and sensitive efforts, like the Monterrey fusion center, soon fell apart.

And in Mexico progress toward strengthening local police forces and courts also stalled. This was highly problematic, since the basic premise of the strategy was that reducing giant crime networks to small "Soprano-like" local crime groups would allow local authorities to go after them. This worked well in some of the largest cities, where the reforms stuck, but far less so in many other parts of the country where police, prosecutors, and courts remained underdeveloped and easily susceptible to corruption or coercion by well-financed and heavily armed crime groups, even smaller ones.

Starting in 2015 homicide rates began to rise again in Mexico, just as Americans started to become aware of the opioid epidemic in the United States. This was no coincidence. Although the opioid crisis began with the misuse of painkillers, it soon led to an increasing de-mand for heroin and synthetic opioids.

Deaths from heroin overdoses in the United States quadrupled between 2010 and 2016, according to the Centers for Disease Control and Prevention. Heroin and other opiates had once comprised a fairly small part of the drug trade between Mexico and the United States—so much so that smaller groups with only loose affiliations with the larger transnational crime organizations generally controlled the business. Most drug money had come from cocaine, with additional profits in methamphetamine and marijuana.

The meteoric rise in heroin addiction in the United States led to a scramble to control poppy production and processing in Mexico and new smuggling routes to reach American consumers. The US State Department believes that heroin production in Mexico more than doubled between 2013 and 2015. And Mexican traffickers have also become key intermediaries for shipments of fentanyl and other synthetic opiates from China, which often arrive by boat in Mexico and then make their way north.

By 2017, homicide rates in Mexico had once again climbed to 2011's levels—and perhaps even higher. The failure to carry through on reforms for rule of law in Mexico, combined with the drift in bilateral cooperation, had led to a return of violence that would have been unthinkable three years before.

Yet this time there are some differences in the violence. For the most part, there are still no large crime groups fighting with each other; rather, a mixture of smaller groups and possibly factions within the Sinaloa Cartel are going to war with each other. From a national security standpoint, this is clearly better, though still equally deadly for local communities.

And, surprisingly, this time other crimes don't appear to be rising in the same way. In fact, citizens report limited or no rise in other criminal activities, according to the country's largest survey of citizens' perceptions of crime. There is some reason to believe that even with the backsliding in security policy, circumstances in most places in Mexico are still better than they were a few years ago.

The reasons for this are clear in cities like Ciudad Juárez, Tijuana, and Monterrey, where citizens pushed for stronger public security institutions. Organized crime violence may have increased, but traffickers are careful to conduct their business—including killing their rivals—out of the public view as much as possible. And they are less engaged in the kind of violent side activities, like kidnapping and extortion, that took place during the earlier period. This represents a major step ahead in parts of the country for rule of law, even if the rise in homicides is still a major source of concern.

But there are other places in Mexico, like the states of Colima and Nayarit—small, seaside regions that never experienced much in the way of violence—where the rise in homicides has been sudden and devastating. And nowhere has it been more destructive than in Guerrero, Mexico's poorest state, home to many of the country's poppy fields and a major seaport that connects to Asia. Guerrero—my wife's home state—has long had some of the country's highest crime rates, but the rise of heroin trafficking has added a new dimension to the horrors people who live there must deal with.

The September 2014 killing of forty-three college students in Iguala, Guerrero, a case that seared the nation's conscience, most likely was tied to heroin trafficking. According to an international commission investigating the case, the students seem to have inadvertently commandeered a bus full of heroin on its way to the United States, which led the small, local organized crime group that controls heroin trafficking in and around the city to go after them.

The case highlighted the continuing complicity of Mexican government officials with organized crime—the local mayor and several state and perhaps federal security agencies appear either to have been involved in the local heroin trade or to have looked the other way. But it also underscored the connections between the violence in Mexico and the demand for illegal narcotics in the United States. The students had become caught up in the shifting contours of drug trade that was becoming focused increasingly on heroin shipments across the border.

More than a decade after Presidents Bush and Calderón decided to deepen security cooperation between the two countries, the ability of law enforcement and security agencies to work with each other—both across the border and within each other's countries—remains deep and consistent, and it's a tribute to what the two countries can accomplish together. Citizen groups continue to push for improvements in rule of law that are slowly but surely starting to take root. Overall, Mexico has better institutions for rule of law today than a decade ago, and crime groups prey far less on average citizens in most parts of the country.

But this is the one area of the bilateral relationship in which the engagement of political decision makers in the two countries matters deeply. And the signs are that the cooperation is drifting—in ways that have deadly consequences.

8

"If I Were to Go Back, I'd Still Be Homesick"

- -

Migrants Reshape Communities on Both Sides of the Border

When Daniel Lubetzky and his family first relocated from Mexico City to San Antonio, Texas, he was still a teenager and had no way of imagining what his adopted country had in store for him. Born and raised in Mexico's capital city, Lubetzky showed an early aptitude for business, selling watches in a local market in San Antonio to make money on the side while he finished high school.

After college at San Antonio's Trinity University and later law school at Stanford, Lubetzky moved to New York City and tried setting up his first business, selling hummus and Middle Eastern sandwich spreads. A few months spent in Israel had inspired him to try to do something that would build peace in the Middle East at the same time that he built a business. The spreads were made jointly by Israelis and Palestinians, with some of the profits funneled back into peace efforts in the region. He called it a "not-just-for-profit" enterprise. It was designed to make money but also to contribute to the social good.

Lubetzky didn't hit on the business idea that would catapult him to much greater success until a few years later. He decided to make nutrition bars from nuts, fruits, and spices, packaged in transparent plastic wrapping to showcase their natural ingredients. He would reinvest some of the profits in social causes, as he had done with the first business. He called the product "KIND Bars" to capture the socially oriented ethos of the business and its focus on health.

Today, KIND is the fastest-growing nutrition bar—by far—in the United States, competing effectively with similar offerings made by major multinational companies like Kellogg's and General Foods. Lubetzky still has a noticeable Spanish accent and retains his love of Mexico, but he is happy in New York as a successful and innovative American entrepreneur and the father of four US-born children.

Without question, Lubetzky is an unusual case among Mexican immigrants. He had a middle-class upbringing in Mexico City, thanks to his father's hard work in starting a profitable business. He also had access to a top-notch education after arriving in the United States, attending leading universities that helped prepare him for his later professional ventures. And Lubetzky also had his father's extraordinary example as a Holocaust survivor, which he still holds up as the most important influence in his life. His father escaped Dachau concentration camp at the end of World War II before resettling in Mexico as a refugee and marrying Lubetzky's mother. Lubetzky is both an immigrant in the United States and the son of a refugee in Mexico.

But his path is, in one crucial way, very similar to that pursued by many other Mexicans who have moved north to the United States.

Mexican immigrants—and, as it turns out, immigrants generally—have an unusually high rate of entrepreneurship in the United States. Most will never be as successful as Lubetzky, whose business generates $727 million a year, but they start businesses at twice the rate that native-born Americans do.

Demetrio Juárez, who runs El Mariachi restaurant in Hazleton, Pennsylvania, is probably far more typical of the average Mexican immigrant entrepreneur. Juárez runs a business that has given his own family a comfortable living and helped employ a few other people locally. In fact, Mexican immigrants tend to be overrepresented among small businesses, especially in the food service, construction, and hospitality industries. But when you add up their combined earnings, Mexican immigrant entrepreneurs pump over $17 billion into the US economy each year.

Immigrants, who make up around a seventh of America's population, just under 14 percent, start over a quarter of all new businesses in the United States. Mexican immigrants, who compose less than 4 percent of the total US population, start around one-tenth of all businesses in the country. It's no surprise that in Hazleton, a city that saw a huge upsurge in Mexican and other Latin American arrivals, immigrants have started most new businesses in recent years. The city's economic revival has largely depended on the risk taking of its newest residents. And over the past decade, average household income in the city has grown in tandem with the rise of immigrant-owned businesses.

American public opinion has been deeply divided about immigration, especially from Mexico, and Donald Trump spoke to these concerns in the 2016 presidential campaign. Many Americans fear job competition from new immigrants, dislike the way their arrival changes cultural patterns, and are concerned about the effect on rule of law of those who arrive without legal status.

Yet, surprisingly, these Americans are actually in the minority. Poll after poll shows that a majority of Americans have positive views of immigration and immigrants. Not surprisingly, as the economy has improved in recent years—and the number of those arriving without authorization has plummeted—public opinion has even grown more positive.

Most Americans recognize that immigrants are vital contributors to the American economy, and they often equate newcomers' stories with those of their own parents, grandparents, and great-grandparents who arrived from abroad. The notion of America as "a nation of immigrants," a phrase made famous by John F. Kennedy's book of the same name, remains deeply embedded in the American consciousness. And today a quarter of all Americans are either immigrants or children of immigrants. Immigration is deeply embedded not only in the historical fabric of American society but in our daily lives. That is especially true in metropolitan areas, but increasingly so in smaller cities, like Hazleton, as well.

Immigration, on balance, has certainly been positive for American society. It's a big part of the country's constant economic vibrancy and renewal, and studies show that over time, immigrants of all skill levels tend to contribute more than they consume in public services. And immigrants commit far fewer crimes than native-born Americans. They even tend to be healthier and live longer.

Today's immigrants also appear to be learning English, improving their education levels, and intermarrying with members of different ethnic groups at much the same rate that earlier immigrant groups from Italy, Ireland, and eastern Europe did a hundred years ago. Although many first-generation immigrants struggle to learn English, almost all children of immigrants speak it. Even more telling, very few grandchildren of immigrants, including those of Mexican descent, remain fluent in their grandparents' language, even though some may continue to have cultural ties to their grandparents' homeland. America's ability to absorb newcomers from other parts of the world and integrate them into American society has stayed robust through the ages.

Immigration also appears to be a net benefit for the economy, but there is some debate about whether it creates wage pressures for lower-skilled workers, especially those without a high school degree. Economists disagree on just how much and who, if anyone, is actually affected. After all, immigrants are not only workers but also consumers and entrepreneurs, so while they fill jobs, they also contribute to creating new ones. But there are some sectors and some places where immigration may exert downward pressures on wages, especially during times of recession.

There is also no question that rapid influxes of immigrants, as in Hazleton, can be far more jarring than slow changes. A sudden population shift can put a strain on schools and hospitals that have to adapt to people with limited English-language skills, and it can sometimes lead to a sense of alienation among native-born residents who feel their traditional way of life is slipping away. And while immigration flows from Mexico slowed to a trickle over the past decade, many immigrants who already lived in the United States left large metropolitan areas for smaller cities and towns—like Hazleton—where they found job opportunities and a better quality of life, creating tensions in areas of the country that hadn't seen much immigration for almost a century.

Yet we are probably at the beginning of the end of debates about Mexican immigration—as hard as this may be to see in the middle of the heated politics of the moment. Most immigrants today come from Asia, not Latin America, and immigrants overall are more likely to have a college degree than even the average native-born American, according to a recent Migration Policy Institute study. Immigration may well remain a contentious issue in the United States, but over time the debates will shift.

Still, the large wave of Mexican immigration that took place over several decades between the 1960s and 2007 will likely leave a major imprint on the character and demographic composition of the United States far into the future, much as the previous waves from northern Europe in the 1800s and from southern and eastern Europe in the early 1900s did. And it will be one of the major factors tying Mexico and the United States together in the coming years.

Efraín Jiménez should have felt proud, but something was bothering him. As he looked around his hometown of Nochistlán, in the southern part of the state of Zacatecas, he could see all the improvements made with the money he and other Zacatecan migrants to Southern California had raised over the past few years. By 2003 the streets were mostly paved, even all the way to his parents' village of La Villita, once an isolated hamlet outside town. "Zacatecas was once completely cut off," he remembers. "But now everything had changed." There were streetlights everywhere at night, just like in the United States. The schools looked surprisingly inviting—nothing like the crumbling buildings in which he had been educated as a child.

But Jiménez also learned that one of the schools he'd helped fix up, in a village right outside town, had been forced to close down for lack of students. When he returned to San Fernando, California, where he works as a mechanic, he raised this issue with the other members of the Zacatecan Federation of Southern California, a group of migrants from the state who live in and around Los Angeles. He realized that they were equally frustrated. Another school, in the large Zacatecan municipality of Jerez, had also closed down, and two clinics weren't being used because there weren't enough people around to pay for a doctor. "It made me sad that clinics couldn't stay open and that schools were closing because there weren't enough children," he says. "People just kept coming [to the United States]." It wasn't enough to improve transportation and the way towns looked—or even to build schools and health clinics—if Zacatecans still felt they had to migrate north to improve their lives.

After many discussions, the Zacatecans in California hit on a plan. For the past few years the local, state, and federal governments had been matching their investments in infrastructure in equal parts, essentially quadrupling the funds they raised in the United States to send home for agreed-upon projects. Jiménez had personally met with President Vicente Fox right after he was elected in 2000 to get his support for the initiative. Now the federation wanted to try something similar, but this time focused on building businesses rather than infrastructure. They proposed to both President Fox and the state governor that if migrants in the United States would invest their savings—often as little as $20,000 or $30,000—in a small business in Zacatecas, the federal and state governments would match investment with a five-year interest-free loan to the business owner. In return, the businesses would have to be registered and pay taxes, a change that would bring them into the formal economy.

Starting in 2006, this program, which matches collective investment dollars raised by the hometown associations three to one with government credit, had funded the first six business initiatives in Zacatecas. In 2009 the federation proposed a new initiative to match *individual* investments by migrants affiliated with Zacatecan hometown associations with government credit. Jiménez shared the idea with Mexican president Felipe Calderón during one of his visits to the United States, and the result was the creation of a new "1 × 1" program that matched individual investments in micro and small businesses with interest-free government credit for five years. Investors would be responsible for developing a business plan and registering the businesses in Mexico for tax purposes—which meant they had to pay taxes but could also become eligible for commercial credit down the road.

Set in motion in 2010, this program has successfully helped start—or expand—dozens of small businesses across the state. Many of them are farms and ranches that can now afford to hire additional workers, but they have also included mezcal producers, a tire shop, a honey-making collective, a water-purifying plant, and even a state-of-the-art candy factory located in a rural hamlet right next to a dilapidated colonial church. All told, these ventures employ hundreds, if not thousands, of people across the state. In precisely the communities people once left for lack of opportunities, there are now jobs. And in 2011, the program expanded to become the "2 × 1" program when the recently elected governor, Miguel Alonso, agreed to use state funds to double the loans that businesses could receive for each dollar invested.

From the 1980s through the 2000s, Mexico saw a vast movement of its population northward across the border. By 2007, 12.8 million people born in Mexico were living in the United States—more than a tenth of the Mexican population. In states like Zacatecas, Jalisco, and Michoacán, as much as a quarter to a third of residents had left. At the height of this migration, almost a half million Mexicans crossed the border without documents each year, emptying entire communities in Mexico and creating tensions in the United States around illegal immigration.

When the beginnings of the US financial crisis started to ripple through the construction and service industries in 2007, unauthorized migration dropped dramatically overnight. This is perhaps unsurprising since jobs in these sectors had been the magnet drawing people across the border in the first place. More surprisingly, the flow of Mexicans northward has never picked up again since then, even after the US economy started to grow. In fact, since 2009, more Mexicans appear to have been leaving the United States than arriving. While many Mexicans still come on legal visas, the number of unauthorized Mexicans north of the border has dropped by more than 1 million over the past decade.

Today there are 11.6 million Mexican-born people in the United States; slightly less than half, around 5.6 million, lack legal documents. Mexicans, once almost two-thirds of the unauthorized population in the United States, probably make up half or less today—and the number keeps dropping. Most Mexicans who cross the border today do so with legal visas.

Long-term growth in Mexico's economy, investments in education and health care, and a huge drop in Mexican fertility rates are critical factors in the vastly reduced number of Mexicans willing to leave their country, but so are remittances from migrants that have given people the ability to remain in their communities and make a living. Studies show that remittances from Mexicans in the United States, which have ranged between $21 billion and $27 billion a year for the past decade, help poor Mexicans improve their livelihoods. Remittances are linked to higher educational achievement, greater investments in health care, improved health outcomes, and reduced poverty in Mexican communities. There is increasing evidence that remittances are also linked to employment creation.

To be certain, migration also drains local economies, often siphoning off some of the most talented and enterprising community members, who decide to start new lives abroad, but the money they send back significantly improves life for those left behind. Much like Demetrio Juárez, the Hazleton restaurant owner who put five of his six siblings through college in the state of Puebla, many Zacatecan migrants have given their family members educational and work opportunities they couldn't have aspired to otherwise.

In Zacatecas, one of Mexico's poorest states, the changes are particularly noticeable. In small towns and rural hamlets, streets are paved, and modern highways connect communities. Schools, including several small regional campuses of the state university, dot the countryside, built in part with money sent back by migrants. Most importantly, after a period of stagnation, the state economy grew for more than a decade after 2003 and at an even faster rate than the country as a whole, thanks in large part to the money sent by Zacatecans living north of the border, and employment expanded exponentially, tripling between 1998 and 2017, according to state statistics.

This process, for the most part, happened naturally as Zacatecan migrants sent money home to their families, but Efraín Jiménez and his colleagues in the federation scaled up the money available for these family businesses and pushed them into the formal economy, allowing them to access credit and scale up further over time.

Now when Jiménez surveys the schools and clinics that he helped build, he's pleased to see they're full. And over the past few years, the Zacatecans in California have contributed to the construction of three new campuses of the state university in smaller towns. They, too, are full.

"My main challenge was the food," says Alejandra Pinzón as she remembers her return to Mexico City six years earlier. She had lived much of her life in Overland Park, Kansas, and Carmel, Indiana, and grown accustomed to small-town life in America. Although she spoke Spanish at home with her aunt and uncle, she was the only Mexican among the 3,000 students in her high school in Carmel. In most ways, her life was as American as that of her classmates. And so was the food she ate.

But as her friends started applying to college, Pinzón realized that she was different—and that she wouldn't be able to follow them. Without legal documentation in the United States, she didn't qualify for in-state tuition, and she couldn't even get a driver's license so that she could commute to school. Frustrated, she finally decided to return to Mexico City, the metropolis in which she had been born eighteen years earlier. "I miss the small towns," she says wistfully, as a truck rolls by in the distance near her home in Mexico City.

After moving back, Pinzón found work with TeleTech, one of several large call centers in Mexico that hire young people who have grown up in the United States to provide service to cable companies, credit card providers, and other corporate clients. Companies like TeleTech used to set up centers mostly in India because of the availability of English-speaking workers, but they have now started tapping Mexico and its growing pool of native English speakers like Pinzón. And Mexico has huge comparative advantages: people like Pinzón speak American English, they live in the same time zone, and they can also serve Spanish-speaking clients in the United States. Tens of thousands of Mexicans now work in call centers—perhaps over 100,000—which is still below the numbers in India and the Philippines but gaining quickly.

"Any area around a call center will have burritos," says Pinzón, turning back to the subject of food. In Mexico City, tacos with homemade corn tortillas, cilantro, onion, and salsa are the quintessential on-the-go lunch food. But people who grew up in the States prefer burritos made of wheat tortillas—the heart of Tex-Mex cuisine. "Instead of tacos, we look for burritos," she says. Within a couple blocks of TeleTech, five or six restaurants now serve burritos to attract workers from the call center. That's one way you can pick TeleTech workers out of the crowds eating in the small restaurants in this busy part of Mexico City. The other way is that they speak English to each other.

Pinzón, who went through the sixth grade in Mexico, speaks fluent Spanish, but she prefers English and says most of her friends do too. She met most of them through the networks of young people who work in call centers; that is also how she met her husband, Chris Chirinos. He speaks Spanish with a marked American accent, having spent most his life in California. At home, the couple mainly speak English to each other, and they are raising their twin sons in English too. Every November they gather with friends to cook a turkey and celebrate

Thanksgiving, as they did growing up—but they also celebrate Mexican Independence Day and other Mexican holidays, fully accepting that their life is a hybrid of traditions from the two countries.

According to separate analyses by the Pew Center and El Colegio de México, more than 1 million Mexicans returned home between 2009 and 2014, most of them immigrants who lacked legal status in the United States. Many were deported, but even more made their way back on their own.

One of the biggest challenges Pinzón faced on returning was getting her high school diploma from Carmel, Indiana, validated so she could attend college. None of the universities she applied to would accept it. To get her studies accredited in Mexico, she needed to go through a complex process of notarizing and apostilling the diploma—essentially getting the Indiana state government to certify that the notarization is valid—which requires being physically present in the United States. After two years of frustration, Pinzón eventually gave up, though she may try again someday. Not having a certified degree has not been much of an impediment to her career in the short-term—she's risen to become a senior manager at TeleTech, even without a degree, on the basis of talent alone.

In March 2017, the Mexican Congress finally changed the law to get rid of onerous requirements that students who had studied abroad faced to get their documents recognized in Mexico. This should streamline the process for most in the future, though the change may have arrived too late for some, like Pinzón, who are already well into their professional lives.

People who follow migration have puzzled over why Mexican immigrants stopped coming to the United States after the Great Recession of 2008 and then started returning to Mexico. This may have to do with the slow return to growth in the US economy, but more than that seems to be at play, since the number of immigrants from other countries, including in Central America and Asia, have increased dramatically since 2009.

Enhanced border security certainly had a dissuasive effect on new arrivals, since it raised the cost of being smuggled across the border. The size of the border patrol increased fourfold over two decades from 1994, and the federal government now spends more on immigration enforcement agencies than it does on all other federal law enforcement agencies put together, according to a Migration Policy Institute study. And the increased number of deportations under President Barack Obama probably added to the return numbers—although most of those removed under Obama were actually recent arrivals caught crossing the border rather than people already inside the country.

The Mexican population is also aging, with fewer and fewer young people between the ages of fifteen and twenty-nine. These are the people who are the most likely to try a dangerous journey north, so this population shift may explain a small part of the drop in migration as well.

But the largest reason appears to be the greater opportunities available to Mexicans who stay in their country compared to the benefits of crossing the border. Mexico has hardly had the kind of dramatic economic growth that some East and Southeast Asian economies have experienced. Yet, added up over more than two decades, the increases in income, educational opportunities, health care, and infrastructure appear to have made a huge difference in the willingness of Mexicans to cross the border to start life anew and increased the attraction of returning home. Even Pinzón and her husband, who often pine for life north of the border, have found a good life in Mexico and never talked seriously about trying to return to the United States.

Economists often refer to the "migration hump" to explain the fact that out-migration rates usually rise as a country's economy improves and then subside as it reaches middle-income levels. The argument is simple: Economic growth initially creates incentives for people to leave home because they have extra money to spend on smuggling themselves into a wealthier country but still limited faith in the future of their own country. The dislocations that come with opening trade and economic change also help convince people to leave. But eventually, as average income grows and the economy develops, more and more people decide that it's worth their while to stay rather than leave. That's exactly what happened in Mexico in the 1990s and early 2000s, and it's not unlike what happened in Italy, Ireland, or Poland in another era.

It's hard to tell what effect this sudden influx of Mexicans who have spent their lives in the United States will have on Mexican society and culture. One group of researchers from both countries followed several hundred returning migrants over five years and found that their experience in the United States gave them intangible skills in entrepreneurship, leadership, and management, which they applied to improve their professional opportunities in Mexico. And in many cases, returning migrants also use money they have saved in the United States to start businesses or invest in property.

Alejandra Pinzón has her own theory about what will happen to Mexico as others like her return. "I think it's going to help them [Mexicans] adapt to the rest of the world a little bit," she says. She thinks her fellow returnees may be adding a new, unexpected dimension to what has often seemed like a homogeneous society. She notes that her friends raised in the United States have greater tolerance for different ways of life than do friends and relatives raised in Mexico. "Call centers are considered a safe zone for gay people," she observes, because "most of the people who have lived in the States don't have a problem with gay and lesbian people." Growing up in the United States, Pinzón and her friends experienced what it was like to be different from others, and she thinks they possess greater openness to diverse lifestyles than many of their relatives who have never left the country.

Despite her struggles to adapt to her country of birth, Pinzón recognizes that she loves much about living in Mexico and is proud that she and Chirinos have made a good life for their family. While she misses the United States—and still doesn't always feel at home in Mexico—she's not sure she would feel any more at home now in the United States either. In the end, both countries have made her who she is.

"If I were to go back," she admits wistfully, "I'd still be homesick."

Today as the flow of Mexicans crossing the border has dropped— and the number of Mexicans returning has increased—Central Americans have begun coming in larger numbers, crossing Mexico to reach the United States. This is not a wholly new flow: Central Americans have been coming in significant numbers since the 1980s, and roughly 3.4 million people born in Central America live in the United States today. But the numbers started rising precipitously in 2014 and include mostly families and unaccompanied children. Almost all come from three of the poorest countries in the hemisphere: El

Salvador, Honduras, and Guatemala. Out-migration from these three countries spiked in tandem with violence linked to drug trafficking in recent years. Ironically and tragically, some of this may have been a result of joint US-Mexican efforts to make it harder for international drug trafficking groups to operate in Mexico, which pushed more of their criminal operations into Central America.

In 2014 and again in 2016 and 2017, more Central Americans crossed the US-Mexican border illegally than Mexicans, a shocking change, given that these countries are together only a quarter the size of Mexico and located more than 1,000 miles away. Right as unauthorized migration from Mexico reached its lowest level in more than four decades—and Mexicans began to return home—Central American migration reached its highest point in history.

Many of the Central Americans apply for asylum when they reach the United States, claiming fear of persecution in their home country. Increasingly some of these migrants—a few thousand each year, but the number is growing rapidly—have started applying for asylum in Mexico rather than trying to reach the United States. Neither the US nor Mexican asylum systems have been able to handle this sudden influx, and asylum seekers find themselves facing long delays—often eighteen months to two years in the United States and a few months in Mexico—before the respective government makes a decision about their cases.

In a strange twist of fate, Mexico has morphed from the United States' principal source of unauthorized immigrants to its first line of defense against the newest unauthorized immigration flows. Since 2015, Mexican authorities have interdicted and returned a majority of the Central American migrants to their home countries before they reached the northern border with the United States.

During the Obama administration, the Mexican and US governments began collaborating to find ways to stem this flow. They coordinated on interdiction strategies at Mexico's southern border and tried to find ways of strengthening police and judicial systems in Guatemala, El Salvador, and Honduras. After some significant disruption in this coordination at the start of the Trump administration, when US officials, including President Trump, angered their Mexican counterparts with negative statements about Mexico, the two countries appear to have found their rhythm again in cooperating on migration. In June 2017, the US and Mexican governments jointly hosted an international summit in Miami to focus on strategies for helping the Central American countries reduce violence and stanch the outflow of their citizens. Hosted by American secretary of state Rex Tillerson and Mexican foreign minister Luis Videgaray, the summit also included a presentation by US Vice President Mike Pence, who seemed eager to assume the coordinating role on this issue that his predecessor, Joe Biden, had played during the Obama administration.

For Mexico, this shift from being a nation of emigrants to receiving and often deporting migrants from Central America has hardly been comfortable. Gustavo Mohar, one of Mexico's most respected analysts of migration and a former undersecretary of migration, notes that the cooperation with the United States is a highly sensitive issue politically, so cooperation has always been "between explicit and implicit." In other words, the two governments have formalized some cooperation agreements on dealing with migrants from Central America and other countries as part of their joint effort to protect their own territories from criminals, traffickers, and human rights abusers, but most of the enforcement policy rests on implicit understandings around the common goal of deterring undocumented flows.

As in the United States, it's taken a long time for mental maps to catch up with reality. Mohar observes with concern that the question of Central American migration through Mexico "has been a subject that has received little interest except from NGOs, religious activists, and human rights advocates in Mexico." Only occasionally has it generated noise in the Mexican Congress, where opposition legislators have raised concerns about their government becoming America's lapdog in enforcing US immigration policies.

Mexicans are also increasingly uncomfortable with the knowledge that thousands of Central Americans each year are subject to serious abuses—from robbery to rape—as they transit through Mexico. In many cases, federal immigration agents and local law enforcement authorities have been suspected of complicity in the crime rings that prey on migrants traveling through Mexico. More than two-thirds of Central American migrants report violent abuse of some kind during their transit through Mexico. The lack of serious public debate has allowed this pattern to continue.

Today, both Mexicans and Americans are struggling to bring their mental maps in line with the changing patterns of migration between the two countries. Americans continue to think that Mexico is the main source of immigration, although most immigration now comes from other countries. Meanwhile, Mexicans too think of Mexico as a migrant-sending country, when, in fact, it is primarily a transit country for Central Americans and, as we'll see in the next chapter, home to increasingly large immigrant communities of its own. Of course, the past wave of migration from Mexico to the United States has left a powerful imprint on both societies, but new patterns are now emerging that people in both countries have yet to come to grips with.

In many ways, Efraín Jiménez's hometown of Nochistlán shares a lot in common with Hazleton, Pennsylvania, which Demetrio Juárez now calls home. Both were aging small towns that younger residents largely abandoned in search of opportunities elsewhere. Today both are growing again and recovering a dynamism lost decades ago. In Hazleton's case, the rebirth is due in large part to the arrival of new immigrants, like Demetrio Juárez, who have injected life and entrepreneurial energy into a greying town. Indeed, most of the growth of America's smaller cities and towns has come from immigrants over the past two decades. In the case of Nochistlán, like many small towns in Mexico, migrants who once left have sent money back to start businesses, and some have even returned home to run them, creating new sources of employment and dynamism.

As migration recedes between the two countries, seeing its legacies and how it's already reshaped both countries and thousands of local communities for the better becomes a lot easier.

9

"I Now Feel Welcome in This Country"

A Million Americans Move to Mexico

When Frank O'Grady was about to turn fifty, he and his wife, Katie, decided they needed a change. Both had jobs they enjoyed—he was a firefighter, she a Spanish teacher—but Frank's work was taking a toll on his health, and Katie's wasn't paying her much more than they were spending on child care for their young twins. And day to day, they didn't see enough of one another or their children. The family lived in its "forever home" in an attractive section of San Diego, with orange and lemon trees in the backyard. But the house, they'd learned, was making their children ill: it had been flooded, and toxic mold was growing in the walls.

The O'Gradys had always enjoyed traveling in Mexico—they considered their vacations there the best part of the year. "The time we spent going to Mexico ingrained in us the notion that life [there] was not just joyful and colorful and textured, but better," says Katie. So they began to wonder, Could they move there?

If they took early retirement, they discovered, they could not just get by in Mexico but actually improve their quality of life in many ways. So in 2012 they moved, first to a small seaside community and then to San Miguel de Allende, a stunningly beautiful colonial city about three hours north of Mexico City that has a large American expatriate community with good bilingual schools and services. Cobblestone streets, colonial-era churches, flower-covered walls, and springlike weather year-round make San Miguel an alluring spot for American expatriates—an authentic Mexican city with many of the amenities of home.

They loved the slower pace of life, the close relationships with their neighbors, the easy access to nature. They went horseback riding in the jungle in Nayarit, climbed pyramids in central Mexico, and studied the martial arts/dance form *capoeira*. Mexico seemed to provide everything they wanted.

Then Katie got sick.

Even after almost three years as residents, the O'Gradys were nervous about relying on the Mexican health-care system for a complicated and risky abdominal surgery. Their friends and family in the United States were shocked that they even considered it. Katie worried about postprocedure pain-management options.

But she found a Mexican doctor and hospital she trusted about an hour away in Celaya, and she decided to have the surgery there. The operation went well, and she was soon on her way to recovery.

But then two of the discs in her back herniated just five months after the abdominal surgery. She found herself paralyzed on the left side of her body, forcing her to have another, even more complicated surgery and then four months of physical therapy to be able to walk again.

She emerged from more than a year of medical ordeals thankful for the treatment she had received in the Mexican health-care system. "The care was accessible, affordable, and high-quality," she says. She loved the "caring, humanistic component of the doctors who treat you like an individual," including hour-long patient visits and frequent check-ins by phone and text message. On her blog, *Los O'Gradys in Mexico*, Katie wrote, "I can assure you that my experiences have been nothing but amazing…life changing, life saving."

Mexico, it turned out, did provide everything the O'Gradys wanted—not only a great quality of life but also all the necessities for when things went wrong. Having provided both the good life and some very tough challenges, Mexico was simply home.

And the O'Grady's are just one family among the million or so Americans who have moved from the United States to Mexico in recent years. Today, almost as many Americans live in Mexico as live in all of Europe. Like the Mexicans who previously traveled north in large numbers, many Americans are heading south primarily for economic opportunity and quality of life. Some take jobs in multinational companies located in Mexico or start small businesses there. But many are recently retired and looking for a better way to live. Some are older, but many, like the O'Gradys, are still in the prime of life. Frank now owns and operates a small solar panel design and installation company, following on studies he did in San Diego and Colorado, and Katie has built a growing relocation consulting business out of her popular blog.

As retiring has become more difficult in the United States, and Mexico has developed a larger middle class and better infrastructure, pursuing the "Mexican Dream" has grown increasingly attractive for many Americans. Their income, savings, and pensions go further in a place where life can also feel less hectic and more fulfilling.

Of course, there have always been Americans in Mexico. But over the past fifteen years, the number of Americans moving south has exploded. The Mexican census registered a doubling of the US-born population between 2000 and 2015, reaching 739,168. This is almost certainly a significant undercount, since many of the retirees move back and forth between the two countries. The US State Department puts the number of American citizens living in Mexico at closer to a million. It's possible, even probable, that the number of Americans in Mexico is growing faster these days than the number of Mexicans in the United States.

Most non-Spanish-speaking Americans who move to Mexico settle in a handful of cities that are either close to the border, such as Rosarito and Ensenada—beachside communities just south of Tijuana—or towns that cater to American expatriates, such as San Miguel, Puerto Vallarta, and those around Lake Chapala near Guadalajara. All have bilingual schools, English-language newspapers, and accessible health care for foreign residents. In addition, tens of thousands of Americans live in Mexico's largest cities, including Mexico City, Guadalajara, and Monterrey, drawn primarily by jobs with global corporations.

So many Americans reside in Mexico today that US migrants now have their own radio broadcasts, popular authors, and even Republican and Democratic political organizations. And while a number of Americans keep to themselves, more and more are assimilating into Mexican society, including a handful of well-known figures in business, the arts, and the media who were born in the United States.

But not all of the people moving south to Mexico are retirees or corporate employees. The Pew Research Center estimates that since 2009 more than a million Mexicans who were living in the United States have returned to Mexico. Many were deported, but even more returned of their own volition. Katie O'Grady has noticed this trend too through her relocation business: most of her clients are Americans seeking to relocate for a better quality of life, but increasingly a few are families with at least one Mexican-born parent who either is being forced to leave the country or wants to "come home."

In fact, the vast majority of Americans who live in Mexico today are family members, mostly children, of Mexicans who have repatriated. Silvia Giorguli, president of the prestigious El Colegio de Mexico and a demographer, notes that the 2015 census recorded 550,402 American-born children in Mexico, comprising a full three-quarters of all American-born people registered in the census. Even if retirees are undercounted, the largest group of Americans in Mexico is unquestionably the children of Mexicans returning home.

Exactly how American migration to Mexico will change the country is difficult to say. The roughly 1 million US-born residents in Mexico constitute only 1 percent of the country's population, while the 12 million Mexican-born residents of the United States make up over 3 percent of the US population. But it's already possible to see some of the impacts, from the advent of large-scale senior-care development around Lake Chapala to the employment of young returnees, like Alejandra Pinzón, in English-language call centers that contract with US companies.

Americans living in Mexico are likely to become crucial bridges between the two countries in the same way that Mexicans living in the United States have been. And their children, whether they stay in

Mexico or move back to the United States, may well play an outsized role in bringing people of the two countries together.

"I remember growing up in a very different Mexico," says David Luhnow, who was raised from early childhood in Mexico City, the son of American parents who fell in love with the country and moved there.

"It was a closed economy," he adds. "Our TV set was a Zonda"—the not very well-made national brand that almost all Mexicans had in the 1970s. "It was like firing up the Wurlitzer every time you wanted to watch a television program."

When his family vacationed in the United States, the variety of products available—the different kinds of cars and breakfast cereals, not to mention the much better-working television sets—astounded him. His American relatives had the latest technology and vast choices in everything from food to toys, products out of reach even for successful middle-class Mexican families.

Although Mexico has experienced a recent explosion of Americans moving south, there have always been Americans in Mexico. Former Mexican president Vicente Fox was fond of telling people about his grandfather who moved to Mexico from Ohio to find good farmland. Former Massachusetts governor and presidential candidate Mitt Romney's great-grandfather founded a Mormon colony in northern Mexico in an effort to find religious freedom, and Romney's father, later a governor of Michigan, was born there. The African American poet Langston Hughes lived for a time in Mexico with his father, who had gone there seeking opportunities in a country with less overt racial discrimination, and Hughes later returned on his own to enjoy the cultural scene of Mexico City. Rural Morelos has a small community of dairy farmers who originally came from the States in the 1940s, and small groups of American leftists moved to Cuernavaca and Mexico City in the 1950s to escape the McCarthy era and stayed.

Despite this long historical presence, Luhnow, like many Americans, never felt entirely sure of his place in Mexican society. "I never felt completely welcome," he remembers. At the time, Mexicans largely distrusted the United States, and they had an ambivalent attitude toward the Americans living among them. Luhnow remembers at times being called names and getting teased for his slight American accent.

To some extent, this is part of an ambivalent attitude that Mexicans hold toward immigrants in general. Although Mexico has had periods of immigration—Jews and Maronite Christians from Syria; refugees from the Spanish Civil War; Afro-descendant immigrants from the Caribbean countries; Jewish and Christian refugees from Europe before, during, and after World War II; South American and later Central American refugees fleeing dictatorships; and smaller groups of Chinese immigrants, many of whom came through the United States—Mexico has never been a country of full-scale immigration like its northern neighbor.

Most Mexicans see themselves as descendants of the native peoples who populated the Americas and the Spanish *conquistadores* and settlers who started arriving in the sixteenth century. José Vasconcelos, perhaps Mexico's premiere philosopher of the early twentieth century and the founder of the national university, wrote about Mexicans as a *raza cosmica* (cosmic race) that incorporated both indigenous and European roots. His idea became the cornerstone of modern Mexican nationalism, emphasizing how this dual heritage distinguished Mexico from other countries, especially the United States.

At the time, the idea of a "cosmic race" was radical. Many Mexicans still saw European blood as superior to native blood, and Vasconcelos established the idea that the blending of the two made Mexicans unique. This notion didn't stamp out racism in Mexico—television and advertising still demonstrate a marked preference for lighter skin and blond hair, which says much about the persistence of subtle beliefs—but it did establish a new sense of identity that dignified Mexico's indigenous as well as Spanish roots.

But while progressive in many ways, this concept of a single blended people also made it harder for Mexicans to acknowledge the distinct traditions of indigenous peoples, Afro-Mexicans, and immigrant groups that had helped build the country and often wanted to keep a sense of unique identity within their "Mexicanness." Interestingly, Mexico's second president in the late 1820s, Vicente Guerrero, was a mulatto, a Mexican of part-African descent, while the country's most revered president in the nineteenth century, Benito Juárez, whose photo stares down at schoolchildren in schools across the country, was a Zapotec Indian. But not until the 1990s did Mexico begin to come to terms with the modern cultures of its indigenous people, who make up anywhere from 8 to 15 percent of the population, and not until the 2010 census were respondents allowed to self-identify as Afro-Mexican, a group that makes up 1 percent of the population.

Questions about whether people born abroad can be fully Mexican still persist. Even today, the Mexican constitution prohibits anyone born in another country from serving as a cabinet minister or ambassador, and public anger has erupted several times when the Mexican Football Federation has tried to include naturalized soccer players—usually from South America—on the national team.

But another factor—Mexico's long, conflicted relationship with the United States—compounds the ambiguity felt toward Americans. Not only did the United States wage a war against Mexico in the 1840s that ended with the loss of a third of Mexico's territory to the United States—today's California, Arizona, New Mexico, Texas, and parts of Nevada and Colorado—but the US government meddled in Mexico's affairs during the latter's civil war, known as the Mexican Revolution. US Ambassador Henry Lane, acting on his own, conspired with the Mexican Army to overthrow the country's elected president, Francisco Madero, in 1911. President Woodrow Wilson removed Ambassador Lane for his conduct and later sent a warship to help the rebels trying to restore democracy, but that naive action was perceived on all sides of the Mexican civil war as yet another instance of international aggression against the country.

The governments that emerged after the Mexican Revolution— the rebels were ultimately victorious—built the modern Mexican state, and they created a sense of national identity in part by imposing a notion of "Mexicanness" that contrasted Mexicans with those who lived north of the border in the United States. Mexican films, painting, and popular culture are replete with cautionary references to American meddling and reminders of past aggression. Until the 1990s, school textbooks went out of their way to emphasize Mexico's victimization at the hands of American invaders.

In a fascinating study from the 1980s on how the two countries relate to each other, Mexican scholar Jorge Castañeda and American scholar Robert Pastor wrote a book about how each country sees the other—after exchanging homes and jobs in each other's country for a year. They started the book with an exploration of school textbooks, highlighting that Mexican school children learned primarily about American aggression, while American children learned next to nothing about Mexico.

Yet in the 1990s things began to change in the way that Mexicans saw the United States—in part because of the increasing commercial relationships, which changed the way that political elites talked about the country next door, and in part because of increasing migration, which gave many-lower income Mexicans a firsthand look at America through the lens of friends and relatives who had moved north. The United States for many Mexicans stopped being a mere symbol of historical oppression and imminent danger and became a real country with opportunities and pitfalls like any other. From friends and relatives they learned about discrimination and hardship north of the border, but also about economic and educational opportunities. And many soon had close relatives who were American citizens.

As the Mexican government began to negotiate the North American Free Trade Agreement, then president Carlos Salinas de Gortari made a controversial decision to modernize the elementary school curriculum and return some balance to the descriptions of Mexico's relationship with the United States. While they still contain the real history of conflict between the two countries, the textbooks today read less like a morality play than they once did.

David Luhnow left Mexico during high school, hoping to get to know his parents' country, and he spent the next few years in the United States, graduating from college and taking a series of reporting jobs with American newspapers. But Mexico kept pulling him back.

He even took a job for a bit with an English-language newspaper in Mexico City between other assignments.

Eventually, while he was living in London and working at Reuters news agency, the *Wall Street Journal* offered him a job as correspondent in Mexico City in 2000, and he jumped at the opportunity. Back in Mexico, Luhnow met and married his wife, a Mexican of British descent, who had grown up in the parallel community of British immigrants in Mexico City. They now have two children who were born in Mexico.

Luhnow remembers that he interviewed Carlos Salinas once, and while he recognizes that Salinas was a controversial president with a contradictory record, he couldn't help thanking him for bringing his two countries, and the two parts of his heritage, closer together. The last two decades have allowed the two countries to discover each other in new ways, and it's become infinitely easier to be both Mexican and American—while living on either side of the border.

Growing up, Luhnow may have felt ambivalent about living in Mexico, but he has no qualms about raising his own children there after the changes of the past twenty years. And his children have been able, in their own ways, to embrace what it means to be both Mexican and American. Says Luhnow, "I now feel welcome in this country, and my kids can grow up feeling both countries are home."

In 2009, when Jennifer Clement was elected president of PEN International's Mexico Chapter, one of the most prestigious associations for writers and artists in Mexico, no one batted an eye. After all, she was one of the Mexico's most established novelists, poets, and es-sayists, whose works dealt with some of the country's most pressing social challenges, from the mistreatment of domestic workers to the way violence affects women in rural Mexico, the kinds of issues that PEN was designed to tackle.

But Clement was born in the United States and came to Mexico when she was a year old. She is an American immigrant in Mexico, and all of her books have been in English, though she is thoroughly bicultural and bilingual and writes articles in Spanish as well.

Twenty years ago, having a US-born immigrant head one of Mex-ico's most visible civic organizations would have caused more than a few ripples—as it still might in the world of soccer. But by 2009 her country of birth didn't seem to matter anymore—at least not in the cosmopolitan world of writers and artists.

In 2015, following on the success of her most recent novel, *Prayers for the Stolen*, an achingly beautiful yet deeply disturbing story about girls fighting to stay out of sex slavery, the Mexican Chapter of PEN International proposed Jennifer Clement as a candidate to head the global body of the organization. In November 2015 she was elected president of PEN International, the first woman ever to lead the orga-nization once headed by H. G. Wells, Thornton Wilder, E. M. Forster, Alberto Moravia, Arthur Miller, and Mario Vargas Llosa. She is the second Mexican to hold the presidency, after the poet and diplomat Homero Aridjis, who was elected to the post in the late 1990s.

It may not be such a surprise that Mexico's writers are a fairly open bunch, far more comfortable overlooking Clement's immigrant status and penchant for English prose than might have been the case if she had been running for public office or hoping to make her mark on the soccer field. But it also helped immensely that Clement has always been deeply integrated into Mexican society. "My parents were more interested in the Mexican world than the expat world," she says. She grew up attending a Mexican-British school and absorbing the country's culture at a time when Mexico City still had relatively few American immigrants.

Not all American immigrants to Mexico succeed at integrating into Mexican life—or even want to—as Clement and her family did. Many see their residence in the country as temporary and feel more at ease congregating with other expatriates in retirement communities, in US-run private schools, and in English-language churches and clubs. They remain a community apart from Mexican society. And some Mexicans are equally content to see this burgeoning group of Americans as a transient community rather than wrestle with the consequences of growing immigration from the north.

But there are signs that at least some Americans are becoming more deeply embedded in Mexican society. An increasing number have married into Mexican families or started businesses, establishing more intimate ties to the country. And a growing number, like Clement, are playing prominent roles in Mexican society.

Today these include a well-known television host, Ana Maria Salazar, who was once a senior US Defense Department official, and Randy Ebright, drummer for the punk rock band Molotov, whose parents once worked at the US embassy. Perhaps most telling, two of the last three US ambassadors to Mexico, Tony Garza and Carlos Pascual, have chosen to remain in the country, starting successful careers in international firms there.

And more than a few prominent Mexicans are essentially bicultural. These include Jesse & Joy, a brother-and-sister pop group that has taken the Mexican music charts by storm. The duo's mother is from Wisconsin, and they occasionally add English lyrics into their Spanish-language songs. And there is Julieta Venegas, a phenomenally successful, Grammy-winning alternative rock singer. She grew up between Tijuana and San Diego, attending schools on both sides of the border and absorbing the musical trends of both countries. Denise Dresser, one of Mexico's most prominent public intellectuals, is also the bicultural daughter of an American father and a Mexican mother, though she was raised exclusively in Mexico.

Jennifer Clement tried living in the United States for a few years, finishing her last two years of high school there and then attending New York University. She loved her time in New York, but she eventually decided that she just felt more connected to her writing when she was in Mexico and so would have to return. "She writes in English, but she dreams in Spanish," the American poet W. S. Merwin once said about her, and the quote captures her well. "There are just layers and layers of history and complexity and sense of humor" in Mexico, Clement says, and they are part of the heritage—her heritage—that inspires her to write. Even when the words flow onto the page in English, much of the inspiration comes in Spanish from the stones and buildings and people around her.

One of her best poems, "Making Love in Spanish," is an English-language tribute to the gendered nature of Spanish and its erotic possibilities. "When I make love to you in English," she writes, "the objects in the room have no gender, and I only hear our voices.... But when I make love to you in Spanish, the chairs—those little girls—chatter, and our shoes want to step, with adoration, on the body of light, lamplight, that falls across the floor." Clement pens works in one language while drawing on the subtle differences in the other language she speaks in her daily life. Her sister, Barbara Sibley, claims, "Her books are in Spanish even though they're in English."

While Clement has stayed in Mexico producing poetry and novels, her sister, a chef and anthropologist, took a different path, staying in New York and founding a Mexican restaurant, La Palapa. Today Jennifer writes English-language novels in Mexico, and Barbara cooks Mexican food in the United States, both products of their dual upbringing as Mexicans of American descent.

In 1997 the sisters decided to honor their shared passion for poetry and their two countries by starting the San Miguel Poetry Week, which brings together Mexican and American poets for several days of poetry readings, writing workshops, and fellowship. It has grown significantly and now attracts prominent poets from both countries. "We started the San Miguel Poetry Week," Clement says, "to create a poetic bridge between the United States and Mexico." But for the two sisters, the event is also a bridge between the two parts of themselves that made them who they are. And it takes place in the country where they both grew up and in which Jennifer Clement still lives as a proud American immigrant.

"Every woman's nightmare," says Hanna Pérez about becoming a successful singer in Mexico. She was suddenly a pop star at the age of fifteen. But that meant going through "the stages of puberty in the public eye."

Hanna and her younger sister Ashley were signed to a record deal in Mexico when they were fifteen and fourteen years old, right in the middle of their teenage years. Now in their early thirties, Hanna looks much older—short, blonde, and serious—while Ashley is wisp-thin and tall, with dark hair and flirtatious eyes. "We had to get adapted to a life of constant movement, long hours, and becoming public figures." Despite these challenges, they were excited and "loved every minute of it" because "our hobby became a job."

But they had to adjust to becoming not just public figures but *Mexican* public figures. Hanna and Ashley Pérez had grown up mostly in Lake Charles, Louisiana, the daughters of a Mexican father and an American mother. They had lived in Mexico briefly as children and then spent summers there once they started school, but most of their life, including their school, church, and friends, was in Lake Charles.

The move was worth it. Today Hanna and Ashley Pérez are known as Ha*Ash, a combination of the first syllables of their two first names, and they have become one of Mexico's most popular music groups, with hit after hit on the radio, a string of successful albums, and sold-out concerts throughout the country. But back then they were just teenagers who had grown up singing gospel at church in Lake Charles and performing country music at county fairs, and the switch to pop stardom in a country where they had not lived since childhood was more than a little daunting.

Their story is unusual. Few kids who dream of becoming pop stars ever actually succeed. But in one way, the story of the Pérez sisters actually resembles that of hundreds of thousands of other Americans who have moved back to Mexico: almost no one realizes they are Americans. Dozens of my Mexican friends and colleagues have all registered surprise when I tell them that one of their country's most recognizable and ubiquitous musical groups is actually American born and raised. Of course, die-hard fans know this—after all, real fans make it their business to find out everything they can about their idols—but my highly informal and completely unscientific polling suggests few average Mexicans who listen to their songs regularly on the radio have any idea that the band known as Ha*Ash is really a duo from small-town Louisiana.

Of the Americans living in Mexico, three-quarters or more are like the Pérez sisters, the children of at least one Mexican parent who were born in the United States and later moved back to Mexico. Few have recording contracts or the luxuries that Hanna and Ashley Pérez do today. But they are a silent and growing presence in Mexico, numbering well over a half million in all.

As Mexicans began coming back to their home country in recent years—and deportation numbers soared—many brought back American-born spouses and children. These kids often spoke Spanish at home and "looked" Mexican, and many had been raised for most of their formative years in the United States and attended American schools. In their identities and cultural attitudes they were often more aligned with other American children than with their Mexican parents.

José Luis Gutiérrez has spent a lot of time trying to help these children adapt to life in their parents' country. After spending thirty years in Chicago—and three years as the director of the Illinois state government's Office of New Americans—Gutiérrez returned to his home state of Michoacán in 2016 to become its secretary of migration, a position created to help migrants deal with the issues of living in a binational world. A dual citizen, Gutiérrez has had the rare privilege of doing essentially the same job on both sides of the border—helping Mexican (and other) immigrants get prepared for life in the United States and now helping American-born immigrants (and Mexicans returning home) adapt to life in Mexico.

"The biggest challenge is the language," says Gutiérrez. "In some communities, these American kids make up 10 percent of the student population," he says, and at least sixty thousand children have come back to Michoacán over the last ten years, constituting maybe 4 or 5 percent of the total student population. He notes that in many cases they have never learned to read or write in Spanish. And he remembers one particular case of a young girl whom everyone thought was mute until a teacher tried speaking to her in English, and she immediately opened up.

But the issues often go beyond language. "Many of these children have adaptation problems because they are in rural areas or poor communities where the living conditions are really precarious," he says. For children who have grown up in cities and towns north of the border, arrival in their parents' rural village can be extremely jarring, and the cultural distance spans not only the United States and Mexico but urban and rural life.

I have met families who have loved the transition to Mexico—whose children adapted well to school and enjoyed the slower pace of life in their parents' hometown—and others whose kids dream about returning to the United States, living for the day they can head off on their own to attend college or go in search of work. And it's hard to know what will happen five, ten, and fifteen years from now as more and more of these children reach an age where they can choose whether they want to stay in Mexico or go back to the United States.

For now, Gutiérrez and his team have their hands full trying to make sure that school principals admit American-born children without hassle—a legislative change in 2014 mandated enrollment of these students with only minimal requirements—and that teachers address their specific learning needs as they become acculturated and get used to reading, writing, and doing mathematics in Spanish. And he and his team spend a lot of time working with the local civil registry office in Michoacán to make sure these children get registered as Mexican citizens, for which any child of a Mexican parent is eligible, as well as with the US embassy in Mexico City to get these children US passports, to which they are entitled as American citizens.

Today roughly 2 percent of Mexico's elementary and middle school students were born outside the country, 90 percent or more of them in the United States, and in some states, like Michoacán, the percentage can be much higher. In fact, most states in Mexico with significant numbers of return migrants now have offices, like the one José Luis Gutiérrez runs in Michoacán, dedicated to this population, and some have special education programs for children raised in the United States.

What other effects will this influx of Americans—including the vast majority who are bicultural and binational—have on Mexico? It's probably too early to tell. At a minimum, they will almost certainly reinforce ties on both sides of the border, as some of these children will use their dual citizenship to move back and forth between the two countries when they become adults.

For their part, the Pérez sisters have made the most of their new-found celebrity status in Mexico without losing their identity as Americans. "As children we were so used to being 'the Mexicans' in Louisiana and 'the Americans' in Mexico," says Hanna Pérez. "This always bothered us because children never want to feel different. Now that we are older, we have learned that being different and cultured is a huge asset." They define their music as a mixture of country, gospel, and Latin pop.

Recently, the Pérez sisters recorded a whole album in Nashville to emphasize and draw on their country roots, and they recorded one of the songs in English with country singer Brandi Carlisle. "We enjoy trying new things and involving different audiences," says Hanna Pérez. Hinting at where they may go next, she adds, "Making an English Album [is] a possibility in the next couple of years." After all, they may be happy with their new life in Mexico, but at heart they are still country singers who started their career in their church's gospel choir and at county fairs in Louisiana.

10

"A Tsunami of Mexican Talent"

- -

How Mexican Filmmakers Went Global

Ben Odell was used to his dinner conversations being interrupted. A successful Hollywood producer, he dined often with actors and actresses, and he had grown accustomed to other diners stopping by their table to ask for photos and autographs. But on the night, a decade ago, that he had dinner at an upscale New York restaurant with Eugenio Derbez, a veteran Mexican actor who was then starring in a Broadway play, not one person seemed to notice them. Anonymity has its benefits too, so they enjoyed the quiet dinner together.

Then, just as they were getting ready to pay the check, a cake arrived unexpectedly, courtesy of the chef. A nice touch, thought Odell.

And then every one of the cooks, sous-chefs, and dishwashers from the kitchen, plus every one of the waiters and busboys, crowded around their table wanting to shake hands with Derbez and asking for a group photo. The entire workings of the restaurant ground to a halt for a few minutes, while the other diners looked on mystified, uncertain what had caused this commotion.

Eugenio Derbez, though almost entirely unknown in New York's social circles, was Mexico's most famous comedian. And he was also well known to audiences throughout Latin America and to many American-born Latinos who watched Spanish-language television from time to time. The other customers might not have known who he was, but the restaurant staff sure did. "At that point," Odell recalls, "I knew I would have to work with him."

Ben Odell had spent his time in Hollywood trying to find out how to market movies to people both in Latin America and the United States, looking for blockbusters that would appeal across borders. A former journalist in Latin America who is married to a Colombian, Odell leads a thoroughly bilingual and bicultural life. He knew that there must be a way to reproduce that on the big screen for others who live in those two worlds, to make films that appeal both to Latin Americans and to American Latinos. But though he'd ended up working on some great movies, that goal had largely eluded him. Movies with a Latin flair either did well north of the border or south of the border but rarely in both places.

Odell knew that harnessing both markets would be a home run. After all, Mexico is now the tenth-largest market for movie ticket sales in the world, and it's the only emerging economy in the top ten, ahead of even Italy, Brazil, and Russia. Mexicans spend almost $1 billion on movie tickets a year. Movie attendance per capita in Mexico grew 59 percent from 2005 to 2015 at the same time that it dropped 21 percent in the United States. The number of movie theaters in Mexico has exploded too, growing from 492 in 2005 to 698 in 2016, whereas the number of theaters in the United States has contracted slightly.

And in the United States too, Latino moviegoers, two-thirds of whom are of Mexican descent, have been keeping the market afloat. US Latinos attend movies anywhere from 40 to 80 percent more often than white Americans, depending on the survey year, suggesting a significantly more active engagement with the cinema.

One of the theater chains that has bucked the trend of declining theaters in the United States is, perhaps not surprisingly, a Mexican company. Cinépolis is the fourth-largest theater company in the world and second globally in ticket sales, and it has a major foothold not only in Mexico but also in India, Brazil, and Colombia, among other countries. In 2011, Cinépolis began an expansion into the United States, buying a single theater in the seaside town of Del Mar, near San Diego, and renovating it to accommodate the company's high-end approach to cinema, which involves waiters, premium beverages, and high-quality food.

"The American market was quite mature, but with little focus on service," says Miguel Rivera, Cinépolis's vice president for programming. "So service was the differentiator," the new ingredient that the Mexican company could bring to the American industry. Soon the Del Mar cinema had the highest ticket sales in the United States for any eight-screen movie theater.

Cinépolis, run by the forty-six-year-old Alejandro Ramírez, has since expanded to eighteen theaters across the United States, up and down both the East and West Coasts. Most of its theaters are in some of America's wealthiest neighborhoods, but the company also offers a slightly less expensive option in a few less wealthy areas, including some mostly Latino areas in California. Although Cinépolis hasn't based its expansion on targeting Latino moviegoers exclusively, it has made sure to have offerings that appeal to Latino audiences.

Hollywood studios are just beginning to discover the growing Latino community in the United States. Although America's Latino movie audience goes to see all kinds of films, evidence suggests that they particularly gravitate toward well-made movies with Latino stars, like the *Fast and Furious* and *Spy Kids* franchises. "If it's Latino and cool, it will overindex with Latinos," says Ben Odell. And these movies do particularly well in Mexico and Latin America as well. The scramble is now on in Hollywood to develop other Latino talent that can headline new movie franchises.

"It's kind of surprising it hasn't happened earlier," says Claudia Puig, former film critic for the *Los Angeles Times* and *USA Today*, who now heads the Los Angeles Film Critics Association.

After several partially successful ventures, Ben Odell finally settled in as the head of production for Pantelion, an unusual joint production company formed by Hollywood's successful Lionsgate Studio and Mexico's largest television network, Televisa, to develop films for a binational market. The idea was to target Latinos in the United States and Latin Americans in their home country. At first, Pantelion made a series of small-budget productions that recovered their investments but achieved limited exposure. "We were the early test for the market," says Odell.

Then Odell helped convince Eugenio Derbez, his dinner companion in New York a few years before, to do a truly binational film in Spanish, which Pantelion distributed. The result of that effort, *Instructions Not Included*, broke records for a Spanish-language production. The bittersweet film, which focuses on a Mexican immigrant, played by

Derbez, who becomes a Hollywood stuntman and single parent raising an American-born daughter, brought in $99 million, $46 million
in Mexico, $44 million in the United States, and another $10 million
elsewhere in the Spanish-speaking world.

Derbez and Odell now have their own production company together, and they launched a second film—this one in English—titled
How to Be a Latin Lover in 2017. Featuring not only Derbez but also
Mexican actress Salma Hayek and American actors Kristen Bell and
Rob Lowe, the lighthearted comedy about an aging Latin lover learning to find meaning in life was wildly successful. It brought in almost
$25 million in Mexico and $32 million in the United States, with Pantelion estimating that 89 percent of the American audience on opening weekend was Latino.

Interestingly enough, the weekend that it opened, *How to Be a Latin
Lover* placed second in ticket sales behind *The Fate of the Furious*, which
had an equally diverse cast, and just ahead of the Bollywood movie
Baahubali 2, which targeted Indian Americans almost exclusively. The
message to Hollywood from that weekend's ratings was resoundingly
clear: movies with ethnically diverse casts are the future.

Ben Odell and Eugenio Derbez are now hard at work on a third
film starting Derbez, but they are also developing several other films
that have partially Latino themes and target markets in both the
United States and Latin America. One is a car-racing-themed movie,
contracted by NASCAR, while others have not yet been publicly
announced.

But Odell thinks of these efforts as opening up the market for
more mainstream ventures that are less specifically Latino themed
but include significant Latino talent and content. "The future is more
mainstream content by and for Latinos," he says. "Professionally

produced, bigger budgets, where you see Latinos as part of the mainstream conversation." The kinds of big-budget movies that Hollywood knows how to make, but with a recognition of America's increasing diversity—and its indelible ties to the countries south of the border.

"I thought my hair was going to fall off," Patricia Riggen recalls about her decision, in 2007, to pull out of her first production arrangement with a major Hollywood studio. Shortly after arriving in Los Angeles, she found a script, *Under the Same Moon*, that she wanted to turn into her first feature-length movie. The story centered on an eight-year-old boy who was migrating north from Mexico to find his mother in Los Angeles, and Riggen had spent a year developing it with the original screen writer and negotiating a production deal. But when she started working with the studio to make the movie, she realized she was losing creative freedom and doubted whether she'd retain control over the film's distribution once it was done.

Turning down the deal—and the millions of dollars in financing that came with it—was risky. Riggen had only made two short films in her life, both as a graduate student, and while they had won some of the industry's top prizes, making a feature film as a Hollywood director was a huge leap forward, especially for a woman and a Mexican. But Riggen had taken risks before and was willing to try it again.

A few years earlier, just as she turned thirty, Riggen had left a successful career working for the Mexican Film Institute, known as Imcine, Mexico's government-run film production agency, and enrolled in Columbia University's MFA film program. She felt there were few opportunities for a woman to become a director in Mexico's film industry and that she'd be better off starting over north of the border.

Although she was self-conscious about having more experience than most of the other students, she soon discovered that it actually gave her a leg up. Her thesis film, *The Cornfield*, about the Mexican Revolution, won the Student Academy Award. She then used the $5,000 in prize money to produce another film, *Family Portrait*, a documentary about a resilient Harlem-based family. The movie went on to win the top prize for short films at the Sundance Film Festival in 2005.

But now, having pulled out of the deal with the production company to make her first feature-length film, Riggen realized that she would have to return home to Mexico—the country she had left for lack of opportunities for a female director—and ask for support from Imcine, her former employer. "I went back to Mexico," she says, "and the beautiful thing was that I got all the support and resources I needed to start my career."

Imcine, which funnels around $30 million a year into films made in Mexico, ended up offering her half the funding she needed. She then leveraged that to get a private equity firm from the United States to put in the other half. This turned out to be one of the first American-Mexican film coproductions.

With this backing, she was able to shoot *Under the Same Moon* in locations both in Mexico and in the United States with a tight budget on a five-week schedule. She used talent recruited from both countries, including one of Mexico's most popular actresses, Kate del Castillo, and—yes—the comedian Eugenio Derbez, whom she cast in his first ever dramatic role. She even found a cameo role for Los Tigres del Norte, Mexico's equivalent of the Rolling Stones, a band that's been popular in Mexico for over four decades. The band was particularly apt for this story about migration, since its members themselves are migrants—all five of them live in San Jose, California, where they migrated as teenagers.

Patricia Riggen was happy with the results of the film. "I controlled it, and I took good care of it," she says with pride.

The film turned out to be a major debut success. Riggen spent $1.7 million making the film, and it brought in $23 million in revenue, $12.5 million in the United States, $9.5 million in Mexico, and the balance in other countries—a healthy margin for a first-time director. The movie became a sentimental favorite for many American Latinos, who identified with its themes about migration, but it also gained huge audiences south of the border in Mexico and even crossed over to English-speaking art film audiences.

Riggen has since gone on to direct several big-budget Hollywood movies, including *Miracles from Heaven*, *The 33*, and *Girl in Progress*, working with stars like Jennifer Garner, Antonio Banderas, Lou Diamond Phillips, and Juliette Binoche. Yet she admits that she has never enjoyed the process as much as she did with *Under the Same Moon*, where she had full creative control.

But Riggen is hardly the only—or even the most famous—Mexican director working in Hollywood today. For three years in a row, from 2013 to 2015, the Oscar for best director went to two Mexican directors who have worked extensively in Hollywood, Alfonso Cuarón and Alejandro González Iñárritu. Cuarón took home the honors for *Gravity*, which brought in more than $750 million in revenue, while González Iñárritu won for both *Birdman* and *The Revenant*, the first a reflective look at Broadway acting and the second a blockbuster starring Leonard DiCaprio as a grizzled fur trapper.

In each of those three years, the Oscar for best cinematography went to the same cameraman, Emmanuel Lubezki, yet another Mexican and a friend of both Cuarón and González Iñárritú. He filmed all three movies using highly experimental techniques, though strikingly different ones in each case. Lubezki has become known for pushing the boundaries of what the camera can do to set the tone of a film.

In many ways, Mexican cinema is also breaking boundaries. Claudia Puig, the film critic, says that Mexican filmmakers have "pushed the envelope" in large part because "they do interesting things cinematically." She notes that they have combined "risk taking" with good "storytelling."

González Iñárritú and Cuarón—along with a third director, Guillermo del Toro, who directed *Hellboy*, *Pacific Rim*, and *Pan's Labyrinth*, for which he was also nominated for an Oscar—have become known as the "Three Amigos," three directors who became successful around the same time in Mexico and later transitioned to making global films. And all three are, in fact, amigos—not just friends but close friends.

Together the three made some of the most experimental and commercially successful films in Mexico in the late 1990s and early 2000s, including Cuarón's *Y tu mama también* (*Your Mother Too*), González Iñárritú's *Amores perros* (*Dog Loves*), and Del Toro's *Cronos*. These movies got them noticed in Hollywood and across the Atlantic in Europe, which allowed them to move into bigger-budget productions financed by international studios. Today they are some of the most highly sought talents in Hollywood, as well as among the most creative and original.

According to Bruce Ramer, one of Hollywood's top entertainment lawyers, the "Three Amigos" have now blazed the trail for other

Mexican and Latin American talent in Hollywood. "They paid their own way with talent," he says, "and opened up an incredible path for others." And the result, he adds, is that there is now "a tsunami of Mexican talent up here."

That new talent includes not only Riggen but also cameraman Guillermo Navarro, who has filmed movies like *Spy Kids*, *Night at the Museum*, the *Twilight* saga, and *Star Trek Discovery*, as well as Del Toro's movie *Pan's Labyrinth*, for which he took home an Oscar. It also includes cameraman Rodrigo Prieto, who has filmed an eclectic set of movies that include *Argo*, *Frida*, *The Wolf of Wall Street*, *Brokeback Mountain*, and *8 Mile*.

And there is no lack of acting talent these days either, including global stars like Salma Hayek, who was nominated for an Oscar for *Frida*; Gael García Bernal, who starred in *Babel*, González Iñárritú´s first international film; Diego Luna, who recently appeared in *Rogue One: A Star Wars Story*; and Damian Bichir, nominated for an Oscar for his role in *A Better Life*. All are veteran actors who continue to appear in Mexican-made films but have now also ventured north of the border quite successfully.

Like Bruce Ramer, Riggen gives credit to the "Three Amigos," who helped open the way for other Mexican filmmakers in Hollywood, saying, "They have broken the mold for what it means to be a director south of the border." She also notes that the Mexican government's decision to invest in filmmaking helped revitalize the industry.

In the end, she says, it comes down to a mix of storytelling and originality. "We have a different and very fresh vision of the world but with a craft as good as anyone else in Hollywood," says Riggen.

As a country that has been going through rapid changes in recent years, Mexico offers an endless source of inspiration for storytelling, but it has also developed an industry with the strength to produce technically skilled filmmaking talent. "When you can combine both the craft and a fresh look at things," she says, "you have a star director."

"I was clear that I would have more freedom in Mexico," says Gabriel Ripstein about his decision to give up a successful career as a Hollywood studio executive and move back to Mexico City a few years ago. "But I keep a foot there, a foot here," he adds.

Ripstein, the son of one of Mexico's most storied directors and the grandson of an equally legendary movie producer, had tried to break away from the family tradition by becoming a business consultant for several years but eventually realized that his heart lay in cinema. He worked at a Mexican-run production company for a bit, then studied for an MBA at Columbia University with a focus on the film industry. He then rose through the ranks at Columbia Pictures in Los Angeles, helping identify and produce films from around the world.

But he realized after a while that he wanted to do more than just be on the business end of filmmaking, and so he came back to Mexico in 2012. Since then, he has directed his own independent film in Mexico, *600 Miles*, which won a prize at the Berlin Film Festival, and produced two independent Mexican films for his friend Michel Franco, *Chronic* and *April's Daughters*, which won top prizes at Cannes in 2015 and 2017.

Ripstein has also kept a hand in Hollywood, working with major studios as a screen writer. Recently he also wrote a historical drama for Televisa, the Mexican television station, about the breakdown of the country's political system in 1968, when the government ordered a massacre of protesting university students and then covered it up.

In one of his most unusual experiences, Ripstein found himself directing the third season of *Narcos*, the wildly successful Netflix series about the rise of the Colombian drug cartels. The series is funded by French and American production companies and written in the United States but features a cast of actors from all over the hemisphere who speak a mixture of Spanish and English onscreen, often with a jumble of different accents. "It was a postmodern effort," he says, reflecting on the months he spent in Colombia filming the series.

Ripstein's career today spans the divide between independent and commercial film; American, Mexican, and truly international productions; and a mix of movies, television, and on-demand distribution. And he himself switches roles between screenwriter, director, and producer—sometimes performing all three at once—depending on the project.

That versatility says something about Ripstein and his diverse skills but also about the way that the film industry is evolving. Today the introduction of new media platforms is making careers in film more mobile and varied. And in many ways Ripstein's life is also a microcosm of what's happening to other filmmakers from Mexico, who are gaining an important presence in the global film industry—and especially in Hollywood—often while remaining firmly anchored in their own country.

Things were quite different for Alfredo Ripstein, Gabriel's grandfather, who became one of the founding fathers of Mexico's modern film industry. The son of a Jewish immigrant from Poland, Alfredo became one of Mexico's first movie producers during the country's golden age of film, a period that stretched roughly from the late 1930s to the early 1960s. The Mexican government invested millions of dollars annually in film production, helping around one hundred films a year reach audiences at the height of that period. Political leaders saw this as part of a strategy to build a true national consciousness, a sense of what it meant to be Mexican.

Ripstein produced some of Mexico's best-loved films starring the most famous actors of the day, including Pedro Infante, Maria Felix, Pedro Armendariz, Silvia Panal, and Antonio Aguilar. They often portrayed hardworking farmers and beautiful but poor women who managed to overcome adversity through their dedication, honesty, and pride in their land. These films sought to build a sense of Mexican national identity shared by people of all social classes.

Mexico's golden age cinema existed in parallel with Hollywood, dominating the global Spanish-language film market in the way that Hollywood did the English-language market. To be sure, a handful of actors and actresses crossed over between the two industries, but for the most part they were separate poles in the filmmaking universe.

Gabriel Ripstein's father, Arturo Ripstein, took a different path, working first as a camera assistant for the Spanish-born filmmaker Luis Buñuel, who lived in Mexico. He then followed in Buñuel's footsteps, becoming a highly regarded international director who experimented with light, addressed challenging social themes, and explored the solitude of interpersonal interactions. Unlike the golden age films, the movies made by Arturo Ripstein and other contemporary directors, like Jorge Fons and Felipe Casals, hewed much closer to European independent cinema, exploring complex themes of individual rather than national identity and questioning prevailing norms in society.

But in the 1990s, the entire Mexican film industry underwent a dramatic transformation. President Carlos Salinas de Gortari

(1988–1994) decided to privatize the film industry and eliminate the government-run theaters that made cinema accessible to all social classes by selling tickets at bargain-basement prices. In their place came large private theater chains that catered to Mexico's middle class. Ticket prices were significantly higher and affordable only for people with middle-class incomes.

At first, this privatization looked like the death of the Mexican film industry—yet it actually helped reinvent it.

Ignacio Sanchez Prado, a leading scholar of Mexican film and professor at Washington University in St. Louis, says, "Movies became very expensive…but they became profitable." He adds that the reform essentially "took the films from the poor and gave them to the middle class." It made moviegoing far less democratic, but for the first time it created a private market for successful films. Privately owned movie theaters and several large movie chains sprung up in the 1990s. The Cinépolis chain, then run by Alejandro Ramírez's father, had its boom in this period.

Perhaps ironically, Gabriel Ripstein's grandfather—the long-time producer of popular government-sponsored films—was one of the first to find the formula for producing privately funded movies that could both succeed commercially and push the boundaries of convention. Two of his movies became icons of this new period and helped launch a new wave of still experimental but also commercially successful cinema in Mexico. One, *El callejón de los milagros* (*Midaq Alley*), explored social conflicts in an urban neighborhood of Mexico City—and launched the career of Salma Hayek, the movie's young protagonist. The other film, *The Crime of Father Amaro*, told a controversial story about complicities between priests, criminals, and the government and helped lift the career of Gael García Bernal. Both films generated pushback in Mexico, *Midaq Alley* because of its portrayal of homosexuality and *The Crime of Father Amaro* because of its discussion of corruption in the church.

In the late 1990s and early 2000s, the "Three Amigos"—Cuarón, González Iñárritú, and Del Toro—also made their first Mexican films, using a mixture of public and private funding. They were, in one sense, beneficiaries of the changes that allowed investors to go looking for innovative, marketable films that might never have fit into government funding priorities. But the three also felt let down by the lack of public investment in film and began to look abroad for funding to make their future movies.

All three eventually moved away—González Iñárritú to Los Angeles, Del Toro to Madrid, and Cuarón to London—where they could access other sources of funding for their films. Increasingly, all three would be drawn to English-language films that they could produce in cooperation with major Hollywood studios.

But then in the early 2000s, the Mexican Congress decided to start financing films again, creating three different funds to help filmmakers realize their projects, including one supported by dedicated corporate tax payments. From 2013 to 2016 anywhere from 79 to 101 long-form films were produced each year with government funding, often complemented with investment from film funds in other countries or by private Mexican and Hollywood funding. Contrary to what many expected when the film industry was privatized, Mexico may actually now be experiencing a second golden age of film.

But there are important differences. To begin with, dozens of movies are produced each year, but not all of them find an audience.

"The fight for screens is fierce," says Gabriel Ripstein, who has spent a great deal of time trying to get movies he's produced and directed into Mexican theaters. Industry consolidation drove the number of major theater chains down to three, with a handful of independent theaters in major cities. Both chains and independents make decisions about what to show based on what they think will generate profits. "It's business," says Ripstein.

Quite unlike government, which often prioritizes quality and originality over commercial potential in its support for film, the theater chains are looking for commercial viability. As a result, there is a mismatch—for better or worse—between the movies produced and those that are actually seen.

Ignacio Sanchez Prado notes that at any given time only 7 to 10 percent of theater screens show Mexican-made movies, with most of the rest dedicated to Hollywood blockbusters and, very occasionally, other international films. Some of the chains and independents have created special theaters for upscale audiences that like to see innovative Mexican and international films, along the lines of the Landmark Theaters in the United States. Cinépolis also sponsors film festivals around the country, using its theaters for independent cinema.

One of the great ironies, of course, is that the Mexican directors who have gone abroad have probably had more success in Mexico by becoming international superstars and gaining access to the generous financing and big studio sets that only Hollywood can provide. But Mexico too remains a seedbed of enormous talent, and the directors who have decided to stay in Mexico continue to push the boundaries of film convention in ways that are gleaning international attention and acclaim.

And increasingly, many Mexican film professionals, like Gabriel Ripstein, move back and forth across the border, creating original content by taking the best they can get from the film industry on both sides.

Pablo Cruz, another producer of Mexican films, found himself on a flight from Spain back across the Atlantic with his friend Gael García Bernal a few years ago, and they got to talking about Mexico's film industry. Cruz had been taking his first steps as a producer of Mexican independent film, while García Bernal was well on his way to becoming one of Mexico's most popular actors—equally at ease in lighthearted comedies as in weightier independent films.

"Gael and I had a conversation on a plane," recalls Cruz. "Why not create a business with a social sensibility...because there are still many faces of Mexico that no one was bothering to look at."

Mexican film, like its counterpart, television, had long favored sentimental melodramas. Change was in the air, however, in the late 1990s and early 2000s, with films that provided social commentary and presented more complex dramatic situations. Many of these movies were made by the "Three Amigos," as well as Gabriel Ripstein's father and grandfather. Gael García Bernal and his close friend Diego Luna, now two of Mexico's best-known actors around the world, starred in many of these films. But the economics of independent film in Mexico was still shaky. Cruz and García Bernal wanted to ensure that quality films would see the light of day.

In 2005, Cruz, García Bernal, and Luna formed Canana Films, a production and distribution company dedicated to promoting movies that grapple with critical social issues and present a picture of the many Mexicos. Over time, this mission would evolve beyond Mexico, looking at the United States and at Mexicans abroad as well. And the company would become a source of innovation in independent film on both sides of the border.

But right as they were planning to launch Canana, they decided that they also needed to do something about documentaries, a kind of film that rarely had any exposure in Mexico, yet perhaps did the best job of looking at Mexico's many different social realities. The three recruited Elena Fortes, a young social activist, to run a parallel project called Ambulante, which means something like "rambling" or "walking around," to support documentary filmmakers.

The two parallel organizations were actually quite different from the outset. Canana was a for-profit production and distribution company dedicated to investing in low-budget, meaningful, independent films and occasionally acquiring distribution rights to films already made. It had a social purpose but used market mechanisms to encourage investment and promote the visibility of films that could tell stories about Mexico in compelling ways. Ambulante, in contrast, was set up as a nonprofit, created to stimulate a documentary film industry that barely existed yet in Mexico and to give it broad visibility around the country.

For Ambulante, they found a key partner in Alejandro Ramírez, CEO of Cinépolis. Ramírez had already helped start the Morelia Film Festival, Mexico's most prestigious venue for screening independent cinema, so he had experience in hosting film festivals. And Ramírez was also the rare business executive who had done graduate work specifically focused on social inequality.

In the 1990s, then in his twenties, Ramírez had followed his mentor, Amartya Sen, the Nobel Prize–winning scholar of human development, from Oxford to Harvard, eventually completing graduate work in the late 1990s focused on poverty issues. He was a coauthor of the United Nations' 1996 Human Development Report, for which Professor Sen served as an outside advisor, and Ramírez himself later served as an advisor on social development to Mexico's government in the early 2000s before he became CEO of Cinépolis in 2006.

Ambulante made business sense for Cinépolis because it offered the company a way to reach out to new audiences but also gave Ramírez an opportunity to use the family business to help generate a broad national discussion about the divisions in Mexican society and what to do about them.

Ambulante would help train documentary filmmakers and produce their films, while Cinépolis would sponsor the film festivals that would ensure Mexicans could see them. It was a brilliant idea and has been phenomenally successful ever since.

Canana, on the other hand, has been behind many of Mexico's most successful independent films for over a decade. These have included *Sin nombre*, a powerful drama about Central American migrants riding the railway in Mexico, which catapulted its director, the American Cary Fukunaga, to prominence; *Miss Bala*, which tells the tale of a young woman in Tijuana who becomes unexpectedly entwined with a drug cartel as she becomes a beauty queen in a local pageant; and *The Chosen Ones*, a masterful but heartrending story about sex slavery, which Netflix later acquired for global distribution. Both *Miss Bala* and *The Chosen Ones* were screened at the Cannes Film Festival.

Their directors, Gerardo Naranjo and David Pablos, are part of an emerging group of young Mexican film directors who have received high critical acclaim at film festivals around the world. This group also includes Michel Franco, Gabriel Ripstein's close friend and frequent collaborator, as well as Amat Escalante, the maker of compelling movies about social conflict, and Carlos Reygadas, known for his innovative use of light and tendency to recruit nonactors to play dramatic roles. All three have received top awards at Cannes.

Groundbreaking Mexican filmmakers have become so prevalent at the world's leading film festivals that Salma Hayek, who in her fifties has become the dean of Mexican actresses and actors, organized a spontaneous Mexican party at the Cannes Film Festival's seventieth anniversary dinner in 2017. She told James Corden on CBS's *Late Late Show* that after a photographer lined up all the Mexican talent at the festival for a photo, it struck her how important Mexican filmmakers had become for the festival. "I realized that out of these hundred people from all over the world, at least ten percent were Latinos, most of the ten percent were Mexican, and they were my friends. And I felt such a sense of pride and I was so moved that I went crazy."

Within hours she had managed to locate a mariachi band in Paris, where she now lives with her French husband, and transported them to the southern coast of France. She and her associates then scoured the restaurants and bars in Cannes for every bit of tequila and mezcal—even half-empty bottles—they could buy for the evening. Later that night, the world's most prominent film talent consumed large quantities of Mexican spirits while trying to sing and dance— not always successfully—to mariachi music. The spontaneous videos of the evening, made by some of the world's best filmmakers on their smartphones, make for an amusing tour of the evening.

In contrast, documentary filmmaking lacks the glitz—and the financial backing—of the rest of the film industry, but it's proved an important part of the original vision that Pablo Cruz and Gael García Bernal laid out on their plane trip many years ago. Paulina Suarez, who took over running Ambulante from Elena Fortes, says it "has helped take documentaries out of the margins and put them in the center" of the Mexican film industry. A few of Ambulante's films have received national attention, thanks largely to the film festivals that Ambulante organizes with Cinépolis. But Ambulante has also organized documentary filmmaking workshops in indigenous and rural communities never reached by film festivals. There they teach young people to film the reality around them and then hold localized film festivals for the communities.

Ambulante even had a small role, together with Cinépolis, in distributing Mexico's most famous documentary of all time, Roberto Hernández and Layda Negrete's film *Presumed Guilty* about the judicial system. It remains one of the few commercially successful documentary films in Mexico, with 1.7 million theater ticket sold, according to Miguel Rivera of Cinépolis, and an equally successful run on DVD.

While Ambulante remains firmly rooted in Mexico—although with occasional film festivals in Los Angeles, Central America, and Colombia—Canana has now moved its center of operations to Hollywood, where Pablo Cruz has his office.

The shift stemmed, in part, from the economics and logistics of the film industry, since Hollywood exerts a powerful gravitational pull. But it also arose from the desire to tell stories about Mexicans north of the border. Cruz says that they were fascinated by "the evolution of the Mexican identity when you cross the border.... How does that transform itself and become a new identity?" And the movies they make increasingly have a binational angle, focusing not just on Mexico but on Mexicans in the United States.

But while speaking of trying to find the binational market for their films, Cruz sounds a note of caution. "We failed every time that we tried to make things for a specific purpose." Instead, the films that become successful on both sides of the border are often unexpected and unpredictable.

Yet Pablo Cruz recognizes that Canana's biggest impact has not been at the box office but in bringing films to light that would never have emerged otherwise. "I have produced films that no one else would have made," he says.

And today Mexican producers and directors—some working in the United States, others in Mexico, and many in both countries—continue to produce fresh, original films that push the boundaries of convention and often tackle pressing social issues. And all signs suggest that they will continue to be a driving force in the global movie industry for the foreseeable future.

11

"We've Gone from Ethnic to Mainstream"

How Mexican Influence Is Changing America from Within

On October 20, 2007, Mark Sanchez demolished Notre Dame. The sophomore University of Southern California (USC) quarterback completed twenty-one of his thirty-eight passes, including four for touchdowns, leading the Trojans to a 38–0 win. It was a historic game: the largest margin of victory for USC in a decades-long rivalry, as well as the worst home-field loss for Notre Dame in more than half a century. Yet some viewers seemed less concerned with what this extraordinary new talent had done on the field than what he wore on his teeth: a mouth guard styled after the Mexican flag, right down to the eagle sitting on a cactus in the middle.

Visitors to online forums posted complaints that Sanchez, who grew up in the United States, the grandson of Mexican immigrants, had "split his loyalty" and was "politicizing his heritage," and

245

a number of op-ed writers and callers on radio shows criticized his decision. Sanchez laughed off the minor controversy, saying that he "didn't know that it was that big of a deal" and explaining that the mouthpiece was simply "a portrayal of love for my heritage."

Sanchez, who had grown up in a comfortable, English-speaking, middle-class family in Orange County, California, decided not to wear the mouthpiece again during his college career. He'd had enough controversy. Instead he went out of his way to learn Spanish, the language of his paternal grandparents, who had immigrated from Mexico, and he began to give interviews to Latino media. Over time, he nurtured a fan base of Mexican Americans who were proud to see one of their own excel in the United States' most popular sport.

USC had been supportive of his efforts to court Latino fans, but when he made the jump to the pros as a quarterback for the New York Jets in 2009, Sanchez quickly discovered that the National Football League (NFL) was not just supportive but eager to market his Mexican heritage. In fact, Sanchez had arrived right as the NFL was in full swing trying to build its Latino fan base, and the sudden crop of Mexican American quarterbacks—Sanchez, the Dallas Cowboys' Tony Romo, the Buffalo Bills' J. P. Lossman, and the San Francisco Forty-Niners' Jeff Garcia—were just what the league needed to build a bridge to Latino fans. Sanchez and Romo would eventually transition from quarterbacks to sports commentators, joining the ranks of the top personalities in the media covering football.

Several years before, the league's executives had realized that although Latino fans watched more sports than the US population at large, they hadn't embraced football as much as other Americans. In 2002 the NFL established a task force to look at this potential new fan base. That same year it began broadcasting games on

Spanish-language radio. In 2005 the league hosted its first game in Mexico City. And in 2014 the Super Bowl was televised for the first time on a US Spanish-language network, Fox Deportes.

"Hispanics have been growing fast as a percentage of our fan base," says NFL director for marketing and fan development Marissa Fernandez—faster, in fact, than any other demographic over the past few years. "Where we've seen most of this growth is with Spanish-language bilingual and bicultural Hispanics," most of them US born and of Mexican descent.

The NFL has used Spanish strategically to reach out to this new fan base. All of the league's marketing data indicate that even second- and third-generation Latinos who speak English fluently "are still consuming content in Spanish," says Fernandez. Although most Americans who are the children of Mexican immigrants primarily speak English in their daily lives, and most grandchildren of immigrants lose their proficiency in Spanish entirely, they still remain familiar with basic Spanish words and phrases and often find advertising in Spanish—at least in simple Spanish—appealing. "They are consuming content [in Spanish] for particular reasons that are emotional, not functional," adds Fernandez.

With that in mind, the NFL has conducted a series of English-language campaigns that incorporate references to Latino heritage. One, "Feel the Orgullo," ran on television and radio and across digital and social media. The Spanglish phrase incorporates the Spanish word for "pride." Another campaign used artwork modeled on the popular Mexican game Lotería, which involves bright cards with pictures of gothic-looking animals. Instead of the usual Lotería images, the NFL substituted figures representing the thirty-two NFL teams to create an emotional connection for Latino fans.

The NFL has also expanded into Mexico. NFL games are broadcast every Sunday on television, and the three games the league has played in Mexico's mammoth Aztec Stadium were among its best attended ever. And the league occasionally even brings in cheerleaders from abroad, according to Steve Ladick, the immigration attorney who works for pro football teams on their visa needs, in hopes of appealing to new audiences in Latin America and Asia.

Of course what's been happening with the NFL has also been happening across the rest of the entertainment industry, as media executives and advertisers have discovered the purchasing power of 57.5 million Latinos, almost two-thirds of them of Mexican descent. Together Latinos comprise a market for consumer goods that, according to Nielsen, grew from $1 trillion in 2010 to around $1.3 trillion in 2015, a massive increase in only five years. This growth is driven less by immigration, which has slowed, than by the greater numbers of both US- and foreign-born Latinos moving into the middle class.

Latinos accounted for 29 percent of real income growth in the decade from 2005 to 2015 and 46 percent of employment growth between 2011 and 2015. Perhaps most strikingly for marketers, the median age of Americans of Latino heritage is twenty-eight, compared to thirty-seven for the population at large and forty-three for non-Hispanic whites. The future—from professional sports to consumer products—lies with this younger, growing consumer base.

Other professional sports, beyond the NFL, have discovered this potential too. NASCAR, once the least diverse of sports (along with hockey), has seen its share of Latino—primarily Mexican-descent—fans grow from only 2 to around 9 percent over the past decade. This is hardly surprising, given the growth of Mexican American populations in the South and Midwest, where NASCAR has long had its strongest base of support. NASCAR has increasingly conducted out-reach campaigns to Latino viewers and even posted Spanish-language signs at some tracks to make Spanish-speaking fans feel more wel-come. And NASCAR recently partnered with Mexican actor Eugenio Derbez and his partner Ben Odell, the duo behind several success-ful Spanish- and English-language movies, to produce a NASCAR-themed movie that they hope will appeal to Latino audiences.

Just in time, NASCAR has also finally gotten its first star driver of Mexican descent in Daniel Suarez, who competes for Joe Gibbs Racing. Initially recruited as part of NASCAR's "Drive for Diversity" campaign, Suarez, already a well-known driver in Mexico, drove a Volkswagen Beatle from his hometown of Monterrey to Charlotte, North Carolina, to join Gibbs's team. After all, he was the son of a Volkswagen mechanic who had sold his auto shop to help pay for his son's career as a racer. In 2016, Suarez, at twenty-five, won the Xfinity Series, becoming the first Latino driver to take home one of the major NASCAR series champion-ships. Suarez has since bought his father a new auto shop in Monterrey in gratitude for jump-starting his racing career.

Major League Baseball (MLB), of course, has a much longer history of reaching out to Latino fans—almost a third of professional players were either born in Latin America or are of Latino heritage. The game is popular in Mexico and much of Caribbean Latin America, especially the Dominican Republic, Cuba, and Venezuela. Mexico has its own pro-fessional baseball league with passionate fans and widespread support.

In the United States, MLB has long broadcast games in Spanish and courted Latino fans, who make up roughly 9 percent of its fan base. MLB even schedules exhibition games—and sometimes regular-season games—in cities around Mexico and has flirted at times with expanding the league to either Mexico City or Monterrey. When the

Montreal Expos were for sale, a Mexico-based consortium briefly considered putting in a formal bid for the team, which eventually ended up in my hometown as the Washington Nationals.

Yet, surprisingly, basketball is actually doing even better with young Latinos, including those of Mexican descent, than baseball. About 12 percent of National Basketball Association (NBA) fans are Latino. Although currently no star players are of Mexican descent, the NBA boasts a few high-profile players born in Brazil, Argentina, and Spain. But more importantly, the NBA simply has done well with younger audiences generally—45 percent of its fans are under thirty-five years old (compared to 24 percent for MLB and only 14 percent for NASCAR)—including young Latinos.

The Women's National Basketball Association (WNBA) also claims that one in five of its fans are of Latin descent. That includes my daughter Lucia, a devoted fan of our local WNBA team. When I once suggested we go see an NBA playoff game, she expressed surprise—with a nine-year-old's wisdom—that men even played basketball and wondered whether anyone would pay to go see them. So you can still count her as part of the WNBA's Latino—and Latina—fan base, though not necessarily because of any specific outreach to Hispanic families.

And then, of course, there is soccer. Although men's soccer remains far behind other professional sports leagues in overall revenue, and women's professional soccer has struggled even to survive, soccer has actually become one of the two most popular amateur sports played in the United States, along with basketball. It's accessible, inexpensive, and relatively safe to play, and both girls and boys can embrace it equally and sometimes even play together. Since 1980, the number of children and youth playing in organized soccer leagues has tripled, from 1 million to over 3 million.

Major League Soccer (MLS), the men's professional league, has been growing steadily over the past decade, with teams worth an average of $185 million each, up 80 percent from 2013 to 2017—and 400 percent from 2008. Over a third of the league's fans identify as Latino, as do many of the best players, and Hispanic fans have helped fuel the game's growing success. In one ESPN poll, young viewers, ages twelve to twenty-four, chose soccer as their second favorite sport to watch after football, with over a quarter of all Hispanics saying it was their favorite sport.

Both English- and Spanish-language media have increasingly televised soccer games, making soccer the fourth most watched sport on television after football, basketball, and baseball—and well ahead of racing, hockey, and tennis. Viewership of the MLS finals jumped to around 2 million in 2016, a 70 percent increase from a year earlier, a strong sign of the sport's growth in popularity.

World soccer is also extremely lucrative for television networks. One World Cup match in 2016, the United States versus Belgium, pulled in 16 million viewers on ESPN alone, outdoing the NBA finals. And that number doesn't include the millions who watched on Spanish-language channels.

Spanish-speaking Latinos—mostly first-generation immigrants—tend to be the most passionate soccer fans, though Latinos who speak English at home, who are more likely to be US born, are also enthusiastic soccer followers. And one of the MLS's original teams, Chivas USA, was actually an American franchise of Guadalajara's famous Chivas team.

The growth of soccer owes a great deal to the influx of Mexicans and other Latin Americans into the United States since the 1980s and to the growing population of American-born Latinos. It would be almost impossible to sustain the growing popularity of the MLS without Latino fans, and the passion of recent arrivals who brought the game with them fueled much of amateur soccer's initial boom. But most soccer fans in America today—not to mention most recreational players—have no Latin heritage. The sport has now simply become part of America's recreational landscape.

The soccer story reminds us of one of the timeless truths about immigration in the United States. Each successive wave of immigrants not only becomes a new target for savvy marketers but also transforms the country in indelible ways. Immigrants and, even more importantly, their descendants become irreversibly American and end up looking and acting much like the rest of the population, but in the process they also subtly influence our tastes and contribute to the country's cultural tapestry.

And there is a similar lesson in those Lotería cards that Marissa Fernandez and her team designed to reach Latino fans. It turns out the NFL actually ended up reaching a much larger fan base than expected through that campaign. "It generated a ton of engagement from fans of the game that weren't Hispanic," remembers Fernandez, not just the Latino fans they were targeting. A marketing tool to reach the children of a specific immigrant group ended up becoming part of the repertoire of symbols that the NFL uses to reach fans of all backgrounds. As so often happens, what starts out as a pastime or a symbol associated with a new immigrant group simply ends up becoming part of our larger American culture.

When Jaime Camill moved to the United States to star in a new drama series on American television, he had no way of knowing what a career-changing move it would turn out to be. A successful soap opera star, game host, and singer in Mexico, Camill had thrown in his lot with an unusual television program, *Jane the Virgin*. To begin with, the show was produced by the little watched CW, a small network mostly aimed at millennials, with none of the big-time prestige of the major networks—NBC, ABC, CBS, and Fox. And the plot itself was more than a little quirky—some might say over the top. It featured a young woman, the protagonist, Jane, who had become pregnant when she was artificially inseminated by accident. The show also included Jane's Venezuelan grandmother, who spoke only Spanish, and her estranged father, a middle-aged Mexican soap opera star, played, of course, by Camill, a middle-aged Mexican soap opera star.

Jane the Virgin went on to become a critical success, garnering a string of Golden Globe, People's Choice, and American Film Institute awards. It also became a commercial hit, regularly attracting around a million viewers per show, a huge accomplishment for a small—and until then not very successful—network. Part of its staying power came from its largely Latino cast, which appealed to young audiences with roots in Latin America, but it was also a surprisingly big hit among young people with no Latin heritage. One survey actually found that *Jane the Virgin* was the most binge-watched streaming show in Kansas, a state with a very small Latino population.

Jane the Virgin wasn't the first Latino-themed show to succeed in mainstream television. *George Lopez*, a series produced and starred in by comedian George Lopez, ran from 2002 to 2007 on ABC, with regular viewership of anywhere from 6 million to 10 million per episode. *Ugly Betty*, executive-produced by Mexican actress Salma Hayek, ran for four seasons from 2006 to 2010, also on ABC, with even larger audiences. Both featured Mexican American families.

Shows with Mexican- and Latin American–origin characters are becoming increasingly mainstream on television. Television executives are hoping to reach Mexican American and Latino viewers by recruiting Latino actors, some of them born in the United States but many of them already established actors and actresses south of the border.

Jaime Camill is only one among many Mexican actors who grace American television sets each night, while many others appear in shows as diverse as *How to Get Away with Murder*, *Fear the Walking Dead*, *Louie*, and *From Dusk to Dawn*.

Patricia Reyes Spíndola, one of Mexico's most celebrated actresses, who was recruited to play a recurring character on *Fear the Walking Dead*, says, "The [Latino] public in the United States wants to see Latinos on the screen, so they've started calling us." Reyes Spíndola has starred in some of her country's best independent cinema, winning four Ariels, Mexico's equivalent of the Oscar, for best actress, but also appeared in several *telenovelas*, or soap operas. Her versatility and name recognition among Mexican-origin audiences made her a natural for the hit series when the producers decided they wanted to attract young Latinos.

And while the English-language networks compete to attract Latino talent and viewers, Spanish-language rivals Univision and Telemundo have been trying to figure out how to hold on to second- and third-generation Latinos who consume most of their entertainment and news in English. Still today, Univision and Telemundo, the two biggest Spanish-language networks, attract millions of viewers nightly. In some major markets, like Los Angeles and Houston, they actually beat out the English-language networks for viewers on some evenings.

But as immigration rates decrease, the Hispanic population is shifting gradually away from the first-generation immigrants who consume entertainment in Spanish to American-born Latinos— children, grandchildren, and great-grandchildren of immigrants— who overwhelmingly speak English at home. They are often still familiar with Spanish, and sometimes will still consume small amounts of Spanish-language programming, especially when around older relatives, but Univision and Telemundo can no longer count on their loyalty in the same way.

León Krauze, a young Mexican journalist who was recruited to be Univision's Los Angeles news anchor, notes that the network "has been adapting to the end of migration" by "evolving to get close not only to immigrants but also those who are bilingual, who have a foot in one culture and language and also in another culture and language." Instead of just relying on language as the primary connection to its viewers, the network is learning to focus on "Hispanic pride," the pride that Mexican- and other Latin American–origin viewers have in the culture of their parents and grandparents. The aim is to tempt second- and third-generation Latinos who might consume most of their news and entertainment in English to check in with Univision periodically for a sense of emotional connection.

Univision has experimented with a channel and web portal in English called Fusion, which targets young Latinos who speak English mostly but still feel connected to their heritage. So far, the experiment has met with mixed success. Disney, once a joint partner, withdrew from the channel in 2016, and Fusion is still struggling to find the right way to attract English-speaking Latinos who care about their heritage but have countless other English-language options to choose from.

León Krauze believes that the current frenzy in the television industry to reach out to Latino consumers—both by English-language and Spanish-language media, though with different challenges for each—is more than just a passing phase that will dissipate as the latest generation of immigrants and their US-born descendants get assimilated into American society.

"I'm convinced that in a couple decades...the pride of 'Hispanicness' will continue among us and be part of an assimilation," says Krauze. The continuation of migration, proximity to countries of heritage, and new technologies that allow people to stay connected internationally enable young Latinos to identify as full Americans and yet remain connected to their roots south of the border. "There is a sense of bicultural belonging" among Latinos, especially among young Mexican Americans. In the end, he says, "You really can be both things."

And television networks will continue to compete to see how they can reach this bicultural though increasingly English-dominant audience.

"I went for a weekend," says Daniela Soto-Innes about her first visit to Pujol restaurant in Mexico City, "and I stayed for six months."

Already an up-and-coming aspiring chef, who had studied cooking at the Le Cordon Bleu in Austin, Texas, and worked at many of the top restaurants in Texas and the American South, Soto-Innes was fascinated with what head chef and owner Enrique Olvera was doing at Pujol. He had taken traditional Mexican cuisine and given it a playful, creative spin, combining flavors and expanding it into new realms.

And he had put Mexican food on par with fine French cuisine, using principles in line with the local food revolution of Noma in Denmark and El Bullí in Spain, in the eyes of the world's restaurateurs and critics. Since 2011 Pujol had been voted a top-fifty restaurant in the world year after year, alongside better-known establishments in New York, Paris, Rome, and London. It is one of two Mexico City–based restaurants on the list, along with a newer venue, Quintonil.

After her apprenticeship at Pujol, Soto-Innes returned to Texas, where her family had lived since she was fourteen, but she remained fascinated with what she had learned there. "It never occurred to me," she admits, that the food she had grown up with in Mexico—quesadillas, tacos, and mole—the same food she enjoyed eating the most with her family, could also be part of fine dining. Yet the evidence had been there at Pujol: an entire meal of artfully crafted tacos, baby corn seasoned with chilis and served on a stick in a gourd, roasted cauliflower with almonds and chilis that tastes almost like meat. "I fell in love with Mexican food again," she says.

And as she dived back into making continental cuisine at another high-end restaurant, she couldn't help but ask herself, "How can it be that I'm Mexican and not doing what I really want to."

So she went back for another six-month apprenticeship at Pujol. As her time there ended once again, Olvera approached her with an offer she couldn't refuse: How did she feel about opening a new restaurant in New York with him? And suddenly Soto-Innes, scarcely twenty-five years old, found herself the head chef at Cosme, Olvera's new restaurant in New York, which also sought to "play with" traditional Mexican food to create something new, original, and sublime, this time using locally sourced ingredients from the New York area.

In 2016 and again in 2017 Cosme—a small venue in Midtown Manhattan—was also voted one of the top fifty restaurants in the world, giving Enrique Olvera his second restaurant in the rankings and becoming the third Mexican-owned restaurant to win that honor. Soto-Innes shared the credit with Olvera as the managing chef and codesigner of the menu. And it's not hard to see why they won the honors. The flavors and the dishes are undeniably Mexican, but they are created in an artful way that takes them to new heights.

And if Pujol is low-key and relaxed—you can just stop by the bar for a selection of tacos if you don't want the twelve-course tasting menu—Cosme is vibrant and moving. Soto-Innes says it's "Enrique's and my personality fused together," a place that is "energetic" in contrast to the tranquil Pujol, which is located on an unusually quiet street in Mexico City. "And go down to the kitchen," she adds, talking about Cosme, "and it's like a market." Everyone is talking and listening to music, with several different nationalities taking part in the festival of preparing the food.

A decade ago, few people would have believed that Mexican food could find its way into the canon of global fine dining, but high-end Mexican restaurants have been springing up everywhere these days, and not only in Mexico City and New York. Chicago, San Francisco, Los Angeles, and Dallas, among others, now all have high-end Mexican restaurants, as do a dozen different cities in Mexico, from Tijuana to Guadalajara to Oaxaca. Mexican cuisine was once thought of as ordinary street food, good for a taco night at home or a quick meal at a cheap restaurant, but hardly on par with European high cuisine. Now that is changing.

Mexican food is easy to prepare, nutritious, and affordable, and it comes in endless related variations, from the simple taco, a tortilla filled with meat, beans, cilantro, onion, and salsa, to cornmeal tamales, filled with bits of meat, cheese, chilis, and even sweet jam, to pozole, a soup with chicken and round bits of hominy floating in a delicious broth seasoned with oregano, onions, and chilis. And then there is mole, the decadent dish, made with chocolate, peanuts, chilis, tomatoes, and often dozens of other ingredients, which has become the signature dish at Olvera's restaurants. One of his moles contains over a hundred ingredients and has been cooked and recooked over months with new ingredients added all the time.

Jeffrey Pilcher, a scholar of global food, describes his first encounter with Mexican food as a "Buddha moment." Raised in Illinois, he was attending a wedding along the US-Mexican border when he bit into a gordita, a thick fried corn tortilla filled with meat, vegetables, and salsa. He says it was as if "I had never tasted anything before, and my taste buds woke up.... [T]hat was my moment of enlightenment."

Pilcher argues that Mexican governments in the early twentieth century played a huge role in pulling together the multiple regional cuisines and creating the concept of a single Mexican national cuisine, as we know it today, as part of an attempt by the country's leaders to create a sense of national unity and pride. But while Mexican food was developing south of the border, it was also evolving north of the border. Mexicans in America's Southwest—Texas, New Mexico, Arizona, California, Nevada, and parts of Utah and Colorado—which had once been part of Mexico, created their own regional cuisines, which were largely forgotten in Mexico.

Anyone who has lived in the Southwest and even parts of the American South will have grown up with some of these regional cuisines. Chili is as Texan as barbecue; burritos can be bought at local stands in Alabama; *sopapillas*, or fried bread, pop up at small restaurants throughout Arizona; fish tacos are part of any beach adventure in Southern California; and you can't order a meal at a New Mexican restaurant without being asked whether you want red sauce or green sauce, *salsa roja* or *salsa verde*, even if you are just having a burger. While corn forms the basis of almost everything from tacos to gorditas in most of Mexico, Mexican food in the United States and in a few of the Mexican border states is often served with flour tortillas.

"You get some regional Mexican cuisine [in the United States] that doesn't even exist in Mexico," says Pati Jinich, who hosts a weekly PBS program on Mexican food called *Pati's Mexican Table*, but it's just as authentically Mexican as the food people in Mexico City or Oaxaca eat. Yet in the twentieth century, as Mexicans established ideas about what their national cuisine was, they overlooked many of these northern regional variants.

Now all of America—not just the Southwest—has embraced Mexican food. "We've gone from ethnic to mainstream," says Jinich. "The same thing that happened with Italian," she adds. She notes that while from time to time she gets effusive letters and emails about her TV show from Mexican immigrants, like herself, most of her viewers are Americans with no prior connection to Mexico.

Statistics certainly support what Jinich says. Chinese, Mexican, and Italian food make up most of the "ethnic cuisines" that Americans consume regularly, according to the National Restaurant Association, with half of Americans saying they consume Mexican food frequently and another third at least occasionally. And most American families have, at some point, probably made a Mexican or Italian meal at home too, regardless of their own background. Tacos have become almost as American as apple pie—or pizza—with #TacoTuesday a common hashtag. And Mexican food has become so much a part of America's food habits that even some newer ethnic cuisines try fusing with it. For instance, Korean barbecue tacos have showed up at food trucks around the country. "That tells you about Americanized food today," says Pilcher, when "American Korean food is in a taco, not a bun."

In the 1950s, a California-based entrepreneur, Glen Bell, decided that America was ripe for the mass introduction of Mexican food. After watching the rise of MacDonald's nearby, he started his first Taco Bell and soon grew his Mexican-themed restaurant into a national empire. He observed Mexican American cooks at taco stands and restaurants to find the best ways to prepare the food and simplify the ingredients for mass production. Most importantly, he learned how to fry tortillas to make them into hard taco shells, a technique that had become common among some Mexican American chefs. According to Jeffrey Pilcher, this became the key to his expansion. And other chain restaurants soon picked up the idea, offering fast-food versions of Mexican food, and supermarket brands, like Old El Paso, started selling hard taco shells and spice packets to make your own Mexican dinner at home.

Taco Bell remains the sixth-biggest restaurant chain in the United States—close behind MacDonald's, Subway, Starbucks, Wendy's, and Burger King. But most of the growth in Mexican food today is elsewhere. Across the country, Mexican immigrants and their children have started small restaurants and local chains, realizing that the American familiarity with Mexican food and growing appetite for authenticity have created a market for a new kind of offering, with fresher ingredients and a few signature dishes that go beyond tacos and burritos.

When my mother-in-law, who grew up in Chilpancingo, Guerrero, stays with us, she has an unusual way of keeping connected to her Mexican tastes in food. Her hometown is known for its *sopes*, round, thick tortillas topped with beans, meat, and sour cream; *huaraches*, long, boatlike tortillas sprinkled with cheese and beans; and white pozole, the town's specialty, a soup with chunks of chicken and round hominy swimming in an aromatic broth. So I've always expected her to find a small, authentic locale to frequent. But instead she likes Chipotle, the new mass-market sensation in Mexican food. It's certainly not the food she grew up with, but there are hints of the taste and freshness she's used to at home, and it's twice as fast.

Founded in Denver by a classically trained chef, Chipotle has been for much of the past fifteen years one of the top growth stories in the fast-food market. It ranks sixteenth in sales, well below Taco Bell, but has twice the sales per store and a growth trajectory that far outstrips that of its older rival. Chipotle grew from 16 stores in 1998 to over 1,800 in 2015 and became the darling of the fast-food market by pitching healthier ingredients.

And it's not just Mexican food that has gone mainstream—through a mixture of small restaurants, big chains, and home cooking in families across the country—but Mexican beer and tequila too. Today Mexican beer—almost entirely made by the two companies that own Corona and Tecate—makes up two-thirds of all imported beer in the United States and about 10 percent of all the beer that Americans consume.

And tequila, that classic Mexican liquor made from the leaves of the agave plant, a kind of low-lying, leafy cactus, has also enjoyed a renaissance in the United States. American bars and restaurants sell over $5 billion worth of tequila each year, and tequila-based cocktails—with margaritas at the top—are the hands-down favorite of American consumers, according to Nielsen, outpacing cocktails made with vodka, whiskey, or gin. America's tequila imports have doubled since 2003 and are now close behind those of whiskey and vodka, which Americans often drink straight.

But as tequila has become an international sensation, Mexicans have been shifting their tastes toward another, humbler Mexican liquor, mezcal. Also made from the agave plant, it has a rougher, smokier taste than tequila, and it's made through a different process that involves months of fermentation in the ground and then distillation in homemade, small-batch stills. And unlike tequila, which can only be made in one part of Mexico, almost every state in Mexico has its own kind of mezcal. It's long been the drink of choice for many rural Mexicans, but now urban professionals have discovered mezcal. It's just as common now to be offered mezcal when visiting someone's home as it is to be offered tequila, and most of the country's top-shelf restaurants and bars serve mezcal. Mezcal production has tripled in five years, and exports to the United States are on the rise too.

Enrique Olvera and Daniela Soto-Innes, of course, also serve a good selection of mezcal in both Pujol and Cosme. There may be a little parallel between their restaurants and that humble peasant liquor. Olvera and his protégée, Soto-Innes, have built their success on a cuisine that few considered more than street food—or fast food—until a few years ago. But they found the artistic soul inside the cuisine that had nourished Mexicans north and south of the border for generations and gave it a twist that could appeal to the most exacting global audiences.

A little over a decade ago, Mexicans were surprised that their own cuisine could be world-class, and it took a while for Pujol to develop a clientele out of those who had once frequented French and Italian restaurants. Now Olvera and Soto-Innes are doing the same thing in

New York with Cosme, showing Americans that Mexican food is part of their own heritage and can be as inventive, earthy, and experimental as the best cuisines of the world.

When Ruben J. Kihuen, now a thirty-seven-year old congressman from Nevada, started his political career, it very nearly didn't get off the ground, much like his first career as a professional soccer player.

In 2006, at the age of twenty-six, Kihuen decided to run for state assemblyman in his home district in Las Vegas, challenging a long-time incumbent. The district was overwhelmingly Latino, but Hispanic voters rarely bothered to vote. So the incumbent, who was white, had held on for two terms without serious challenges. And this was part of the pattern across the state. Nevada had a growing Latino population, which was already fairly successful in the small-business community and influential in the local labor unions, but there was only a single elected official of Latino descent in the state, Mo Dennis, a Cuban American assemblyman and cousin of Senator Marco Rubio.

"The only way I knew I could win this race was by doubling Latino turnout," says Kihuen. But first he had to convince Latino voters to go to the polls. And he also had to convince them that even with his strange last name—his paternal grandparents had emigrated from Lebanon to Mexico—he was one of them. Kihuen knocked on every door of his target group at least three times. One constituent even told him that he'd refuse to vote for Kihuen if he showed up one more time.

Kihuen hadn't started out wanting to get involved in politics. He first love was soccer. He was recruited to be part of the Olympic Development Program but wasn't selected because he wasn't yet an

American citizen. Kihuen had come to the country with a visa, following his father, a farmworker, but he had overstayed it and spent several years as an unauthorized immigrant. He only legalized his status thanks to the amnesty offered by Ronald Reagan in 1986 as part of the Immigration Reform and Control Act, a deal that brought 3.1 million unauthorized immigrants, a majority of them Mexicans, out of the shadows. It's "thanks to Ronald Reagan, a Republican, that I'm here in the United States," says Kihuen, a Democrat.

While he didn't make the US Olympic Team, the owner of one of Mexico's top teams, Chivas, spotted him and invited him to Guadalajara, the city he'd grown up in as a boy, to try out for the Mexican professional league. But before the tryouts started, Kihuen broke his foot badly and had to abandon his hopes of playing professionally. He ended up back in Las Vegas instead, finishing college, working on political campaigns, and eventually serving as the Latino outreach coordinator for Harry Reid, then the Senate Democratic leader.

His decision to run for state assemblyman turned out to be a good gamble. The Latino share of the vote tripled, and he won the primary with 61 percent and the general election with even more support. The key, he says, was to "effectively reach out to the Latino community and share a story that resonates with them."

Now in the assembly, he and Mo Dennis, the only Latinos among the sixty-three members, teamed up to create the Nevada Hispanic Legislative Caucus, an effort to recruit and train Latino candidates to run for the state legislature. He and Dennis both decided to run for the Nevada Senate in 2010—and both won—and they managed to help six other Latino candidates run successfully for the assembly. "We quadrupled the Hispanic Legislative Caucus in one election," he says, noting that they went from two to eight Latino legislators.

Today it's actually hard to imagine that Nevada once had so few Latino representatives. Barely a decade past Kihuen's first foray into electoral politics, many of the state's leaders now trace their heritage to Latin America, and most of those to Mexico. The governor, a Republican who is widely respected on both sides of the aisle, is Brian Sandoval, who is of Mexican descent. But unlike Kihuen, who came to Nevada from Mexico, with a brief stop in California on the way, Sandoval grew up in the smaller city of Reno in a family several generations removed from Mexico.

Kihuen ran for the US House of Representatives in 2016 and now serves his state as a freshman congressman. That same year, Nevada's longtime attorney general, Catherine Cortez Masto, a Democrat and the granddaughter of Mexican immigrants, won the race to replace Harry Reid in the Senate.

Latinos, overwhelmingly of Mexican descent, make up 20 percent of Nevada's population today—and around 17 percent of eligible voters—but they have actually become unusually prominent, both as Republicans and Democrats, in the state's politics.

Something similar has happened in two of Nevada's neighboring states, California and New Mexico. The current governor of New Mexico, Republican Susana Martinez, and her predecessor, Democrat Bill Richardson, are both of Mexican descent. California has yet to elect a Latino governor, but at least two lieutenant governors, Abel Maldonado, a Republican, and Cruz Bustamante, a Democrat, are Latinos, as are the last two mayors of the state's largest city, Los Angeles, Antonio Villaraigosa and Eric Garcetti. So too are five of the last nine Speakers of the assembly and the current president pro tempore of the state senate.

But this growth in certain states shouldn't be confused with a massive national wave. Every presidential election cycle, pundits predict that the Hispanic vote will be "decisive" in the upcoming contest, and yet it never actually has been. The National Association of Latino Elected Officials estimates that only 1 percent of all elected officials in the country identify as Hispanic.

There's no question that Latino voters are increasing in number and influence in each election cycle, but they have yet to determine the fate of a national election. Although Latinos make up 17.8 percent of the population, they comprise only 11.9 percent of eligible voters and only 9.2 percent of those who voted in the 2016 election.

The influence of Latinos—especially those of Mexican descent—is growing much quicker and more steadily in consumer markets than in politics. It's reshaping sports, television, and food and influencing the tastes of the rest of us in the process, but the impact on politics has been slower to develop and far less even across the country. While all Latinos matter equally to marketers, entertainment executives, and even religious leaders, only those who are likely to show up at the voting booth matter to politicians at election time. That's why Ruben Kihuen spent so much time working to turn Latino citizens into Latino voters to win his first election.

But the picture at the state level is quite different. States like Nevada, California, and New Mexico have very significant Latino (and mostly Mexican-descent) influence in local politics, as does Florida (where the influence is mostly Cuban American and Puerto Rican but becoming much more diverse). Other states, including Texas, Illinois, and Arizona have growing numbers of Latino voters and elected officials. And in many major cities—from Houston, Dallas, and San Antonio to Phoenix, San Jose, and Los Angeles—Latino voters have been a major force.

But Ruben Kihuen has since learned another truth about being an elected official. When he first ran for office, he did so as a Latino candidate, trying to energize and connect with voters like him. He then built his early career on trying to lift up other Latino politicians, because they were in such short supply. Now he represents a congressional district where Latinos are not a majority, just as Nevada's Governor Brian Sandoval and Senator Catherine Cortez Masto represent a diverse state in which Latinos are but one part of the overall demographics.

For Kihuen, his heritage as a young Mexican immigrant who once dreamed of playing soccer still informs who he is, but it's only one piece of what he talks about today. He also knows that to be a successful political leader, he has to broaden beyond any specific constituency and communicate a larger message that resonates with all of his constituents. In the end, he's a thoroughly American politician more than he's a Latino politician or one of Mexican descent. He may have been born in Mexico, but he grew up in the United States and developed his political consciousness here—and he now represents a diverse group of Americans of different backgrounds whom it's his duty to serve.

"You cannot run as the Latino candidate," he says, "or just on one issue."

12

Vanishing Frontiers

- -

What the Future Holds

Two days after being sworn in as president of the United States, Donald Trump announced that he would either renegotiate the North American Free Trade Agreement (NAFTA) or withdraw from it entirely. Three days later he signed an executive order to begin construction of a wall with Mexico. The same day he signed another executive order mandating that the Department of Homeland Security expedite its activities to detain and deport unauthorized immigrants.

North Korea threatened to use nuclear weapons. Syria was imploding. And China was rising on the world stage as America's leading economic and political competitor, but the new president had identified a looming threat south of the border that he was determined to home in on in his first days in office.

The pendulum seemed to have finally swung in the other direction. After two decades of growing ties between Mexico and the

United States, the official policy of the US government was to cut back on these ties and begin to wall the two countries off from each other—both literally and figuratively.

But that's only part of the story.

While the political relationship between the two countries was going off the rails, the forces driving them together continued at full pace, giving people in each country new ways to engage with each other.

Right as the president was signing his executive orders, the soccer federations in the United States, Canada, and Mexico were negotiating a joint bid to host the 2026 World Cup, and they eventually announced it in April. This marks the first try by sports federations in the three NAFTA countries to hold a joint region-wide sporting event, and it seems almost certain to succeed.

And while politicians discussed building a longer wall across the border, the airport bridge that connects San Diego and Tijuana—and crosses over the existing wall—was completing its first year of operation, bringing the two cities closer together. It had been used 1.3 million times, far more than anyone had predicted at the outset, and was on target for 2 million crossings in 2017. The bridge had become both a real and a metaphorical anchor tying together the two halves of this growing metropolitan region.

As the president debated whether to withdraw from NAFTA and eventually opted to renegotiate it, trade between Mexico and the United States continued to boom. So too did the joint production of cars and other heavy machinery, which had reached an all-time high in 2016 and continued to expand.

In January, Ford Motor Company, under pressure from the new president, had cancelled plans to build a new plant in San Luis Potosí,

Mexico, pledging to expand one in Flat Rock, Michigan, instead, but toward the end of the year the company quietly announced that construction would continue in Mexico after all—although at a different location just north of Mexico City. Auto production was going so well that Ford could afford both to expand the Michigan plant—even more than originally thought—and build the Mexican one too.

And while Ford was upping its investment in Mexico, Mexican companies continued to pour money into small cities and towns across the United States, creating jobs for American workers. Their investments more than doubled over eight years, growing even during the first year of the Trump administration.

American energy exports to Mexico—one of the most surprising trends of recent years—also reached a new high in 2016, $20.2 billion, and then continued to climb after Trump took office, with more than half of America's gasoline and natural gas exports headed across the border to Mexico in 2017.

Meanwhile, in October 2017—just as NAFTA negotiators took a break because they couldn't reach agreement—the Motion Picture Academy announced a special achievement award for Mexican filmmaker Alejandro González Iñárritú, the first such award the academy had given since John Lasseter received one for *Toy Story* in 1996. The following month, *Coco*, an animated film based on Mexico's Day of the Dead, swept the box office ratings over Thanksgiving, and then *The Shape of Water*, the cinematically rich film by Guillermo del Toro, took home seven Golden Globe nominations in December. The connections between the film industries of the two countries remained intact—and growing—despite the turbulence in Washington.

So too did the relationship between the tech communities on both sides of the border. Bismarck Lepe expanded his Silicon

Valley–based company's operations in Guadalajara, while venture capitalist Lynne Bairstow saw one of the Mexican start-ups she had supported enter production with a lifesaving medical technology. Mexican and American innovators and venture capitalists were certainly aware of the political firestorm between the two governments, but it didn't affect them directly in any way.

And as 2017 drew to a close, a rash of sports stories again highlighted the close connections between the two countries. The National Basketball Association played a total of four regular-season games in Mexico City in 2017, the last two in December, making an effort to expand its fan base south of the border. In November, the National Football League too held a regular-season game in Mexico City's mammoth Aztec Stadium, the second year in a row it had done that, and then announced that it would hold at least one regular-season game in Mexico City each year for four more years. Not to be outdone, Major League Baseball announced that it would hold a three-game series in Monterrey, Mexico, in the spring of 2018.

And baseball brought us an even more surprising story that highlighted the ties between the two countries, right as NAFTA negotiators were getting bogged down in mutual recriminations. This time, Joe Maddon, the Chicago Cubs manager who has done so much for his hometown of Hazleton, didn't quite make it back to the World Series, though he took his team as far as the National League Championship Series.

Instead, this was the Houston Astro's year. After the tragic floods that had tested the mettle of America's fourth-largest city, there was more than a bit of poetic justice in the Astros bringing the World Series title to their hometown for the first time in history.

Much of the credit for the Houston Astros' amazing championship run goes to its general manger, Jeff Luhnow, who had thoroughly gutted and then rebuilt the team's roster over the previous six years. Luhnow had been a risky pick as the Astros' GM, since he'd spent most of his career as a business consultant, with only one previous job in baseball, as a scout and later head of talent acquisition for the St. Louis Cardinals.

But the Astros' owners could see something in Luhnow, and they thought that part of it came down to his "bicultural" and "bilingual" upbringing. Luhnow is an American citizen and the son of American parents, but he grew up in Mexico. In fact, he's the brother of David Luhnow, the *Wall Street Journal* bureau chief in Mexico City whom we met in a previous chapter. Both brothers were born and raised in Mexico City after their parents fell in love with it and decided to move there. David still lives in that metropolis, and Jeff visits frequently, usually just to see family, but occasionally to watch his team play exhibition games.

So in 2016, the World Series champion Chicago Cubs featured a manager, Joe Maddon, who has been trying to build bridges between Americans and America's newcomers from Mexico and Latin America. In 2017, the World Series champion Houston Astros had a general manager, Jeff Luhnow, who represents the growing number of Americans who have been born and grown up in Mexico. Sports remains one of the best lenses through which to see the real changes going on between the two countries.

With all this real—and growing—engagement across the border, it's perhaps no surprise that right as the White House was issuing orders to weaken ties between the two countries, Americans' feelings about Mexico actually continued to improve. Despite the political rhetoric about trade and immigration from Mexico hurting the United States, the vast majority of Americans express positive attitudes toward Mexico in public opinion surveys—and the percentage of favorable responses has actually climbed noticeably in recent years.

Polling company Gallup, which has followed Americans' attitudes toward Mexico consistently for years, has recorded a 17 percent increase over four years—jumping from 47 to 64 percent between 2013 and 2016—in the number of Americans who have a very favorable or mostly favorable opinion of Mexico. Other polls show similar favorable opinions of Mexico. One that asks about its importance to the United States finds that 69 percent of Americans rate Mexico highly. The Chicago Council on Global Affairs also finds that Mexico is among the top ten countries Americans like best and that positive feelings have grown significantly since 2010.

These generally positive results hide some greater complexity in how Americans view Mexico. When asked what comes to mind when they think about Mexico, Americans mention drugs, violence, and crime as top issues, which suggests that Americans may like Mexico but also worry about some of its very real problems. In that regard, Americans' feelings about Mexico differ from those they have for Canada or the United Kingdom, which are perhaps less deep but also far less complicated.

There is no question that Mexico's very real struggles with poverty, corruption, and rule of law continue to affect its image abroad and give even Americans who feel positively toward their neighbors more than a bit of concern. It is almost impossible to imagine the relationship between the two countries growing as close as that between the United States and Canada without Mexico coming to terms with its own internal problems. The fact that Americans still earn, on average, four times what Mexicans do suggests that the gaps between the two countries remain quite real, even if there is a growing appreciation of Mexico's advances and its presence in American life.

There are also growing signs of political polarization, with Democrats and Independents increasingly expressing more positive views of Mexico in public opinion surveys than Republicans—an unusual shift, since traditionally Republican rather than Democratic presidents have engaged most closely with Mexico.

This polarization is likely both a cause and an effect of Trump's decision to focus on the border wall as a central campaign theme. Trump found a genuine skepticism toward Mexico among a sector of the American public in small and medium-size cities that were experiencing both rapid demographic change and declining industrial employment, and he played to them by offering the border wall as a powerful visual metaphor for the way he would hold these forces at bay. While most Americans continue to see Mexico with better eyes, a fifth to a quarter of the population expresses strong negative feelings toward the country next door, and that number hasn't shifted appreciably.

Yet generational differences also suggest that younger Americans have much more positive views of Mexico than older Americans, a tribute to the changing nature of the relationship in recent years. This augurs especially well for future ties between the countries. Younger Americans have grown up thinking of Mexico not as a distant neighbor but as a country intimately involved in their lives in multiple ways.

What is perhaps most surprising is that the current tensions around relations with Mexico—NAFTA, the border wall, and immigration enforcement—come at a time when most Americans express increasingly positive feelings toward their next-door neighbor and even toward Mexican immigrants. Members of the president's most loyal political base, who worry about immigration and trade—with Mexico and the world—contrast with most Americans, who are increasingly bullish on global engagement and an expanded relationship with Mexico. These are tensions that are likely to play out over the coming years in American politics.

Over the past two decades, Mexicans too have grown far more positive about the United States, which they initially distrusted as an overbearing and unreliable neighbor that might try to bully them or control their future. Little by little, that old distrust has evaporated, according to multiple public opinion polls, and Mexicans have grown warmer in their feelings toward the United States. The shift is particularly noticeable among younger generations, as it is in the United States.

But President Trump's rhetorical attacks on Mexico as a source of America's problems have dramatically shifted Mexican public opinion against the United States. Polls show an almost universal dislike of Trump and his proposal for a border wall, and they have also begun to show a gradual shift toward less positive views of the United States as a whole. It's hard to tell whether this reversion to a more defensive position will last or is just driven by current events.

One of the clearest signs of this shift is the growing political support for Andrés Manuel López Obrador as a presidential candidate in the July 2018 elections. While most Mexican politicians have long expressed support for greater integration with the United States, López Obrador—a former Mexico City mayor and two-time presidential candidate who formed his own political party—has always been much more skeptical of it. Like Trump, López Obrador wants a more self-contained Mexico, one less subject to the vagaries of the global market and global politics. His views might be labeled "Mexico First" in the same way that Trump and his allies talk about "America First."

In other ways, of course, the two men couldn't be more different. López Obrador is a leftist politician who cut his teeth in protest movements with indigenous communities in his home state of Tabasco back in the 1980s. Overall, he is concerned less with foreign policy and Mexico's relationship with the United States than with social policy in his own country. According to the historian Lorenzo Meyer, one of Mexico's most respected scholars, who has been close to López Obrador, "His focus is the social question, [on] inequality in Mexico."

When I asked López Obrador, shortly before he launched his official campaign, how he would engage with Trump, he minimized any possible conflicts. "I think we can have a good relationship, a respectful one, [with] mutual cooperation." He highlighted his desire to engage Trump on developing Mexico's poorest regions but otherwise offered few specifics on how he would go about tackling an increasingly complicated political agenda with the White House. Still, he made clear that he wasn't in the mood for confrontation.

López Obrador's rise has less to do with his views of the United States than with his perceived commitment to fighting inequality and tackling pervasive corruption. Though himself a career politician, he has ably positioned himself as an outsider who will clean up a corrupt political system, even if his policy proposals for how to do this often seem vague. And he's cultivated the image of someone who keeps a modest, almost austere, lifestyle, in contrast to other politicians who flaunt their often quite inexplicable wealth. While some Mexicans worry that he's a demagogue who will overturn the country's gradual but continuous economic progress, others see him as the only politician who can shake up the country's political system and speed up change.

For many Mexicans, corruption has become the country's overarching issue. Sergio Aguayo, perhaps the most visible leader of Mexico's democratic movement in the 1990s and one of the country's most prominent political analysts today, calls it "the tragedy of Mexico's electoral democracy," the cancer that eats at what would otherwise be a successful political system that has opened itself up to intense, multiparty competition over the past two decades. Democracy successfully created new expectations among citizens about how their political leaders should behave, but leaders have lagged behind average citizens in changing their behavior.

"Today corruption has a lot of public visibility but less social tolerance," says José Woldenberg, former head of the country's Federal Electoral Institute, who like Aguayo played a major role in Mexico's transition to democracy. Both agree that average Mexicans have embraced the notion of good governance and become personally frustrated by corruption, but this has only led to disappointment as politicians have betrayed voters' faith with a series of very public corruption scandals touching every political party. There are signs that citizen frustration is now driving some very tangible changes in how corruption is dealt with in Mexico, such as the appointment of an anticorruption prosecutor in Nuevo León as we saw in chapter 7, but it's a slow process of change.

Rossana Fuentes-Berain, one of Mexico's most widely respected journalist, likes to say that there are increasingly two Mexicos, one that lives in the shadow of the government and the other that doesn't. Two decades ago, the Mexican state—and its corruption—stretched into everything from politics to business to cultural industries. But today, much of Mexico—from the technology and innovation community to cultural industries, from civil society to business—operates largely separately from the government, and there are increasingly parts of the government that are partly or largely insulated from corruption. Of course, there are intersections and interferences, but not everything revolves around the public sector in the way it once did. And while corruption often plagues whatever the government touches, much of Mexico lies beyond its reach in an increasingly creative, demanding, and entrepreneurial realm. The Mexico that lies beyond government has changed dramatically over the past two decades, even if the politicians haven't always kept up.

López Obrador has made fighting corruption—the central frustration most Mexicans feel—the most potent component of his campaign platform, but he has also subtly tapped into the vein of anxiety that Mexicans feel about Donald Trump and the US government. After basing the future of their country on closer relations with the United States, suddenly Mexicans are wondering if that was the right gamble. Most had started to believe that the United States was a reliable partner—and largely good for their economy—only to find that the American government wanted to cut back the ties that bind the two countries together.

By raising his skepticism about NAFTA—telling a recent audience, "It's not true that it's cheaper to buy outside [the country] than to produce inside [it]"—López Obrador's started channeling the fears of many Mexicans that maybe they need to pursue a more inward-looking future, since the United States is doing the same thing.

There is no certainty that López Obrador will win the election, of course. Many Mexicans feel the country has progressed dramatically over the past two decades. Whatever their frustrations about the pace of change and the honesty of their leaders, they may choose a candidate from one of the traditional parties in order to stay the course. And there will be plenty of options.

But no matter who is elected, the next Mexican government will almost certainly be more skeptical of the United States than past administrations have been, in reaction to the actions from the Trump administration. The next administration, no matter who heads it, will be looking for alternatives to dependence on the neighbor to the north, from buying grain in South America to signing a trade agreement with the European Union to courting closer ties with China. The political relationship is in for its rockiest period in modern history—and strong gusts will come from both sides of the border.

The forces driving Mexico and the United States together will ultimately be stronger than any decisions made by politicians in Washington, DC, or Mexico City, but we are entering a period in which governments may become bystanders to the growing engagement among people in the two countries—or even a drag on it.

At Big Bend National Park in South Texas, it's almost impossible to tell where the border between Mexico and the United States lies. The differences between the two countries blend together amid the rocks and the mountains, the trees, shrubs, and cacti, and the winding river that runs down the middle.

In 2010, the US and Mexican governments reached an agreement to manage the ecosystem of Big Bend jointly, bringing the National Park Service on the American side together with its Mexican counterparts to find ways of preserving the natural environment. In 2013, the two countries opened the first virtual border crossing, which allows people to get prior online approval to visit the other country and then just scan their passport at a kiosk immediately prior to entering. There are no immigration or customs agents in sight—though they do monitor the crossing by video remotely.

In many ways, despite the political noise we hear today, much of the relationship between the United States and Mexico looks a lot like the way the two countries come together at Big Bend. There is a boundary—it hasn't disappeared, though at Big Bend it's somewhere in the middle of the river—but the interaction between people on both sides of the border is so fluid and frequent that it's easy sometimes to forget where the border lies. People and products, investments and ideas flow north and south in ways that would have been unimaginable a little over two decades ago. The frontiers that once separated people from the two countries appear to be vanishing as powerful economic, cultural, and social forces drive the two nations together.

When I moved to Tijuana from St. Louis, Missouri, in 1992, well over two decades ago, this would have been unimaginable. I lived scarcely six miles south of the border, but the real distance that separated us—cultural, economic, and political—was enormous.

Yet in the space of a little more than a generation, Tijuana and San Diego have become part of a single metropolitan area that shares everything from economic foundations to entertainment venues and is building a shared vision of the future. And though a wall does separate the two cities from each other, making it easy to see where one country ends and the other begins, city leaders have built a bridge over it so that they can get things done faster.

When I lived in Tijuana we used to go to the border in the evening to watch the thousands of people who lined up to cross over at night. During the day we scanned the newspapers and airwaves to follow the negotiations for a free trade agreement, which seemed almost unthinkable at the time, given the real differences between the two economies.

Today there isn't much to see at the Tijuana border at night since few, if any, try to cross there. That's partially because the level of border security has made it next to impossible to get into San Diego, but it's also because there are just so few border crossers these days in general. Whereas several thousand people once tried to cross out of Tijuana each night, perhaps only a few hundred try each day now along the entire 2,000-mile border between the countries.

And as migration is vanishing between the two countries, NAFTA may follow suit. It was once a powerful economic force that increased trade between the two countries and eventually spawned shared production and cross-border investment.

Yet it may not make much of a difference—at least in the long-term—in the way the two countries interact. While a withdrawal from NAFTA would certainly hurt farmers and small producers and could even trigger a trade war between the countries, it's almost certain that even without the trade agreement, the two countries would continue to have an active commercial exchange. Industries that have integrated their production across the border would carry on, even if they had to deal with some greater inefficiencies in doing business. After all, they have all made significant investments that are costly and complicated to undo.

And migration, while it became one of the toughest issues in the relationship between the two countries, has actually reshaped both countries in profound and irreversible ways. Today Mexicans and Americans have formed close and personal bonds across the border and have influenced each other's tastes in food, sports, and entertainment to a point where they are likely to grow closer even as migration ebbs. The growing positive views that Americans express about Mexico are partly a result of this greater personal familiarity with the people and culture of the country next door and partly a recognition of its strategic importance in our lives.

No matter what happens in our current political moment, the direction of the future seems clear. The frontiers that once separated us will continue to vanish as forces stronger and more dynamic than any presidential order or trade agreement continue to bring us closer together. The push to separate the two countries is, if anything, a reaction against what people in the two countries have already built together—and what they will continue to build in the future.

Acknowledgments

While the responsibility for the content of this book is mine alone, it could never have been written without friends and colleagues who have made important contributions to my thinking about the book—and sometimes even specific ideas and stories—that found their way into these pages. Among these are Rossana Fuentes-Berain, Duncan Wood, Chris Wilson, Alfredo Corchado, Shannon O'Neil, Antonio Ortiz Mena, Lázaro Cárdenas, Alan Bersin, Jill Anderson, Luis de la Calle, Luis Rubio, Raúl Rodríguez Barocio, Johanna Mendelsohn, Diana Negroponte, Kino Arteaga, Miguel Salazar, Guadalupe Correa, Joy Olson, Cinny Kennard, Roberta Jacobson, John Feeley, Silvia Giorguli, Rodrigo Gallegos, Jonathan Schorr, Tonatiuh Guillén, Ginger Thompson, Amy Glover, Ricardo Alday, Mary Wallace, Lorena Montes de Oca, Bobby Mandell, Jim Dickmeyer, Greg Houston, Andrea Tanco, and Angela Robertson.

Above all, I owe a special thanks to everyone who agreed to be interviewed and to tell their stories through these pages. I hope to have represented their views and their lives faithfully.

Jonathan Nelson, Jorge Zavala, Mak Gutierrez, and Alexa Clark helped educate me on technology innovation, while Carlos Aguilar, Elena Fortes, Paulina Suarez, Patricia Reyes Spíndola, and Rossana Fuentes-Berain provided guidance on film.

In Hazleton, Pennsylvania, I am grateful to Demetrio Juarez, Charles McElwee, Francisco Torres-Aranda, Kent Jackson, Amilcar Arroyo, Father Victor León, David Sosar, and Elaine and Bob Curry, while in the San Diego/Tijuana metro area, help from Sandra Dibble, Jorge D'Garay, Denise Moreno Ducheny, James Clark, Hector Vanegas, Rodrigo Caballero, Mary Walshok, and Mario López proved invaluable. So too the friendship, hospitality, and insight of Carlos Mendoza, Concepción Aguilar, and their son Andrés, and of Amparo Cortés, Elizabeth Sandoval, and Israel Ponce.

Collaborations on earlier written projects with Peter H. Smith, David Shirk, Eric Olson, Jonathan Fox, Jacqueline Peschard, Raúl Benítez, Gaspar Rivera-Salgado, David Ayón, Xochitl Bada, Alberto Díaz-Cayeros, Joe Tulchin, Cindy Arnson, Chris Wilson, Katie Putnam, Heidy Servin-Baez, Leticia Santín, Enrique Peruzzotti, and Philip Oxhorn were particular helpful in refining my thinking through the years, as were several other collaborations with Andrés Rozental, Rafael Fernández de Castro, Carlos Heredia, Lorenzo Meyer, Luis Rubio, Rossana Fuentes-Berain, Roderic Ai Camp, Arturo Alvarado, Sidney Weintraub, Mariclaire Acosta, Enrique Krauze, Sergio Aguayo, Jim Kolbe, Dan Restrepo, Javier Treviño, Kate Brick, and Diana Rodriguez. None of these colleagues, of course, bear any responsibility for the specific conclusions in this book.

I was privileged to work for seventeen years at the Woodrow Wilson Center, and I owe a special debt of gratitude to José Antonio Fernández and Roger Wallace, who provided leadership as the co-chairs of the Center's Mexico Institute, and to everyone who has served on the Mexico Institute's board, and to all my Center colleagues there through the years—staff, fellows, and members of the board of trustees and cabinet—and especially to Megan Geckle and Liz Byers.

For many years I have collaborated with colleagues at the Migration Policy Institute (MPI) on projects to elevate the debate around migration issues and develop creative new ideas for migration policymaking, and in August 2017 I was fortunate to join MPI full-time. There I am especially grateful to Demetri Papademetriou, Doris Meissner, and Marc Rosenblum, who have helped shape my thinking about migration and borders through the years. Since joining MPI, I owe special thanks to Michelle Mittlestadt, who commented on parts of the manuscript, and board members Gustavo Mohar and Jim Ziglar, who provided key insights, as well as to all many other colleagues who have provided inspiration and new ideas.

Gabriel Lesser, my principal research assistant and careful editor, deserves special mention. An author in his own right in three languages, he has a good eye for making ideas come to life. Jeffrey Hallock took over from him in the final months, and provided both key research assistance and a good editing eye on the final manuscript. Ana Ortega Romeu, Gina Hinojosa, and Andrea Marín Serrano all contributed important research along the way. Leonard Roberge was a very talented editor for the early book proposal, and Caroline Scullin provided a careful review of the whole manuscript at a key point near the end.

This book wouldn't exist without Bonnie Nadell, my agent, and John Mahaney, my editor at PublicAffairs. Bonnie was one of the first people to believe in the book—but she made me rethink it and work on my storytelling before she would take me on as a client—something that ended up vastly improving the final product. John Mahaney is simply an extraordinary editor, who constantly questioned my assumptions and improved my prose. And a special thanks to everyone at PublicAffairs for their efforts to get this book out and into the hands of readers.

The Carnegie Corporation and its President Vartan Gregorian offered me the Andrew Carnegie Fellowship in 2017, which made it possible to dedicate several months full-time to the book and to conduct far more research than would have been possible otherwise. It would have been a far less polished effort without their support. Geri Manion at the Carnegie Corporation has been a source of wisdom, and Greta Essig and Zoe Ingalls guided me through the fellowship process.

Finally—and most importantly—this book would not exist without my wife, Alejandra Vallejo, who has lived with this project for almost a decade since it was first just the seed of an idea. Over the years, she has read and commented on hundreds of pages of drafts, as well as pitched me many of the best ideas that ended up the book. She has been not only endlessly supportive of my time away to research and write, but also a creative partner in coming up with many of the concepts and stories in the book.

Our daughter Lucia, who has just turned ten, has grown up with this book too, knowing that her father was trying to write something to explain the connection between her two countries. For her, the argument in this book—that Mexico and the United States are deeply connected in ways that most people on both side of the border don't even realize—is just intuitively obvious. After all, she has moved back and forth between these two countries since she was born. Lucia has been immensely tolerant of her dad's occasional disappearances to research and write, and she's been a great traveling companion on quite a few of the research trips.

This book is dedicated to Alejandra and Lucia and to our two youngest children, Elena and Alexander, twins who were born while I was writing the book. My hope is that by the time the twins are old enough to really read this book—still many, many years away—most of the ideas about the connections between their two countries will be so well understood that they'll wonder why I even bothered to write about these things in the first place....

Notes

Introduction

3 **Hazleton, almost 2,000 miles:** I have chosen to use the term "America" and "American" in this book to refer to the United States and its people—in line with common usage in this country. While Mexicans and others in the Western Hemisphere rightly point out that the entire hemisphere should be called "the Americas" and its people "Americans," for stylistic reasons I've tried to hew closely to standard usage in the United States in using these terms with their US-specific meaning.

8 **And he realized that night:** Based on interviews with Elaine and Bob Curry. Direct quote from "Going Home: Joe Maddon on His Plans to Unite His Divided Hometown," *Sunday Night with Megyn Kelly*, NBCNews.com, July 23, 2017, https://www.nbcnews.com /megyn-kelly/video/going-home-joe-maddon-and-his-plans-to-reunite-his-divided -hometown-1007470147784.

10 **After all, immigrants drive much:** "Startup Activity Swings Upward for Third Consecutive Year, Annual Kauffman Index Reports," Ewing Marion Kauffman Foundation, May 18, 2017, http://www.kauffman.org/newsroom/2017/05/startup -activity-swings-upward-for-third-consecutive-year-annual-kauffman-index-reports. See also Robert W. Fairlie, *Open for Business: How Immigrants Are Driving Small Business Creation in the United States* (New York: Partnership for a New American Economy, 2012).

10 **In fact, they have incarceration rates:** National Academies of Sciences, Engineering, and Medicine, *The Economic and Fiscal Consequences of Immigration* (Washington, DC: National Academies Press, 2016); Robert J. Sampson, "Rethinking Crime and Immigration," *Contexts* 7 (winter 2008): 28–33; Robert J. Sampson, "Open Doors Don't Invite Criminals," *New York Times*, March 11, 2006, http://www.nytimes.com/2006/03/11 /opinion/open-doors-dont-invite-criminals.html; Kristin F. Butcher and Anne Morrison Piehl, "Why Are Immigrants' Incarceration Rates So Low? Evidence on Selective Immigration, Deterrence, and Deportation" (Working Paper No. 13229, National Bureau of Economic Research, 2007).

12 **The owners have a new Spanish-language menu:** Based on a statement by the owner's daughter in "Going Home," *Sunday Night with Megyn Kelly*.

13 **History may not repeat itself:** This wise saying—or variations of it—is often attributed to Mark Twain, but it's unclear if he actually coined the phrase. I've borrowed it from my colleague Aaron David Miller, who often uses it—and it's a fair representation of the way history actually behaves, not in repetition but rhyme.

13　**Almost all population growth:** Patrick J. Carr, Daniel T. Licther, and Maria J. Kefalas, "Can Immigration Save Small-Town America? Hispanic Boomtowns and the Uneasy Path to Renewal," *Annals of the American Academy of Political and Social Science* 641, no. 1 (May 2012): 38–57.

13　**The Downtown Hazleton Alliance for Progress:** See, for example, Downtown Hazleton Alliance for Progress, "Downtown Hazleton: Strategic Plans for Continued Revitalization," Version 1.0, April 2015. Available at http://nebula.wsimg.com /921f559720036b4614fe0ae97790bf9a?AccessKeyId=275C8FC43D202EBF7120 &disposition=0&alloworigin=1.

17　**Social spending in Mexico almost doubled:** John Scott, *Gasto público y desarrollo humano en México: Análisis de incidencia y equidad*, Mexico City: United Nations Development Program, 2009.

18　**Today Mexico produces more engineers:** Cebr, "Engineering and Economic Growth: A Global View," *Royal Academy of Engineering*, September 2016. Available at http://www .raeng.org.uk/publications/reports/engineering-and-economic-growth-a-global -view.

18　**Today a quarter of all young people:** Secretaría de Educación Pública: Sistema Nacional de Información Estadística y Educativa, *Estadísticas históricas 1893–2015*. Available and downloadable at http://www.snie.sep.gob.mx/ estadisticas_educativas.html.

18　**The Mexican economy is now:** Will Martin, "These Will Be the 32 Most Powerful Economies in the World by 2050," *Independent*, February 18, 2017, http://www .independent.co.uk/news/business/these-will-be-the-32-most-powerful-economies-in -the-world-by-2050-a7587401.html.

18　**Mexico is gradually becoming:** On Mexico's growing middle class generally, see Shannon O'Neil, *Two Nations Indivisible: Mexico, the United States, and the Road Ahead* (New York: Oxford University Press, 2013). For two different approaches that lead to similar conclusions about the size of the middle class, see *Cuantificando la clase media Mexicana: Un ejercicio exploratorio*, Instituto Nacional de Estadística y Geografíca (INEGI), 2011, http://www.inegi.org.mx/inegi/contenidos/investigacion/ experimentales/clase_media/presentacion.aspx; *Clases medias en México*, INEGI, June 12, 2013, http://usmex2024.uscmediacurator.com/wp-content/uploads/2013/08/ Clases-Medias-en-Mexico.pdf. For sources considering the existence of a "vulnerable" class (between the lower and middle classes), see *Perfil de estratos sociales en América Latina: Pobres, vulnerables y clases medias*, Programa de las Naciones Unidas para el Desarrollo, Dirección Regional para América Latina y el Caribe, 2014, accessed May 10, 2017, http://www.undp.org/content/dam/rblac/docs/Research%20and%20Publications/ Poverty%20Reduction/UNDP-RBLAC-Grupos_sociales_AL-2014.PDF; Luis F. López-Calva et al., "Clases medias y vulnerabilidad a la pobreza: Reflexiones desde América Latina," *El trimestre económico* 81, no. 322 (2014), http://eltrimestreeconomico. com.mx/index.php/te/article/view/115/351.

18　**Life expectancy—a useful indicator:** "Life Expectancy at Birth, Total (Years)," World Bank, https://data.worldbank.org/indicator/SP.DYN.LE00.IN.

22　**This jump of nine points:** Republicans did show a very slight uptick of support for Mexico—two points over two years—far less than the nine-point jump in favorability among all Americans in those two years. See Justin McCarthy, "Americans' Favorable Views of Mexico Highest Since 2006," Gallup, February 22, 2017, http://www.gallup .com/poll/204212/americans-favorable-views-mexico-highest-2006.aspx. The conclusion to this book discusses these public opinion trends in more depth.

Chapter 1

32 **It was originally the inspiration:** See the chapter on the Tijuana opera week in Sam Quinones, *True Tales from Another Mexico* (Albuquerque: University of New Mexico Press, 2001).

38 **Engineers in San Diego and Tijuana:** Interview with Rodrigo Caballero, Caballero Consulting, San Diego, December 23, 2015, and with Idalia Bernal, Parker Hannifin, January 27, 2016.

44 **Three years later, a second poll:** Chapter 3 of "Our Greater San Diego Vision," San Diego Foundation, July 8, 2012, https://issuu.com/thesandiegofoundation/docs/ogsdv -final-hires; Jean Guerrero, "Survey Says San Diegans, Tijuanans Want More Cross-Border Collaboration," *KPBS*, June 19, 2015, http://www.kpbs.org/news/2015/jun/19 /survey-says-san-diegans-and-tijuanans-want-more-cr.

45 **No one knows for sure:** HDR/HLB Decision Economics, "Economic Impacts of Wait Times at the San Diego–Baja California Border," San Diego Association of Governments and California Department of Transportation, District 11, January 19, 2006, viii. Available at http://www.sandag.org/index.asp?projectid=253&fuseaction=projects. detail.

46 **The board of the Smart Border Coalition:** Burnham cochaired the board for its first years and remains chairman emeritus.

Chapter 2

50 **Over a third of all American exports:** By contrast, China receives 7.9 percent of US exports, Japan 4.3 percent, and the United Kingdom only 3.6 percent. These percentages are for US exports in fiscal year 2017, from October 2016 through August 2017. Data available at "Top Trading Partners—October 2017," US Census Bureau, Foreign Trade, https://www.census.gov/foreign-trade/statistics/highlights/toppartners.html.

50 **This is not surprising:** Christopher Wilson, *Growing Together: Economic Ties Between the United States and Mexico* (Washington, DC: Woodrow Wilson Center, 2017). Based on author's calculation of the data presented in the state-by-state analysis in the appendices.

51 **A decade before, American president:** The original idea was developed by Sidney Weintraub, an innovative economist and former government official, who had started writing about the possibilities of a North American market in the 1970s, long before anyone else even thought something like that could be possible. See, for example, Sidney Weintraub, *United States–Latin American Trade and Financial Relations: Some Policy Recommendations* (Santiago, Chile: CEPAL, 1977). In his memoirs, former president Salinas says that President Bush had also raised the idea of NAFTA with him in 1988 but that he had wanted to pursue free trade with Europe. Not until the Berlin Wall came down and Salinas realized that Europe's focus would be elsewhere did he come back to President Bush to suggest the idea from the Mexican side. See Carlos Salinas de Gortiari, *México: Un paso difícil a la modernidad* (Mexico City: Plaza y Janés, 2000).

52 **In fact, it only passed:** Frederick Mayer, *Interpreting NAFTA: The Art and Science of Political Analysis* (New York: Columbia University Press, 1998).

52 **Shared manufacturing across the three:** See, among others, David H. Autor, David Dorn, and Gordon H. Hanson, "The China Syndrome: Local Labor Market Effects of Import Competition in the United States," *American Economic Review* 103, no. 6 (2013): 2121–2168; Robert A. Blecker and Gerardo Esquivel, "NAFTA and the Development

Gap," in *Mexico and the United States: The Politics of Partnership*, ed. Peter H. Smith and Andrew Selee (Boulder, CO: Lynne Rienner, 2013); Theodore H. Moran and Lindsay Oldenski, "How US Investments in Mexico Have Increased Investment and Jobs at Home," Peterson Institute for International Economics, July 11, 2014, https://piie.com /blogs/realtime-economic-issues-watch/how-us-investments-mexico-have-increased -investment-and-jobs; Justino De La Cruz and David Riker, "The Impact of NAFTA on U.S. Labor Markets" (Office of Economics Working Paper No. 2014-06A, US International Trade Commission, June 2014).

53   **This political calculus appears:** Danielle Kurtzleben, "Rural Voters Played a Big Part in Helping Trump Defeat Clinton," NPR, November 14, 2016, http://www.npr.org/2016/11/14 /501737150/rural-voters-played-a-big-part-in-helping-trump-defeat-clinton.

55   **And while Mexico and Canada:** Thomas Klier and James Rubenstein, "The Changing Geography of North American Motor Vehicle Production," *Cambridge Journal of Regions, Economy and Society* 3 (2010): 335–347. US tariffs and quotas on imported automobiles in the 1980s also contributed to this shift. See Lorraine Eden and Maureen Appel Molot, "Made in America? The US Auto Industry, 1955–95," *International Executive* 38, no. 4 (1996): 501–541.

55   **Exports of cars from the NAFTA:** Author's analysis of data in "Auto and Truck Seasonal Adjustment," Bureau of Economic Analysis of the US Department of Commerce, December 4, 2017, https://www.bea.gov/national/xls/gap_hist.xlsx.

55   **The Chevy Silverado, one of the toughest:** Interview with Juan Pablo Rosas, general counsel, Rassini, April 27, 2017.

55   **So does the Tesla Model X:** "Steadily Advancing: 2015 Annual Report," Rassini, 2015, http://www.rassini.com/en/documents/IA_Rassini_2015_Eng.pdf, 17.

56   **By the time a single car:** Wilson, *Growing Together.*

57   **In fact, Nemak is the only:** Interview with Adrian Althoff, investor relations associate, Nemak, April 2017.

57   **Despite fears in the 1970s and 1980s:** "Table 1-15: Annual U.S. Motor Vehicle Production and Factory (Wholesale) Sales (Thousands of Units)," Bureau of Transportation Statistics, US Department of Transportation, https://www.rita.dot.gov /bts/sites/rita.dot.gov.bts/files/publications/national_transportation_statistics/html /table_01_15.html_mfd.

57   **And 2 million of these cars:** International Trade Administration, *Trends in U.S. Vehicle Exports* (Washington, DC: US Department of Commerce, August 2015).

58   **It's taken two decades:** Interview with Dave Andrew and Kristen Dziczek, Center for Automotive Research, April 11, 2017.

59   **This contrasts with China:** Robert Koopman et al., "Give Credit Where Credit Is Due: Tracing Value Added in Global Production Chains" (Working Paper No. 16426, National Bureau of Economic Research, September 2010, revised September 2011).

59   **In fact, US manufacturers have shed:** See data in Federica Cocco, "Most U.S. Manufacturing Jobs Lost to Technology, Not Trade," *Financial Times*, June 12, 2017. For similar findings with slightly different dates (1987 to 2017), see also "Manufacturing Sector: Real Output," Federal Reserve Bank of St. Louis, https://fred.stlouisfed.org/series /OUTMS.

59   **The American car industry, for example:** Data calculated from "Table 1-23: World Motor Vehicle Production, Selected Countries (Thousands of vehicles)," Bureau of Transportation Statistics, US Department of Transportation, https://www.rita.dot.gov /bts/sites/rita.dot.gov.bts/files/publications/national_transportation_statistics/html /table_01_23.html_mfd; "Production Statistics," International Organization of Motor Vehicle Manufacturers, http://www.oica.net/category/production-statistics/2016 -statistics; "All Employees (in Thousands) in USA, Motor Vehicles and Parts, Seasonally

Adjusted," Bureau of Labor Statistics, https://data.bls.gov. See also Justin Fox, "The Auto Jobs Boomlet," *Bloomberg*, September 1, 2017, https://www.bloomberg.com/view/articles /2017-09-01/the-auto-jobs-boomlet.

60 **One study estimates that 85 percent:** Michael J. Hicks and Srikant Devaraj, "The Myth and Reality of Manufacturing in America," Center for Business and Economics Research, Ball State University, April 2017, https://conexus.cberdata.org/files/MfgReality.pdf.

60 **Other studies see slightly higher:** Autor, Dorn, and Hanson, "The China Syndrome"; Blecker and Esquivel, "NAFTA and the Development Gap."

60 **Currently most foreign investors in Mexico:** See, for example, Harley Shaiken, "In Whose Interest? Inclusive Trade vs. Corporate Protectionism," *Berkeley Review of Latin American Studies* (spring-fall 2016): 12–45; David Welch and Nacha Cattan, "How Mexico's Unions Sell Out Autoworkers," *Bloomberg*, May 5, 2017, https://www.bloom berg.com/news/articles/2017-05-05/how-mexico-s-unions-sell-out-autoworkers.

61 **One industry estimate suggests:** "NAFTA Briefing: Trade Benefits to the Automotive Industry and Potential Consequences of Withdrawal from the Agreement," Center for Automotive Research, January 2017, http://www.cargroup.org/wp-content/uploads /2017/01/nafta_briefing_january_2017_public_version-final.pdf.

63 **Since 2005, the number of aerospace companies:** Employment data from Instituto Nacional de Estadística y Geografíca (INEGI), Encuesta Anual de la Industria Manufacturera (online database, accessed July 2017). Company data tabulated from data provided by the Mexican economy secretary, accessed through ProMexico and International Expansion Services, July 2017.

64 **These industries have also helped spur:** For two different approaches that lead to similar conclusions about the size of the middle class, see *Cuantificando la clase media Mexicana: Un ejercicio exploratorio*, INEGI, 2011, http://www.inegi.org.mx/inegi/contenidos /investigacion/experimentales/clase_media/presentacion.aspx; *Clases medias en México*, INEGI, June 12, 2013, http://usmex2024.uscmediacurator.com/wp-content/uploads /2013/08/Clases-Medias-en-Mexico.pdf. For sources considering the existence of a "vulnerable" class (between the lower and middle classes), see *Perfil de estratos sociales en América Latina: Pobres, vulnerables y clases medias*, Programa de las Naciones Unidas para el Desarrollo, Dirección Regional para América Latina y el Caribe, 2014, accessed May 10, 2017, http://www.undp.org/content/dam/rblac/docs/Research%20and%20 Publications/Poverty%20Reduction/UNDP-RBLAC-Grupos_sociales_AL-2014.PDF; Luis F. López-Calva et al., "Clases medias y vulnerabilidad a la pobreza: Reflexiones desde América Latina," *El Trimestre Económico* 81, no. 322 (2014), http://eltrimestreeconomico .com.mx/index.php/te/article/view/115/351.

64 **But defining the middle class:** For different approaches to the middle class, see Luis de la Calle and Luis Rubio, *Mexico: A Middle Class Society, Poor No More, Developed Not Yet* (Washington, DC: Woodrow Wilson Center, 2012); Gerardo Esquivel. "La verdad sobre la clase media en México: Respuesta a Roger Bartra," *Horizontal*, July 20, 2015, http:// horizontal.mx/la-verdad-sobre-la-clase-media-en-mexico-respuesta-a-roger-bartra; López-Calva et al., "Clases medias y vulnerabilidad a la pobreza"; Luis F. López-Calva and Eduardo Ortiz-Juárez, *A Vulnerability Approach to the Definition of the Middle Class* (Policy Research Working Paper 5902, World Bank, 2011), http://documents.worldbank.org /curated/en/553321468297271070/pdf/WPS5902.pdf.

64 **The number of cars on the street:** "Consulta general: Vehículos de motor registrados y en circulación," INEGI, http://www.inegi.org.mx/lib/olap/consulta/general_ver4 /MDXQueryDatos.asp?proy=.

64 **Movie theaters too have expanded:** Vicente Gutiérrez, "Cinépolis y Cinemex: Dueños de la exhibición del cine en México," *El Economista*, June 28, 2017; *Estadísticas básicas de la cultura en Mexico* (Mexico City: Conaculta, 2006).

64   **Home mortgages have tripled in coverage:** Organization for Economic Co-operation and Development, *México: Transformando la política urbana y el financiamiento de la vivienda* (Paris: OECD, 2015).

65   **To be sure, there is far less:** Coneval, *Medición de la pobreza en Mexico y en las entidades federativas 2016* (Mexico: Coneval, 2016), http://www.coneval.org.mx/Medicion/MP /Documents/Pobreza_16/Pobreza_2016_CONEVAL.pdf.

65   **But while income inequality has dropped:** Mexico still has a higher Gini coefficient, around .48, while the United States' Gini coefficient is .39, according to the Organization for Economic Cooperation and Development in 2016. However, the US rate has expanded in recent years, while the Mexican rate dropped noticeably over two decades but still remained high. See Mark Deen, "Chile, Mexico, U.S. Have Highest Inequality Rates, OECD Says," *Bloomberg*, November 24, 2016. On growing inequality in the United States, see Thomas Piketty, *Capital in the Twenty-First Century* (Cambridge, MA: Harvard University Press, 2014). On Mexico, see Gerardo Esquivel, *Desigualdad extrema en Mexico* (Mexico City: Oxfam, 2015).

65   **Medium enterprises with more:** Eduardo Bolio et al., "A Tale of Two Mexicos: Growth and Prosperity in a Two-Speed Economy," McKinsey Global Institute, March 2014, http://www.mckinsey.com/global-themes/americas/a-tale-of-two-mexicos (podcast also available).

66   **Over half of Mexico's nonagricultural workers:** Gerardo Esquivel, "Buenas intenciones/malos resultados: Política social, informalidad y crecimiento económico en México; and Santiago Levy," *Letras Libres*, November 30, 2010, http://www.letraslibres .com/mexico/libros/buenas-intenciones-malos-resultados-politica-social-informalidad -y-crecimiento-economico-en-mexico-santiago-levy.

66   **In a country where average wages:** Bolio et al., "A Tale of Two Mexicos."

66   **On average gross national income:** On the increase in gross national income (GNI)/capita of slightly more than a third between 2005 and 2015, see *Mexico Human Development Report 2016* (New York: United Nations Development Program, 2017). For GDP per capita comparisons, see the World Bank DataBank, https://data.worldbank .org/indicator/NY.GDP.PCAP.CD?year_high_desc=true. The United Nations Development Program measures GNI/capita, while the World Bank prefers GDP/capita, but these numbers are closely aligned with each other.

66   **And today average educational attainment:** Secretaría de Educación Pública: Sistema Nacional de Información Estadística y Educativa. *Estadísticas históricas 1893–2015*. Available and downloadable at http://www.snie.sep.gob.mx/estadisticas_educativas. html.

66   **Over the same period life expectancy:** "Life Expectancy at Birth, Total (Years)," World Bank, https://data.worldbank.org/indicator/SP.DYN.LE00.IN; "GDP per Capita (Current US$)," World Bank, https://data.worldbank.org/indicator/NY.GDP.PCAP.CD?end=2015 &start=1960&view=chart.

67   **And perhaps as a hallmark:** Alex Gray, "The World's 10 Biggest Economies in 2017," World Economic Forum, March 9, 2017, https://www.weforum.org/agenda/2017/03 /worlds-biggest-economies-in-2017; Will Martin, "These Will Be the 32 Most Powerful Economies in the World by 2050," *Independent*, February 18, 2017, http://www.indepen dent.co.uk/news/business/these-will-be-the-32-most-powerful-economies-in-the -world-by-2050-a7587401.html.

68   **Doug Ducey, the Republican governor of Arizona:** Doug Ducey, quoted in Paulina Pineda, "CBP Takes Binational Inspection Program to Next Phase," *Nogales International*, December 16, 2016, http://www.nogalesinternational.com/news/cbp-takes-binational -inspection-program-to-next-phase/article_1153d07c-c195-11e6-9037-77cee984ae02 .html.

69 **"Mexico is Arizona's largest trading partner":** Quote from the presentation of Governor Doug Ducey at the Woodrow Wilson Center's fourth annual "Building a Competitive U.S.-Mexico Border" conference, Washington, DC, June 14, 2017.

69 **But at the state and local levels:** For a poll of border residents on this, see Alfredo Corchado, "Poll Finds U.S.-Mexico Border Residents Overwhelmingly Value Mobility, Oppose Wall," *Dallas Morning News*, July 18, 2016, http://interactives.dallasnews.com/2016/border-poll. For public opinion of the US public at large, see Rob Suls, "Less Than Half the Public Views Border Wall as an Important Goal for U.S. Immigration Policy," Pew Research Center, January 6, 2017, http://www.pewresearch.org/fact-tank/2017/01/06/less-than-half-the-public-views-border-wall-as-an-important-goal-for-u-s-immigration-policy.

72 **"Mexico is our partner":** Governor Doug Ducey, presentation at the Wilson Center, June 14, 2017.

Chapter 3

76 **This is more than investment:** *Foreign Direct Investment in the United States 2016* (Washington, DC: Organization for International Investment, 2016), http://ofii.org/sites/default/files/Foreign%20Direct%20Investment%20in%20the%20United%20States%202016%20Report.pdf.

81 **While Bimbo remains a household name:** Bimbo comprises 20.7 percent of the total bakery market in the United States, well ahead of Flower Foods at 14.3 percent. In fresh bread, Bimbo has a 26 percent market share versus 19.3 percent for Flowers, which now includes Wonder Bread. See Vince Bamford, "Bakery Products 2015: The Top 10 Suppliers in Key US Industry Sectors," Bakeryandsnacks.com, March 10, 2016, http://www.bakeryandsnacks.com/Markets/Bakery-products-2015-top-10-suppliers-in-key-US-industry-sectors.

87 **Today Bimbo has more than sixty plants:** Christopher Wilson, *Growing Together: Economic Ties Between the United States and Mexico* (Washington, DC: Woodrow Wilson Center, 2017), 25.

88 **Almost a quarter of graduates go on:** Twenty-two percent go on to run a company within three months of graduating, and 67 percent do so within twenty-five years of graduating. Communications with Raul Rodriguez Barocio and Hernán David Montfort of Monterrey Tec.

88 **And Monterrey Tec has succeeded:** "Instituto Tecnológico y de Estudios Superiores de Monterrey," Quacquarelli Symonds Top Universities, accessed October 22, 2017. https://www.topuniversities.com/universities/instituto-tecnol%C3%B3gico-y-de-estudios-superiores-de-monterrey.

88 **Together they employ at least 123,000:** Wilson, *Growing Together*, 2017.

90 **Theodore Moran and Lindsay Oldenski:** Theodore H. Moran and Lindsay Oldenski, "How US Investments in Mexico Have Increased Investment and Jobs at Home," Peterson Institute for International Economics, July 11, 2014, https://piie.com/blogs/realtime-economic-issues-watch/how-us-investments-mexico-have-increased-investment-and-jobs.

Chapter 4

103 **Users go online to buy an item:** On innovation start-ups in Mexico, see also the special edition of *Expansión* magazine, March 1, 2017, which profiles several of the companies.

Chapter 5

115   **It employed almost twice as many:** "Crude Oil Production," OECD, https://data.oecd
.org/energy/crude-oil-production.htm; "Mexico Crude Oil Production: 1994–2018,"
Trading Economics, https://tradingeconomics.com/mexico/crude-oil-production;
"Brazil Crude Oil Production: 1994–2018," Trading Economics, https://tradingeconomics
.com/brazil/crude-oil-production; Nayeli González, "La nómina de Pemex, el doble de la
de Petrobras," *Milenio*, July 17, 2013, http://www.milenio.com/negocios/nomina-Pemex
-doble-Petrobras_0_118188512.html.

115   **And Mexico's oil production:** Diana Villiers Negroponte, ed., *The End of Nostalgia:
Mexico Confronts the Challenges of Global Competition* (Washington DC: Brookings
Institution Press, 2013).

116   **One report predicts that if:** See, for example, the Raymond James estimate on North
American energy independence by 2020, something echoed by several other analysts I
have asked. See Matt Egan, "U.S. Energy Independence 'Tatalizingly Close,'" *CNN Money*,
August 9, 2016, http://money.cnn.com/2016/08/09/investing/us-energy-independence
-oil-opec/index.html.

119   **Today around half of American:** The exact figure is 45 percent. See "U.S. Natural Gas
Exports and Re-exports by Country," US Energy Information Administration, June 30,
2016, https://www.eia.gov/dnav/ng/ng_move_expc_s1_a.htm.

119   **roughly 4 percent of all:** The actual figure is 3.7 percent. See "U.S. Natural Gas
Marketed Production," US Energy Information Administration, June 30, 2017, https://
www.eia.gov/dnav/ng/hist/n9050us2a.htm.

119   **Sixteen pipelines currently cross the border:** See SENER document *Prospectiva de Gas
L.P. 2016–2030*, Mexico City: Secretaria de Energía, 2015.

120   **For the first time, the United States:** Energy comprised 8.71 percent of US exports
to Mexico in 2016, according to "U.S. Exports to Mexico by 5-Digit End-Use Code," US
Census Bureau, Foreign Trade, https://www.census.gov/foreign-trade/statistics/product
/enduse/exports/c2010.html.

120   **Today most of the cheap natural gas:** Teresa Macías, "Promueve CFE la construcción de
16 gasoductos," *El Financiero*, May 22, 2017, http://www.elfinanciero.com.mx/monterrey
/promueve-cfe-la-construccion-de-16-gasoductos.html.

122   **Instead it developed an interconnected:** Border Energy Strategy Committee,
"Energy Issues in the California-Baja California Binational Region," San Diego State
University, November 2002, www.sci.sdsu.edu/ces/CES_RES_6/BESC%20report%20
final2.doc.

123   **In 2016, over 15 percent:** Secretaría de Energía, "Reporte de avance de energias
limpias, primer semestre 2016," gob.mx, 2016, https://www.gob.mx/cms/uploads
/attachment/file/177519/Reporte_Avance_Energ_as_Limpias_1er_sem_2016_VFinal
_28122016.pdf. Duncan Wood notes that it may be closer to 19 percent today. These
figures exclude hydropower, which generates another 10 percent or so of Mexican energy
but is highly controversial in parts of the country because of the effects of dam building
on local communities.

129   **He died in the same:** In interviews, Cantarell variously dates the discovery to 1958 and
1961, but he doesn't tell others for years, and Pemex doesn't finally come to examine
his find until 1971. For interviews with Rudesindo Canterrel, see Ignacio Ramirez, "A
Rudesindo Cantarell, descubridor de petróleo en Campeche, Pemex no le dio ni empleo
de planta," *Proceso*, August 6, 1983, http://www.proceso.com.mx/136664/a-rudecindo
-cantarell-descubridor-de-petroleo-en-campeche-pemex-no-le-dio-ni-empleo-de
-planta; "Rudesindo Cantarell, de la gloria a la ignominia," *Campeche Hoy*, March 19, 2014,
http://campechehoy.mx/notas/index.php?ID=182736.

129   **The United States had 2,366 oil platforms:** Emily Patsy, "OTC 2017: Mexico's Deep Water Is Open for Business," *E&P*, May 2, 2017.

129   **Since 2004, Mexico's oil production:** "PEMEX_Factsheet, Operating Summary, Investor Relations, December 31, 2016," PEMEX, http://www.pemex.com/en/investors /investor-tools/Documents/PEMEX_Factsheet_i.pdf.

130   **As of early 2017, there were commitments:** Patsy, "OTC 2017."

131   **A second, the Italian energy company Eni:** Stanley Reed, "Oil Discoveries Suggest Mexico's Bet to Open Energy Sector Is Paying Off," *New York Times*, July 12, 2017, https:// www.nytimes.com/2017/07/12/business/energy-environment/mexico-energy-gas-oil .html?mcubz=0.

Chapter 6

138   **More than 45,000 Mexicans died:** Kimberly Heinle, Octavio Rodriguez Ferreira, and David A. Shirk, *Drug Violence in Mexico: Analysis Through 2016* (San Diego, CA: Justice in Mexico Project, University of San Diego, 2017).

138   **More than a hundred reporters:** According to the Special Prosecutor's Office on Crimes against Freedom of Expression within the Attorney General's Office, 105 reporters were killed between 2000 and 2016. See Redacción, "Recuento. Asesinatos de periodistas en 2017," *El Universal*, May 15, 2017, http://www.eluniversal.com.mx/articulo /nacion/sociedad/2017/05/15/recuento-asesinatos-de-periodistas-en-2017.

142   **He would later consider the incident:** David Luhnow and Nicholas Casey, "Felipe Calderón—Interview Transcript," *Wall Street Journal*, May 19, 2010, https://www.wsj.com /articles/SB10001424052748703957904575252551548498376.

144   **When Bush had asked him:** The quote comes via former ambassador Antonio O. (Tony) Garza. For a longer description of the discussion during the Oval Office meeting, see Alfredo Corchado, *Midnight in Mexico: A Reporter's Journey Through a Country's Descent into Darkness* (New York: Penguin, 2013).

150   **Between 2008 and 2017 the Merida Initiative:** Clare Seelke and Kristin Finklea, *U.S.-Mexican Security Cooperation: The Merida Initiative and Beyond* (Washington, DC: Congressional Research Service, June 29, 2017).

Chapter 7

156   **And they would be surprised:** I base this statement on multiple interviews with government leaders, heads of law enforcement agencies, and frontline officers in the two countries.

162   **The movie that emerged:** Notimex, "'Presunto culpable,' la tercer película más vista," *El Economista*, January 2, 2017, http://eleconomista.com.mx/entretenimiento/2012/01/02 /presunto-culpable-tercer-pelicula-mas-vista.

168   **Drawing on the expertise:** The document that emerged from this meeting, called "Ciudad Juárez—the Center of Gravity in Combating Organized Crime," was never made public, but it was widely circulated inside the two governments. I have reviewed the document.

168   **The two governments also launched:** The Barrio Azteca committed another major and tragic misstep after the Villas de Salvárcar massacre, shooting an employee of the US consulate and her husband in Ciudad Juárez in front of their infant child. This led to a massive law enforcement response against the gang on the US side of the border in the search for their killers—a campaign that yielded quite a bit of actionable intelligence against the Juárez Cartel itself, according to law enforcement officials who spoke with me.

168   **After three years as the most violent city:** Elyssa Pacheco, "Tasa de homicidios
       en Juárez llega a su nivel más bajo en cinco años," *Insight Crime*, January 4, 2013. For
       monthly comparisons, see Alfredo Limas Hernández and Myrna Limas Hernández,
       "Crímenes en Juárez 2009 y homicidios 2008–2012," Observatorio de Violencia Social
       y de Género, Universidad Autónoma de Ciudad Juárez, 2014; Observatorio Ciudadano
       de Chihuahua, "Reporte de incidencia delictiva en Ciudad Juárez, Agosto 2017," No. 27,
       September 2017.

Chapter 8

184   **It was designed to make money:** On Lubetzky's life and career, see his autobiography:
       Daniel Lubetzky, *Do the KIND Thing: Think Boundlessly, Work Purposefully, Live Passionately*
       (New York: Ballantine Books, 2015).
185   **Most will never be as successful:** Lauren Hirsch, "Snack Bar Company Kind Explores
       Stake Sale: Sources," Reuters, July 7, 2017, https://www.reuters.com/article/us-kind
       -llc-m-a/snack-bar-company-kind-explores-stake-sale-sources-idUSKBN19S214.
185   **but they start businesses at twice:** "Startup Activity Swings Upward for Third
       Consecutive Year, Annual Kauffman Index Reports," Ewing Marion Kauffman
       Foundation, May 18, 2017, http://www.kauffman.org/newsroom/2017/05/startup
       -activity-swings-upward-for-third-consecutive-year-annual-kauffman-index-reports.
       See also Robert W. Fairlie, *Open for Business: How Immigrants Are Driving Small Business
       Creation in the United States* (New York: Partnership for a New American Economy,
       2012), esp. 23. See also Peter Vandor and Nikolaus Franke, "Why Are Immigrants More
       Entrepreneurial?," *Harvard Business Review*, October 27, 2016, https://hbr.org/2016/10
       /why-are-immigrants-more-entrepreneurial.
185   **But when you add up:** Fairlie, *Open for Business*.
185   **Mexican immigrants, who compose less:** Fairlie, *Open for Business*.
186   **Not surprisingly, as the economy:** For example, the Gallup poll, which tracks US
       attitudes on immigration, finds that the number of Americans who feel that immigration
       should be decreased has dropped from around half—sometimes a little more—to
       around 40 percent in recent years, with a majority of Americans indicating that they'd
       like to keep immigration levels constant or increase them. For a time sequence of the
       Gallup poll, see Andrew Selee, *A New Migration Agenda Between the United States and Mexico*
       (Washington, DC: Woodrow Wilson Center, 2017), 13.
186   **And today a third of all:** Mary C. Waters and Marisa G. Pineau, *The Integration of
       Immigrants into American Society* (Washington, DC: National Academies Press, 2015); see,
       for example, 22.
186   **It's a big part:** For the most comprehensive discussion of the evidence, see National
       Academies of Sciences, Engineering, and Medicine, *The Economic and Fiscal Consequences of
       Immigration* (Washington, DC: National Academies Press, 2016). For another discussion
       of the evidence, see also Richard Florida, "Immigrants Boost Wages for Everyone,"
       Citylab, June 27, 2017, https://www.citylab.com/equity/2017/06/immigration-wages
       -economics/530301.
186   **They even tend to be:** See the summary of the evidence on both health and
       incarceration in Waters and Pineau, *The Integration of Immigrants into American Society*.
186   **Today's immigrants also appear:** Waters and Pineau, *The Integration of Immigrants
       into American Society*. On crime, see also Robert J. Sampson, "Rethinking Crime and
       Immigration," *Contexts* 7 (winter 2008): 28–33; Robert J. Sampson, "Open Doors Don't
       Invite Criminals," *New York Times*, March 11, 2006, http://www.nytimes.com/2006
       /03/11/opinion/open-doors-dont-invite-criminals.html.

187 **Even more telling, very few grandchildren:** On language use, see Paul Taylor et al., "When Labels Don't Fit: Hispanics and Their Views of Identity," Washington, DC: Pew Research Center, April 4, 2012. Tomas Jimenez, a professor at Stanford, offers an interesting look at how ongoing immigration from Mexico has helped replenish third-generation Mexican Americans' emotional ties to Mexico and the way that non-Latinos see them. See Tomas Jimenez, *Replenished Ethnicity: Mexican-Americans, Immigration, and Identity* (Berkeley: University of California Press, 2009).

187 **Economists disagree on just how much:** On competition with low-wage workers, see George Borjas, *We Wanted Workers: Unravelling the Immigration Narrative* (New York: Norton, 2016). For contrasting views, see Giovanni Perri and David Card, "Immigration Economics by George Borjas: A Review Essay," *Journal of Economic Literature* 54, no. 4 (December 2016): 1333–1349; David Card and Steven Raphael, eds., *Immigration, Poverty, and Socioeconomic Inequality* (New York: Russell Sage, 2013); Thomas Kemeny and Abigail Cook, "Spillovers for Immigration Diversity in Cities," *Journal of Economic Geography*, May 31, 2017, https://doi.org/10.1093/jeg/lbx012. For research suggesting that immigration creates benefits for most workers during times of economic expansion but can be more harmful during economic downturns, see Giovanni Peri, "The Impact of Immigrants During Recession and Economic Expansion," Migration Policy Institute, June 2010, https://www.migrationpolicy.org/research/impact-immigrants-recession-and -economic-expansion.

187 **And while immigration flows:** Thomas B. Edsall, "How Immigration Foiled Hillary," *New York Times*, October 5, 2017, https://www.nytimes.com/2017/10/05/opinion/clinton -trump-immigration.html.

188 **Most immigrants today come from Asia:** Jeanne Batalova, Michael Fix, and James D. Bachmeier, *Untapped Talent: The Costs of Brain Waste Among Highly Skilled Immigrants in the United States* (Washington, DC: Migration Policy Institute, December 2016), 26. Overall, 48 percent of immigrants who arrived in the 2011–2015 period had a college degree versus only 31 percent for native-born Americans. For Mexican immigrants, more than one in six of those who arrived in that period had a college degree (17 percent), almost double the 9 percent who did in the 2006–2010 period. Jeanne Batalova and Michael Fix, "New Brain Gain: Rising Education Levels Among Recent Immigrants to the United States," Fact Sheet, Migration Policy Institute, May 2017.

190 **By 2007, 12.8 million people:** Ana González Barrera, "More Mexicans Leaving Than Coming to the U.S.," Pew Research Center, November 19, 2015, http://www.pewhispanic .org/2015/11/19/more-mexicans-leaving-than-coming-to-the-u-s.

190 **In states like Zacatecas, Jalisco:** For Zacatecas, one study found that 38 percent of those born in the state now live in the United States, one of the highest rates anywhere in Mexico. See Miguel Moctezuma Longoria, "La migración internacional de Zacatecas y su relación con el desarrollo y la biodiversidad," Universidad Autónoma de Zacatecas, 2013.

191 **In fact, since 2009, more Mexicans:** González Barrera, "More Mexicans Leaving Than Coming to the U.S."

191 **Today there are 11.6 million:** Gustavo Lopez and Kristen Bialik, "Key Findings About U.S. Immigrants," Pew Research Center, May 3, 2017, http://www.pewresearch.org/fact -tank/2017/05/03/key-findings-about-u-s-immigrants; González Barrera, "More Mexicans Leaving Than Coming to the U.S."

191 **Mexicans, once almost two-thirds:** Jens Manuel Krogstad, Jeffrey S. Passel, and D'vera Cohn, "5 Facts About Illegal Immigration in the U.S.," Pew Research Center, April 27, 2017, http://www.pewresearch.org/fact-tank/2017/04/27/5-facts-about-illegal -immigration-in-the-u-s. Many of those who crossed without papers, including Efrain Jimenez and Demetrio Juárez in Hazleton, later legalized their status through work

visas sponsored by American employers or, in some cases, marriage to an American citizen or legal resident. As of this writing, roughly 548,000 unauthorized Mexicans had been accepted into the Deferred Action for Childhood Arrivals (DACA) program, giving them legal protection from deportation. With the program set to expire in March 2018, Congress was looking at long-term legislative fixes to legalize this population. That leaves roughly 5 million Mexicans, out of 11.6 million in the United States, who lack any legal documentation at all, roughly 43 percent of the total. On DACA numbers, see "Approximate Active DACA Recipients: Country of Birth," U.S. Citizenship and Immigration Service, September 4, 2017, https://www.uscis.gov/sites/default/files/USCIS /Resources/Reports%20and%20Studies/Immigration%20Forms%20Data/All%20 Form%20Types/DACA/daca_population_data.pdf; Randy Capps, Michael Fix, and Jie Zong, *The Education and Work Profiles of the DACA Population* (Washington, DC: Migration Policy Institute, August 2017).

191 **Studies show that remittances:** For an analysis of remittance patterns, see Manuel Orozco, "Las remesas a Mexico durante 2016," Inter-American Dialogue, 2017, https:// www.thedialogue.org/wp-content/uploads/2017/03/Las-remesas-a-M%C3%A9xico -durante-el-2016.pdf.

191 **Remittances are linked to higher:** Gerardo Esquivel and Alejandra Huerta-Pineda, "Remittances and Poverty in Mexico: A Propensity Score Matching Approach," *Integration and Trade* 11, no. 27 (July–December 2007): 45–71; Dilip Ratha, "The Impact of Remittances on Economic Growth and Poverty Reduction" (Policy Brief No. 8, Migration Policy Institute, Washington, DC, October 2013), https://www.migrationpolicy.org/sites /default/files/publications/Remittances-PovertyReduction.pdf; Ramón A. Castillo Ponce and Anayatzin Larios Candelas, "Remesas y desarrollo humano: El caso de Zacatecas," *Región y sociedad* 20, no. 41 (January–April 2008): 117–144; Silvia E. Giorguli and Itzam Serratos López, "El impacto de la migración internacional sobre la asistencia escolar en México," in *El estado de la migración: Las políticas públicas ante los retos de la migración mexicana a Estados Unidos*, edited by Paula Leite and Silvia E. Giorguli (México, DF: Consejo Nacional de Población, 2009).

191 **There is increasing evidence:** Christopher Woodruff, "Mexican Microenterprise Investment and Employment: The Role of Remittances," *Integration and Trade* 11, no. 27 (July–December 2007): 159–184.

192 **Schools, including several small regional campuses:** Studies find that most collective remittances—the ones where migrant groups gather their funds together to help the community—generally fund infrastructure, education, and health care. See Katrina Burgess, "Collective Remittances and Migrant-State Collaboration in Mexico and El Salvador," *Latin American Politics and Society* 54, no. 4 (winter 2012): 119–146.

192 **Most importantly, after a period:** Zacatecas's local economy (state GDP) grew 56 percent between 2003 and 2016, while the average for all Mexican states was 35.5 percent. Instituto de Información Estadística y Geográfica de Jalisco, based on data from Instituto Nacional de Estadística y Geografíca (INEGI), 2016. Available at http://iieg.gob .mx/contenido/Economia/pib_comparativo_entidades.xls.

192 **employment expanded exponentially, tripling:** INEGI, *National Survey of Occupation and Employment*, 2008, and Mexican Ministry of Employment and Social Prevention, *Zacatecas Job Information*, June 2017. Employment grew from around 200,000 to over 600,000 in this nineteen-year period.

194 **According to separate analyses:** González Barrera, "More Mexicans Leaving Than Coming to the U.S."; Silvia E. Giorguli Saucedo, Víctor M. García Guerrero, and Claudia Masferrer, "A Migration System in the Making: Demographic Dynamics and Migration Policies in North America and the Northern Triangle of Central-America," Center for Demographic, Urban and Environmental Studies, El Colegio de México, 2016.

195 **In March 2017, the Mexican Congress:** Email correspondence with Jesús Lopez Macedo, Mexico's National Association of Universities and Higher Education Institutions (ANUIES), June 30, 2017.

195 **Enhanced border security certainly had:** Office of Immigration Statistics, "Efforts by DHS to Estimate Southwest Border Security Between Ports of Entry," Department of Homeland Security, September 2017, https://www.dhs.gov/sites/default/files/publications /17_0914_estimates-of-border-security.pdf.

195 **The size of the border patrol increased:** According to the study, expenditure on immigration enforcement agencies is greater than expenditures on all federal agencies for which law enforcement is the central mission (i.e., the Federal Bureau of Investigation, Secret Service, US Marshals Service, Drug Enforcement Agency, and Bureau of Alcohol, Tobacco, Firearms, and Explosives). Dorris Meissner et al., *Immigration Enforcement in the United States: The Rise of a Formidable Machinery* (Washington, DC: Migration Policy Institute, January 2013).

195 **And the increased number of deportations:** Muzaffar Chishti, Sarah Pierce, and Jessica Bolter, "The Obama Record on Deportations: Deporter in Chief or Not?" Migration Policy Institute, January 26, 2017, https://www.migrationpolicy.org/article/obama-record -deportations-deporter-chief-or-not. The authors find that "eighty-five percent of all removals and returns during fiscal year (FY) 2016 were of noncitizens who had recently crossed the U.S. border unlawfully.... Of the remainder, who were removed from the U.S. interior, more than 90 percent had been convicted of what DHS defines as serious crimes."

196 **These are the people who:** Aaron Terrazas, Demetrios G. Papademetriou, and Marc R. Rosenblum, *Evolving Demographic and Human-Capital Trends in Mexico and Central America and Their Implications for Regional Migration* (Washington, DC: Migration Policy Institute and the Woodrow Wilson Center, May 2011).

196 **But the largest reason appears to be:** Gordon Hanson, Chen Liu, and Craig McIntosh, "Along the Watchtower: The Rise and Fall of U.S. Low-Skilled Immigration," Brookings Papers on Economic Activity, March 23, 2017, https://www.brookings.edu/bpea -articles/along-the-watchtower-the-rise-and-fall-of-u-s-low-skilled-immigration.

196 **Economists often refer to the "migration hump":** See, for example, Philip L. Martin, *Trade and Migration: NAFTA and Agriculture* (Washington, DC: Institute for International Economics, 1993). Martin expected an initial outflow of Mexicans as the Mexican economy improved—which is what happened.

197 **That's exactly what happened in Mexico:** For a review of the literature on this, see Michael Clemens, *Does Development Reduce Migration?* (Washington, DC: Center for Global Development, October 2014); Hein de Haas, "Turning the Tide? Why Development Will Not Stop Migration" (Working Paper 2, International Migration Institute, University of Oxford, 2006).

197 **One group of researchers from both countries:** Jacqueline Hagan, Ruben Hernandez-Leon, and Jean-Luc Demonsant, *Skills of the "Unskilled": Work and Mobility Among Mexican Migrants* (Berkeley: University of California Press, 2015).

198 **This is not a wholly new flow:** Gabriel Lesser and Jeanne Batalova, "Central American Immigrants in the United States," Migration Policy Institute, April 5, 2017, https://www .migrationpolicy.org/article/central-american-immigrants-united-states.

198 **Almost all come from three:** Michael Clemens, "Violence, Development, and Migration Waves: Evidence from Central American Child Migrant Apprehensions" (Working Paper 459, Center for Global Development, July 27, 2017).

198 **In 2014 and again in 2016 and 2017:** "Statement by Secretary Johnson on Southwest Border Security," Department of Homeland Security Press Office, October 17, 2016, accessed July 6, 2017, https://www.dhs.gov/news/2016/10/17/statement-secretary -johnson-southwest-border-security.

199   **Increasingly some of these migrants:** The number of Central Americans applying
       for asylum in Mexico is still small—8,781 in 2016—but that's more than double the
       3,500 applications of the year before, and the Mexican government estimates the
       number may double or triple in 2017. See Gabriel Stargardter, "Asylum Applications in
       Mexico Surge After Trump Election Win," Reuters, April 18, 2017, https://www
       .reuters.com/article/us-usa-immigration-mexico-exclusive/exclusive-asylum
       -applications-in-mexico-surge-after-trump-election-win-idUSKBN17K2CE;
       "Estadísticas 2013 a Agosto 2017," Comisión Mexicana de Ayuda a Refugiados, http:
       //www.comar.gob.mx/work/models/COMAR/Resource/267/6/images/
       ESTADISTICAS_2013-agosto2017.pdf.

199   **Neither the US nor the Mexican asylum system:** Jie Zong and Jeanne Batalova,
       "Refugees and Asylees in the United States," Migration Policy Institute, June 7, 2017,
       https://www.migrationpolicy.org/article/refugees-and-asylees-united-states.

201   **More than two-thirds of Central American migrants:** See "Forced to Flee Central
       America's Northern Triangle: A Neglected Humanitarian Crisis," Medecins Sans
       Frontiers, May 2017, https://www.doctorswithoutborders.org/sites/usa/files/msf
       _forced-to-flee-central-americas-northern-triangle.pdf. For a firsthand recounting of
       these experiences, see Oscar Martinez, *The Beast: Riding the Rails and Dodging Narcos on
       the Migrant Trail* (New York: Verso, 2013). See also "Personas en detención migratoria
       en México: Misión de Monitoreo de Estaciones Migratorias y Estancias Provisionales
       del Instituto Nacional de Migración," Consejo Ciudadano del Instituto Nacional de
       Migración, July 2017.

201   **Indeed, most of the growth:** Over the past two decades, immigrants have driven
       growth in the suburban areas of America's metro areas and in the small cities and
       towns in the nonmetro areas. This growth slowed slightly for nonmetro areas after the
       2008–2009 economic crisis but increased in suburban and exurban areas of metro areas.
       Among other sources, see William H. Frey, "U.S. Immigration Levels Continue to Fuel
       Most Community Demographic Gains," Brookings Institution, August 3, 2017, https://
       www.brookings.edu/blog/the-avenue/2017/08/03/u-s-immigration-levels-continue
       -to-fuel-most-community-demographic-gains; Jill H. Wilson and Nicole Prchal
       Svajlenka, "Immigrants Continue to Disperse, with Fastest Growth in the Suburbs,"
       Brookings Institution, October 29, 2014, https://www.brookings.edu/research
       /immigrants-continue-to-disperse-with-fastest-growth-in-the-suburbs; Renee Stepler
       and Mark Hugo Lopez, "U.S. Latino Population Growth and Dispersion Has Slowed
       Since Onset of the Great Recession," Pew Research Center, September 8, 2016, http://
       www.pewhispanic.org/2016/09/08/latino-population-growth-and-dispersion-has
       -slowed-since-the-onset-of-the-great-recession.

Chapter 9

210   **But not until the 1990s:** "Perfil sociodemográfico de la población afrodescendiente
       en México," Instituto Nacional de Estadística y Geografía, Comisión Nacional de los
       Derechos Humanos, Consejo Nacional para Prevenir la Discriminación, Comunicado de
       Prensa Número 135/17, March 27, 2017, http://www.inegi.org.mx/saladeprensa/boletines
       /2017/especiales/especiales2017_03_04.pdf.

211   **President Woodrow Wilson removed Ambassador Lane:** John Milton Cooper,
       Woodrow Wilson: A Biography (New York: Knopf Doubleday, 2011).

212   **They started the book:** Robert A. Pastor and Jorge G. Castañeda, *Limits to Friendship: The
       United States and Mexico* (New York: Vintage Books, 1988).

214   **In 2015, following on the success:** Her candidacy was also proposed by the Swedish
       and South African affiliates of PEN International.

220 **"The biggest challenge is the language":** There are roughly 1.4 million children in Michoacán schools (preschool through high school), according to state education statistics. See "Estadística del sistema educativo Michoacán ciclo escolar 2015–2016," Sistema Nacional de Información Estadística Educativa, October 2016, http://www .snie.sep.gob.mx/descargas/estadistica_e_indicadores/estadistica_e_indicadores _educativos_16MICH.pdf.

221 **Today roughly 2 percent of Mexico's:** According to one report from Mexico's Public Education Secretariat, there are four hundred thousand students in primary and secondary education born abroad. Daniel Blancas Madrigal, "Cursan 400 mil niños repatriados este ciclo de educación básica," *Cronica*, February 3, 2017, http://www.cronica.com.mx/notas /2017/1012501.html. The Institute for Migrant Women (IMUME) puts the number at 307, 125, using official figures. See "En Mexico, la educación básica no es para todos," *Animal Politico*, March 4, 2015, http://www.animalpolitico.com/blogueros-blog-invitado/2015 /03/04/en-mexico-la-educacion-basica-es-para-todos-sera.

Chapter 10

224 **Mexicans spend almost $1 billion:** The number is usually between 800 million and 900 million, according to "Theatrical Market Statistics 2016," Motion Picture Association of America (MPAA), March 2017, https://www.mpaa.org/wp-content /uploads/2017/03/MPAA-Theatrical-Market-Statistics-2016_Final.pdf.

224 **Movie attendance per capita in Mexico:** "Feature Films Attendance Frequency Data," UNESCO Institute for Statistics, 2017.

225 **US Latinos attend movies anywhere:** "Theatrical Market Statistics 2016."

226 **The bittersweet film, which focuses:** "Instructions Not Included," Box Office Mojo, http://www.boxofficemojo.com/movies/?id=instructionsnotincluded.htm.

227 **It brought in almost $25 million:** Brooks Barns, "'How to Be a Latin Lover' and 'Baahubali 2' Show Power at Box Office," *New York Times*, April 30, 2017, https://www .nytimes.com/2017/04/30/movies/how-to-be-a-latin-lover-baahubali-2-box-office.html.

227 **One is a car-racing-themed movie:** Anna Marie de la Fuente, "NASCAR Teams with Eugenio Derbez for Comedy Film," *Variety*, August 17, 2015, http://variety.com/2015 /film/news/nascar-eugenio-derbez-comedy-1201571330.

235 **To be sure, a handful of actors:** At least one prominent cameraman, Gabriel Figueroa, became one of the most sought-after talents in both countries, filming movies like *The Fugitive* and *The Night of the Iguana*, for which he was nominated for an Oscar.

235 **Unlike the golden age films:** On the history of Mexican cinema, see Ignacio Sanchez Prado, *Screening Neoliberalism: Transforming Mexican Cinema, 1988–2012* (Nashville, TN: Vanderbilt University Press, 2014); Charles Ramírez Berg, *The Classical Mexican Cinema: The Poetics of the Exceptional Golden Age Films* (Austin: University of Texas, 2015).

236 **At first, this privatization looked:** On this point, see Sanchez Prado, *Screening Neoliberalism*.

237 **From 2013 to 2016 anywhere:** *Anuario estadístico de cine mexicano 2016/ Statistical Yearbook of Mexican Cinema 2016* (Mexico, DF: Secretaría de Cultura, Instituto Mexicano de Cinematografía, 2017).

242 **"I realized that out of these hundred people":** "Salma Hayek Pinault Will Never Dive That Deep Again," *The Late Late Show with James Corden*, CBS, June 12, 2017, http://www .cbs.com/shows/late-late-show/video/D070F330-CA14-5DF8-A9CF-9F4BA01D67F8 /salma-hayek-pinault-will-never-dive-that-deep-again. See also Rebecca Ford, "How Salma Hayek Pulled Off a Cannes Mariachi Stunt," *Hollywood Reporter*, May 31, 2017, http:// www.hollywoodreporter.com/rambling-reporter/how-salma-hayek-pulled-a-cannes -mariachi-stunt-1008646.

Chapter 11

246   **In fact, Sanchez had arrived right:** Both Garcia and Sanchez would go on to play for other teams after the Forty-Niners and Jets, and Garcia played some of his best football with the Eagles in Philadelphia.

247   **Although most Americans who are the children:** Jens Manuel Krogstad and Ana González Barrera, "A Majority of English-Speaking Hispanics in the United States are Bilingual," Pew Research Center, March 24, 2015, http://www.pewresearch.org /fact-tank/2015/03/24/a-majority-of-english-speaking-hispanics-in-the-u-s-are-bilingual.

248   **This growth is driven less:** "From the Ballot Box to the Grocery Store: A 2015 Perspective on Growing Hispanic Influence in America," Nielsen Holdings, 2016, 6. Full report available at http://www.nielsen.com/us/en/insights/reports/2016/from-the -ballot-box-to-the-grocery-store-hispanic-influence-in-america.html.

248   **Perhaps most strikingly for marketers:** Jeffrey A. Eisenach, "Making America Rich Again: The Latino Effect on Economic Growth," NERA Economic Consulting, December 2016, http://www.nera.com/content/dam/nera/publications/2016/PUB_LDC_Prosperity _1216.pdf, 1.

248   **NASCAR, once the least diverse:** Scarborough Research, "NASCAR Fan Base Demographics," 2011, downloaded from Brent Sherman Racing, http://www.brentsherman .com/PDFS/NASCAR.pdf.

249   **Suarez has since bought:** Kelly Crandall, "Xfinity Series Spotlight: Daniel Suarez," *NBC Sports*, October 6, 2016, http://nascar.nbcsports.com/2016/10/06/xfinity-series-spotlight -daniel-suarez.

249   **Major League Baseball (MLB), of course:** In 2017, 31.9 percent of all MLB players were Hispanic. See Richard Lapchick, "MLB Race and Gender Report Card Shows Progress Still Needed," ESPN, April 19, 2017, http://www.espn.com/mlb/story/_/id/19185242/mlb -race-gender-report-card-shows-progress-needed.

249   **In the United States, MLB has long:** Derek Thompson, "Which Sports Have the Whitest/Richest/Oldest Fans?," *Atlantic*, February 10, 2014, https://www.theatlantic.com /business/archive/2014/02/which-sports-have-the-whitest-richest-oldest-fans/283626.

249   **MLB even schedules exhibition games:** See Dennis Lin, "Padres to Play Astros in Mexico City," *San Diego Union Tribune*, January 13, 2016, http://www.sandiegouniontribune .com/sports/padres/sdut-padres-astros-spring-training-games-mexico-city-2016jan13 -story.html; Jay Jaffe, "MLB Expansion? These Cities in U.S. and Abroad Make Sense," *Sports Illustrated*, April 22, 2016, https://www.si.com/mlb/2016/04/22/mlb-expansion-montreal -mexico-city-charlotte-portland.

249   **When the Montreal Expos were for sale:** Steve Popper, "Mexican Group Is Latest to Seek to Draw the Expos," *New York Times*, August 5, 2003, http://www.nytimes.com/2003/08/05 /sports/baseball-mexican-group-is-latest-to-seek-to-draw-the-expos.html.

250   **But more importantly, the NBA simply:** Thompson, "Which Sports Have the Whitest/Richest/Oldest Fans?"

250   **The Women's National Basketball Association:** Max Meyer, "WNBA Begins LGBT Marketing Campaign," The Cauldron, June 11, 2014, https://the-cauldron.com/wnba -begins-lgbt-marketing-campaign-5bf9e37e579a.

250   **Although men's soccer remains far behind:** Allen St. John, "The Soccer Mom Paradox or Why American Kids Play Soccer but Only Watch at World Cup Time," *Forbes*, June 26, 2014, https://www.forbes.com/sites/allenstjohn/2014/06/26/the-soccer-mom-paradox-or-why- american-kids-play-soccer-but-only-watch-at-world-cup-time/#39187b112352.

250   **Since 1980, the number of children:** Alex Johnson, "Soccer by the Numbers: A Look at the Game in the U.S.," *NBC News*, May 27, 2015, https://www.nbcnews.com/storyline /fifa-corruption-scandal/soccer-numbers-look-game-u-s-n365601.

251 **Major League Soccer (MLS), the men's:** Ahiza Garcia, "Major League Soccer's Plan to Become Truly Major," *CNN Money,* March 3, 2017, http://money.cnn.com/2017/03/03 /news/mls-growth-don-garber/index.html. That value is a 400 percent increase from the 2008 value of $37 million. See Mark J. Burns, "MLS Records Banner Year in 2016, Cements Position Among Top U.S. Pro Sports Leagues," *Forbes,* October 26, 2016, https://www.forbes.com/sites/markjburns/2016/10/26/mls-records-banner-year -in-2016-cements-position-among-top-u-s-pro-sports-leagues/#4575299178a2.

251 **In one ESPN poll:** Roger Bennett, "MLS Equals MLB in Popularity with Kids," *ESPN FC,* March 7, 2014, http://www.espnfc.us/major-league-soccer/story/1740529/mls-catches -mlb-in-popularity-with-kids-says-espn-poll. For an infographic of the data, see "Soccer Popularity Continues to Climb," Sports Path E-learning Blog, http://sportspath.typepadv .com/files/soccer-popularity-continues-to-climb.pdf.

251 **And that number doesn't include:** Cork Gaines, "Soccer Popularity Is on the Rise in the US, but English Football Is Benefiting More Than MLS," *Business Insider,* July 2, 2014, http://www.businessinsider.com/soccer-popularity-english-football-mls-2014-7.

251 **Spanish-speaking Latinos—mostly first-generation immigrants:** Stephen Master, "Year in Sports Media Report 2016," Nielsen, 2017, http://www.nielsen.com/content /dam/corporate/us/en/reports-downloads/2017-reports/nielsen-year-in-sports-media -2016.pdf.

253 **One survey actually found:** Christine Clarridge, "State by State, Map Shows Most Binge-Watched TV Shows," *Seattle Times,* January 12, 2017, http://www.seattletimes.com /entertainment/tv/state-by-state-map-shows-most-binge-watched-tv-shows.

253 *Ugly Betty,* **executive-produced by Mexican:** Of course, all these shows were preceded by *I Love Lucy* in the 1950s, which Cuban American Desi Arnaz coproduced and in which he also costarred with Lucille Ball.

255 **Disney, once a joint partner:** Meg James, "Walt Disney Co.'s ABC Sells Its Fusion Stake to Univision, Exits Joint Venture," *Los Angeles Times,* April 21, 2016, http://www.latimes .com/entertainment/envelope/cotown/la-et-ct-disney-abc-ends-fusion-univision -20160421-story.html.

260 **Yet in the twentieth century:** My father, an ardent amateur chef, often made us *sopapillas,* a kind of fried bread common in the American Southwest, which he had learned to make while working with the Yaqui people of Arizona, an indigenous group from northern Mexico that had fled to the United States at the end of the nineteenth century after a war with the Mexican government. I've never yet encountered them in Mexico, though they are a staple among Mexican-origin groups in the American Southwest; there are also popular regional variants, with similar names, in Spain and other parts of Latin America.

260 **Chinese, Mexican, and Italian food make up:** National Restaurant Association, *Global Palates: Ethnic Cuisines and Flavors in America* (Washington, DC: National Restaurant Association, August 19, 2015). Full report available at http://www.restaurant.org/News -Research/Research/Global-Palates.

261 **According to Jeffrey Pilcher:** Jeffrey Pilcher, *Planet Taco: A Global History of Mexican Food* (Oxford: Oxford University Press, 2012).

262 **Chipotle grew from 16 stores:** An E. coli outbreak at some of its restaurants led to a decline in sales in 2016, but signs are that it's poised for growth again. See John Edwards, "Understanding Chipotle's Recent and Exponential Growth (CMG)," *Investopedia,* September 23, 2015, http://www.investopedia.com/articles/markets/092315/under standing-chipotles-recent-and-exponential-growth.asp; Trefis Team, "How Chipotle Mexican Grill Plans to Drive Revenues in 2017," *Forbes,* January 13, 2017, https://www .forbes.com/sites/greatspeculations/2017/01/13/how-chipotle-mexican-grill-plans -to-drive-revenues-in-2017.

262 **And tequila, that classic Mexican liquor:** "Americans Spice Up Flavor Palates and Beverages for Cinco de Mayo," Nielsen, May 3, 2017, http://www.nielsen.com/us/en /insights/news/2017/americans-spice-up-flavor-palates-and-beverages-for-cinco -de-mayo.html.

262 **outpacing cocktails made with vodka:** "Nielsen CGA Releases First On-Premise Consumer Survey for U.S. Market," Nielsen, May 9, 2016, http://www.nielsen.com/us /en/press-room/2016/nielsen-cga-releases-first-on-premise-consumer-survey-for -us-market.html.

263 **Mezcal production has tripled:** Hipócrates Nolasco Cancino, "Informe 201," Mezcal Consejo Regulador, 2017, http://www.crm.org.mx/PDF/INF_ACTIVIDADES /INFORME2016.pdf, 25, 46.

266 **around 17 percent of eligible voters:** Gustavo López and Renee Stepler, "Latinos in the 2016 Election: Nevada," Pew Research Center, January 19, 2016, http://www .pewhispanic.org/fact-sheet/latinos-in-the-2016-election-nevada.

266 **The current governor of New Mexico:** Bill Richardson's mother is Mexican, and he spent many of his early years in Mexico City.

267 **The National Association of Latino Elected Officials estimates:** Jessica Weiss and María Sánchez Díez, "The Latino Struggle to Reach Public Office," *Univision News*, October 13, 2016, http://www.univision.com/univision-news/the-latino-struggle-to -reach-public-office.

267 **Although Latinos make up 17.8 percent:** Antonio Flores, "How the U.S. Hispanic Population Is Changing," Pew Research Center, September 18, 2017, http://www .pewresearch.org/fact-tank/2017/09/18/how-the-u-s-hispanic-population-is-changing; "The Nation's Older Population Is Still Growing, Census Bureau Reports," United States Census Bureau, June 22, 2017, https://www.census.gov/newsroom/press-releases/2017 /cb17-100.html.

267 **they comprise only 11.9 percent:** US Census Bureau, Current Population Survey, November 2016.

Chapter 12

270 **Right as the president was signing:** "United States, Canada, and Mexico Declare Intention to Submit Unified Bid to Host 2026 FIFA World Cup," US Soccer, April 10, 2017.

270 **It had been used 1.3 million times:** Data from Luis Palacios, director, Cross-Border Express, via email, October 16, 2017.

270 **So too did the joint production:** Jesse Snyder, "U.S. Auto Production Undergoes a Decade of Transformation," *Automotive News*, October 1, 2010, http://www.autonews .com/article/20171001/OEM01/171009995/auto-production-recession.

270 **And Mexican investment—the money:** See US Department of Commerce, Bureau of Economic Statistics, "Foreign Direct Investment by Country," https://www.bea.gov /international/xls/fdius-current/FDIUS-DetailedCountry-2008-2016.xlsx.

271 **Their investments more than doubled:** "Foreign Direct Investment by Country," US Department of Commerce, Bureau of Economic Statistics, https://www.bea.gov /international/xls/fdius-current/FDIUS-DetailedCountry-2008-2016.xlsx.

271 **with more than half of America's gasoline:** "Crude Oil and Petroleum Product Exports Reach Record Levels in the First Half of 2017," US Energy Information Administration, October 18, 2017; "U.S. Energy Trade with Mexico: U.S. Export Value More Than Twice Import Value in 2016," US Energy Information Administration, February 9, 2017.

271 **Meanwhile, in October 2017—just as NAFTA:** Kristopher Tapley, "Oscars: Alejandro G. Inarritu's Virtual Reality Installation 'Carne y Arena' to Receive Special Award," *Variety*, October 27, 2017.

272 **Not to be outdone, Major League Baseball:** See Randall Archibold, "A Big NFL Game Comes to Mexico City: These Guys Have It Covered," *New York Times*, November 19, 2017. See also "NBA to Play Two Regular Season Games in Mexico," NBA press release, August 9, 2017; "Dodgers, Padres to Play Series in Mexico," MLB press release, November 13, 2017; and Kevin Seifert, "NFL to Play At Least Three More Regular-Season Games in Mexico City Through 2021," ESPN, November 19, 2017.

273 **But the Astros' owners could see:** Houston Astros, press release, December 7, 2011.

274 **Polling company Gallup, which has followed:** Author's analysis of Gallup Poll data from 1989 to 2017: Gallup News Service, "Gallup Poll Social Series: World Affairs," February 1–5, 2017, http://news.gallup.com/file/poll/204221/170222Mexico.pdf.

274 **One that asks about its importance:** For a comprehensive comparison of multiple polls, see Christopher Wilson, Pablo Parás, and Enrique Enriquez, "A Critical Juncture: Public Opinion in U.S.-Mexico Relations," Woodrow Wilson Center Working Paper, October 2017. The poll that cites 69 percent is a survey by Data Opinion Publica y Mercados, Omnibus Survey MX, 2017, cited in ibid., "A Critical Juncture," which surveys both border communities and the public at large in the United States and Mexico.

274 **The Chicago Council on Global Affairs:** Author's analysis of the biennial public opinion surveys of the Chicago Council on Global Affairs.

274 **When asked what comes to mind:** The best breakout of what words Americans associate with Mexico comes from a public opinion poll conducted by the firm Vianovo. Overall, the poll finds much lower positive views of Mexico than all other recent polling, but the break-out of reasons points to some real underlying unease among Americans. James S. Taylor, "Vianovo-GSD&M Poll Shows Mexico's Brand in U.S. Remains Battered," Vianovo, June 28, 2016. They have a comparison poll from 2012 as well.

275 **There are also growing signs:** Gallup, "Gallup Poll Social Series: World Affairs." Republican Presidents, including Ronald Reagan, George H. W. Bush, and especially George W. Bush, had been some of the most active promoters of closer relations with Mexico during their presidencies. But today Republicans appear to be the most skeptical toward Mexico. This polarization is also evident on Americans feelings about immigration and immigration policy, as the Gallup poll's tracking on this issue suggests, and how Americans feel about Mexican immigrants specifically, as recent polling by the Chicago Council on Global Affairs has shown. Dina Smeltz et al., *What Americans Think About America First: Results of the 2017 Chicago Council Survey of American Public Opinion and US Foreign Policy* (Chicago: Chicago Council on Global Affairs, 2017).

275 **Yet generational differences also suggest:** This is a key finding of the Vianovo poll, but it also emerges in the Chicago Council's findings on American public opinion toward Mexican immigrants. Taylor, "Vianovo-GSD&M Poll," and Smeltz et al., *What Americans Think*.

276 **The shift is particularly noticeable:** See CIDE, "Americas and the World," several editions from 2002 through 2016 available at https://www.lasamericasyelmundo.cide.edu, and Latinobarometro's annual polling. See also Wilson, Parás, and Enriquez, "A Critical Juncture."

276 **Polls show an almost universal dislike:** See CIDE, "Americas and the World." Source: "Trump arrastra imagen de EU en México," Consulta Mitosfky/*El Economista*, 2017, http://eleconomista.com.mx/infografias/2017/03/01/trump-arrastra-imagen-eu-mexico; "Tracking U.S. Favorability and Confidence in the U.S. President, 2002 to 2017," Pew Research Center, http://www.pewglobal.org/2017/06/26/u-s-image-suffers-as-publics-around-world-question-trumps-leadership.

279 **By raising his skepticism about NAFTA:** Presentation by Andrés Manuel López
     Obrador at the Reagan Building in Washington, DC, sponsored by the Wilson Center's
     Mexico Institute and the Inter-American Dialogue, September 5, 2017. The author
     spoke with him before the meeting and also hosted López Obrador for his first public
     presentation in Washington on a previous visit in 2011.

Index

Andrew Selee, president of the Migration Policy Institute, is former executive vice president of the Woodrow Wilson Center and founder of its Mexico Institute. An Andrew Carnegie Fellow, Dr. Selee's articles have appeared in the *Wall Street Journal*, the *Washington Post*, and the *Los Angeles Times*, and he writes a regular column in Mexico's largest newspaper, *El Universal*.